PAN-AFRICAN EDUCATION
The Last Stage of Educational Developments in Africa

John K. Marah

Studies in African Education
Volume 2

The Edwin Mellen Press
Lewiston●Queenston●Lampeter

Library of Congress Cataloging-in-Publication Data

Marah, John Karefah.
  Pan-African education : the last stage of educational developments
in Africa / by John K. Marah.
      p. cm. -- (Studies in African education ; v. 2)
      Bibliography: p.
      Includes index.
      ISBN 0-88946-186-4
      1. Education--African--History. 2. Pan-Africanism. I. Title.
II. Series: Studies in African education (Lewiston, N.Y.) ; v. 2.
LA1501.M34 1989
370'.96--dc19   88-1696
  ()   CIP

This is volume 2 in the continuing series
Studies in African Education
Volume 2 ISBN 0-88946-186-4
SAE Series ISBN 0-88946-380-8

The Edwin Mellen Press
Box 450   Box 67
Lewiston, New York   Queenston, Ontario
U.S.A. 14092   CANADA L0S 1L0

Mellen House
Lampeter, Dyfed, Wales
UNITED KINGDOM SA48 7DY

Printed in the United States of America

TABLE OF CONTENTS

List of Tables:

Preface:

What are some of the things that come to your mind
when you hear the name Africa? Indeed, this would
depend upon the times, the person you are with respect
to your knowledge about Africa, your psychological attitudes towards Africa and African peoples, and also
your knowledge about and attitudes towards the world in
general.

During the 1960's Africa was chaotic because these
were the years when many nations 'rushed' into independence. There were coups and counter coups. African
leaders spoke of African unity, nation-building, national integration and many other concepts associated
with development. The late 1960's saw many African
states as independent nations and there were hopes of
immediate prosperity for the masses of the people;
schools, colleges, and universities proliferated on the
African continent with each country establishing its
own national university, often as a symbol of pride,
independence, and to perpetuate particular political
ideologies, or for various other reasons that do not
lend themselves to complete comprehension.

The 1950's could be termed as the preparatory
stage for the 1960's when Africans' desire for more
western education was mounting and preparations were
being made for the independence of several African
countries.

The 1950's were prepared by the 1940's especially
in connection with the return of the ex-servicemen of
World War II. These men had gone abroad and had seen
Europeans in their own countries, some of whom were
street sweepers, prostitutes, and some were not terribly intelligent; some were not Christians and some
were socialists and even disapproved of colonialism.

If these servicemen could fight in outlandish places for the people who were colonizing them, they could also fight for their own freedom in Africa.

There was an intensification of colonialism in the 1920's and 30's, but even these times were affected by World War I and the formation of mandated states under the League of Nations. Educational adaptation was suggested and implemented in several African countries such as Kenya, Liberia, Central and South Africa.

From 1884 to the early 1900's Africa was being actively balkanized by several European countries. The remaining African empires were completely subjugated and colonialism entrenched itself.

Before the Europeans, there were the Arabs and they dominated several North African countries and penetrated, with their religion, several West African countries, the coast of Eastern Africa, and participated in the transportation of African slaves into Arabia, Iraq, and Egypt.

Certain periods of Egyptian history, the Empires of Mali, Songhai, Ghana, the Kingdom of Shaka, the Zulu, etc., are known as spectacular examples of African civilizations.

Thus, the question of what comes to your mind when you hear the name Africa can now be partially answered. The above could be included as some of the myriad of things that might come to mind. In addition to these are of course slavery in America, black Americans, the Dark Continent, Kwame Nkrumah, Julius Nyerere, Kenneth Kaunda, Jomo Kenyattah, Patrice Lumumba, Sekou Toure, Senghor, the Nigerian Civil War, South Africa, Ethiopia and Liberia, the formation of the Organization of African Unity, underdevelopment, starvation in Ethiopia, etc.

What might not vividly come to the reader's mind is the concept of a complete United African States under a federal government - the supreme power to all the African national governments. The idea for a United African States has been branded a dream, a good, but an impossible idea, an idealistic concept which would not be practical because of so many languages in Africa, and a myriad of other rationalizations.

This book is an attempt to describe and explain how Africa's educational institutions, teachers, and politicians have perpetuated the concept of African unity and how they can materialize that unity. This is not an original subject, and it indeed is a vast subject; the major emphasis here, however, is that African educational institutions, especially those designed specifically for the achievement and maintenance of African unity, will not fail. This should become even more optimistic when the African leadership, African teachers and other cultural agents support the concept ideologically and practically.

Now that 1984 has been upon us a hundred years after the balkanization of Africa at the Berlin Conference, is it not timely that we should ask whether Africa would remain divided for another hundred years, or whether it would unite at all? In asking such questions, we could also search for means of achieving African unity, or determine factors keeping Africa divided. This book suggests ways for the achievement of African unity with particular emphasis on Africa's educational institutions, teachers, and African political leaders.

I must acknowledge a great debt to Dr. Vincent Tinto, Dr. John Mallan, and Dr. Thomas Clayton, all of Syracuse University, for their intellectual support and

vii

encouragement.   I am indebted to Reverend Dick
Breuninger, who was a Peace Corps volunteer in Sierra
Leone and who sponsored my study in the United States.
Thanks must also go to the Putnam family in Southwick,
Massachusetts, for their adoption of me into their
family.   I must also acknowledge a great debt to Mrs.
Jean Baum and Mrs. Torrelli for their counseling, moral
and financial support during exigent times at Syracuse
University.

John Karefah Marah
1984

Introduction

Educate the people irrespective of ability, interest, class, national or tribal origin, sex, or academic
promise. Serious and more education should in fact be
for those who need it most. Current educational
schemes in Africa emphasize academic education for
those who have already proven themselves capable of
succeeding anywhere and could easily pursue their own
additional education outside of the formal school
systems; those who need educating the most are left in
the rural areas or roaming the city streets draining
the meager resources of the urban and the larger national resources with no hope of being able to contribute to effective production.

Variety of resources and agencies can be used to
educate various groups of people, students, or clients
of education. One of the major objectives of Pan-
African Education is to improve the conditions of the
lots of people, not just the bourgeoisies and their
families and friends and tribal affiliations. If
African governments do not educate the people in a concerted format and rapidly, the people will 'educate'
the governments massively in individual African
countries and regions.

Tribal systems of education have proven themselves
inadequate for modern technological societies. Tribal
educational systems functioned well at particular
points in history and stage of development and still
function in certain areas and considerations, but at
the national and Pan-African levels, they must be com-
plimented with more vigorous and broader concepts and
practice of education.

Islamic education functioned well for the purpose of perpetuating Mohammedanism to certain groups of Africans who converted and believed in the religion. Not all Africans ascribe to Islam nor can Islamic education be imposed.

West European colonial educational systems came hand in hand with capitalism, colonialism and the spread of Christianity.

Pan-African education is a secular educational system that will respond and perpetuate the concept of African unity, implement the ideology of Pan-Africanism practically and could become the nucleus for the establishment of other fundamental institutions for larger African unity and the achievement of complete African integration. Until Pan-African educational institutions are built specifically for the achievement of African unity, the Organization of African Unity will waste millions of its various African currencies in vain.

This book is a bold one and challenges any concerned African to refute the position that Pan-African Educational Institutions are not necessary for the achievement of African unity. Above all, it encourages criticisms and other opinions that cannot be so easily categorized. It is the author's firm belief that Pan-African Educational Institutions would be authentic and are development oriented institutions. They would conduct valuable researches that are currently 'unheard of' and also create political, social, economic, and psychological attitudes that will revolutionize African economics, politics, and social psychology.

Schools are the main institutions where boys and girls, whites and blacks, Jews and Gentiles, the beautiful and ugly ones meet. If Africa as a whole wants to integrate, the schools are the starting point and with the help of effective and dedicated teachers, administrators, and other school personnel, a Pan-African character can be formed and the balkanized African Continent can become a United Africa.

Education only in one African country narrows one's intellectual, cultural, and psychological dimensions. Above all, it confirms the political balkanization of African states and substantiates the entrenchment of nationalistic and provincial sentiments; it confirms the notion that these are Nigerians and those are Ghanians; these are East and those are West Africans; these are North and those over there are South Africans.

The balkanization of African states promotes the entrenchment of small African communities which feel that they are different, and therefore their problems are different from other African communities, and they begin to see themselves and act in these lights. The people become (are made to become) intimately familiar with mostly their own national heroes of politics, literature, sports and other cultural figures at the expense of other agents, heroes and figures in the other African countries or regions.

Each balkanized African country could, in this predicament, be easily persuaded by outside powers to fight against a neighboring African country. A good example is the recent case between poor Chad and Libya, which is like New York making war on Massachusetts, using weapons from balkanized European countries.

It was easy in the 1960's, and it still is not difficult, to blame Europeans for balkanizing Africa. While this remains true, it is even truer that the current African states have been thoroughly balkanized by the very African leaders who were outspoken in support of African unity in the 1960's. They have further divided Africa into 'self-contained' nations economically, politically, and have solidified the boundaries that were set up by Europeans during the scramble for Africa.

The balkanization of Africa by Africans themselves is excruciating. In a sense, the Europeans did not balkanize Africa to the extent the Africans themselves have done. For instance, the European settlers in East Africa integrated Kenya, Uganda, and Tanganyika with respect to transportation, communication, educational systems, and the administrative infrastructure. Makerere University College produced some of the African nationalists of Kenya, Uganda, and the present day Tanzania. Makerere served as a regional college in a similar way Fourah Bay College served as a West African university. William Ponty in Senegal recruited students from most of the other French West African countries. During colonial times, Cameroonians worked in Ivory Coast and didn't need work permits. The Common colonial power could move workers from one African country into another without fear of crossing boundaries. There were many Nigerian traders in Ghana during colonial times, but it was Nkrumah's regime that implemented the Alien Registration Law. Even though Nkrumah himself supported the Free Movement of African peoples between African countries, Ghanians in general, came to view themselves as Ghanians first and 'Africans' second, especially during the Cocoa crises when the Ghanian economy was at its most trying stage. The Yorubas in Ghana were viewed as strangers now that Ghana had its own national identity and hero. In times of economic crises, strangers are usually viewed, in part, as responsible for the economic chaos, especially when the strangers are traders and/or occupy high positions in the administration. The belief is that when the strangers are gone, the national economy will improve and at least the citizens will get the jobs. In the cases of Ghana, Uganda, and even Nigeria, this belief has not been substantiated. What has been accomplished is that each African nation has defined itself as an entity on to itself and the process of the entrenchment of each African country's identity is almost complete.

This entrenchment is happening in many ways. As African leaders were talking of African unity in the 1960's, they were also pre-occupied with building national universities in their respective African states. Indeed, it became fashionable for each African leader to build a national university; this subsequently reduced the presence of various African nationalities in one regionally located university. In 1963, Selassie recommended the establishment of an all-African university, but this didn't and has not materialized.

Each leader has institutionalized himself or his ideology in the country he governs. Tanzanians can now be called African socialists, Kenyans and Nigerians could be called capitalists, while some African countries can be said to have no clearly defined ideology. Regardless of leadership and political ideology, African countries compete with each other in the world market instead of putting their eggs in one basket for a higher or more appropriate prize. As they disagree on economic issues, so also do they on political issues, for the two go hand in hand.

The separate development of each African state can be viewed with respect to citizenship. As leaders entrench themselves and their political ideologies and economic infrastructure, the citizens within each nation get accustomed to seeing themselves as different from their next door neighbors. In this way, differences between African countries and peoples become entrenched. Nigerians begin to see Tanzanian problems as primarily Tanzanian, and so on and so forth; the citizens of each nation get accustomed to identifying with their immediate national heroes and other symbols. Thus, a Zambia thinks first of Kaunda, a Guinean of Sekou Toure; a Nigerian feels proud of Chinua Achebe, a Kenyan of James Ngugu, a Senegalese of Leopold Senghor. These national symbols are very difficult to transcend especially when they are taught in the nation's schools which transmit cultural, political, and other social values. In addition, each African leader is abundantly portrayed in his nation's newspapers and in the other mediums, making him the most prominent authority.

Even though the entrenchment of each African nation doesn't obliterate the possibility of African unity, it does make it very difficult for African countries to unite. Obviously, it is the African leadership that must be determined to attain African unity and it must be borne in mind that those who benefit from African disunity will always work to maintain the present, balkanized, African predicament. It will be Africans who will unite Africa; they are the ones, in the long run, who would benefit the most. To accomplish that feat, African educational institutions must be geared specifically towards African unity. African schools must be integrated. The curriculum in African schools must be changed in accordance to the principles of African unity, that is the social, political and economic development and integration of Africa. African teachers must be trained in integrated school settings. An all African university, such as Selassie suggested in 1963, must be institutionalized. With support from the African leadership, school administrators and teachers, established pertinent institutions such as specific training outfits, language training institutes, intensive language training programs, etc., the way for a complete African unity based on Nkrumah's Charter would be near realization. Until African countries build educational institutions specifically for the achievement of African unity, present and past talks about African unity are practically useless. African countries will remain balkanized until massive efforts are made to educate the African masses in the direction of Pan-African education which posits that Nigerian problems are African problems, that the problems of Blacks in America are indeed African problems. Pan-African education will teach the African youth, in the words of Kenneth Kaunda, "to see Africa whole."

CHAPTER ONE
A VAST CONTINENT WITH NUMEROUS PROBLEMS

The vastness of the African continent and the diversities primordial in it would seem to suggest that no single study concerned with any aspect of African education should boast of conclusiveness. This caution is made at the outset in cognizance of the various tribes and races in Africa and the different histories and aspirations African countries have gone through. Kenya alone has more than thirty tribes; and Sierra Leone, a small country of not more than four million inhabitants, has more than sixteen tribes; some of these so-called tribes are linguistically related but they are distinct in certain cultural aspects. The presence of multiple tribes in Africa cannot be underestimated even though some progressive African nationalists have tried to undermine tribalism for the sake of nationalism and pan-Africanism.

In addition to the presence of multiple tribes in Africa, the South, East and Central regions are peopled by various racial groups which have rarely lived in

harmony with one another. Moreover, they have participated in different types of educational systems
frequently based on antagonistic philosophies. The
Bantu Educational System, for instance, cannot be said
to be in harmony with African nationalism or pan-
Africanism; the Jeanes School System in Kenya in the
1920's cannot be said to have been in line with African
aspirations for political and cultural dominance of the
African majority. Although the Jeanes School System
can now be said to be an 'anachronism', it was nonetheless implemented at Kabete and trained a good number
of teachers and their families.[1] The Jeanes School was
a practical expression of the philosophy of educational
adaptation, imported from the United States of America,
approved by the various colonial powers in Africa, and
modifications of such schools were established in
Liberia,[2] Tanganyika[3] and in several other African
countries.

One must also add the varied traditional and
colonial political practices and their concomitant
diverse educational, linguistic, bureaucratic, economic
and cultural systems that up to date remain persistent.
In addition to this seeming Tower of Babel, there are
the rapid economic, political, and technical changes
that are sweeping through the continent; and these
changes are destined to make certain alterations some
of which can hardly be predicted with certainty, while
others can only be speculated. As Williams and Polier
(1964) have observed, "In an age of rapid technical
change...the only certainty is the fact of change itself..."[4]

Aside from technical changes and their subsequent
ramifications, North African countries are basically
Arabic in religion, history, geographical proximity to

the larger Arab world and in their ideological commitment to Arab nationalism.[5] In this respect, their commitment to the African Continent is naturally geographical and fragmentary.[6] They cannot commit themselves a hundred percent to Black Africa, nor can they neglect South of the Sahara to any significant degree for this region has a large Islamic population.

There are specific racial problems in those African countries that are multiracial. The Northern Sudanese, who are mainly Arabic, for instance, refer to the Southern Sudanese, who are mostly Black Africans, as "those are just Africans."[7] The Southern portion of Sudan is less developed with respect to industrial establishments and the Northerners are over-represented in the house of Parliament.[8] The Northern dominance in politics and industry will have to be rectified before these institutions take on antagonistic racial, religious and cultural connotations.

The dominance of the white minority race in former Rhodesia "...has resulted in a clamor of international protests and a racial animosity...that still smolders underground like a deadly hidden mine fire."[9] Even though a Black majority now holds political power in Zimbabwe, old racial animosities are not obliterated overnight especially with the fact that South Africa exists as an apartheid state, and so proximitously to Zimbabwe.

The case of the Union of South Africa is too blatant and obvious to deserve any detailed discussion here. It must, however, be pointed out that any genuine movement for total African integration cannot leave South Africa out of the picture. The white

3

suprematists in South Africa should never see themselves immune to any genuine movement for complete, continental African integration.

The problem of the various tribal languages in Africa cannot be underestimated in any movement for genuine African unity; the various European languages have added to the premordial polyglot predicament of Africa. Indeed, the language problem in Africa has been pointed out by almost all writers concerned with Africa, and especially with pan-Africanism, as one of the monumental problems delaying or preventing African unity.

The various political ideologies held by the numerous African leaders have prevented African countries from uniting.[10] In the 1960's, there were ideological clashes between the radicals and the moderates even though the two 'extreme' camps approved of some form of African integration.[11] Some intellectual Africans advocate scientific, or Marxist socialism,[12] while others stress African socialism,[13] or authenticity,[14] or Negritude,[15] or Humanism;[16] there are other African leaders who do not have any clearly defined political ideology and are content with nonalignment, one party state governments, or neocolonialist relationship with their ex-colonial powers. Some African leaders publicly advocate democracy without fully understanding the nature of democracy as practiced in the United States, the foremost exponent of that form of government. These ideological differences, which could be called ideological immaturities, have, and continue to make it difficult for African leaders to make concerted African policy and

have served, in no small measure, to highlight antagonisms and suspicions between African leaders within
and outside of Africa.

Closely related to ideological differences are the
diverse external relations different African countries
pursue. These external relations follow closely the
previous colonial paradigm. Some former French
colonies are still culturally, educationally, politically and economically associated, exploited, by their
ex-colonizers. The former British colonies are also in
a similar predicament. Since the 1960's, America's
presence in certain African countries has been
phenomenal. America's presence in Kenya, Nigeria,
Liberia, etc. is spectacular. Nigeria has even changed
its constitution to closely resemble that of America;
Kenya has changed its educational format to closely
resemble that of America. There is also a good number
of African countries that claim to be socialists or
communists and Russian and Chinese influences are expected to be found within these countries. Cuba has
aided some African countries in their bids for freedom
from colonial domination and Castro spearheaded the
nonaligned nations, and thus Cuban influence is not to
be unexpected in these and other African countries.

The unequal development of African countries poses
another problem. Some African countries such as
Nigeria, Zaire, Ivory Coast, and the Union of South
Africa are well endowed with natural resources and
capacities for agricultural production, mining, hydro-
electric power and have an educated manpower, especially in the case of Nigeria with its numerous fine
universities and the large number of highly educated
personnel. South Africa is technologically more advanced than the rest of Africa, but with its apartheid

5

regime, there would be few African leaders who would join hands with that union until the minority regime is dissolved, (by any means necessary), and power handed to a popularly elected leadership.

Another problem arises in connection with the move for regional or pan-African unity as richer nations would be reluctant to unite with poorer nations such as Chad or Tanzania in light of the fact that they would have to share their resources and facilities, especially when community feeling between African nations cannot, at this point, be taken for granted. Indeed, New York will not be willing to share or undertake a joint project with Connecticut or New Jersey if they viewed each other suspiciously or are ideologically antagonistic to each other. The case between Kenya and Tanzania serves a prime example. Because of the absence of strong community feeling between African nations, at least not sufficient enough to culminate into regional or continental unity, Chad would rather ask for the aid of France in times of economic or military exigencies than that of Kenya, for the former has more community feeling for France than for Kenya. This is beside the plausible counter argument that France would be in a more advanced technical position to provide such an aid. If it were not for the lack in community feeling sufficient to dispel suspicions, mistrusts, etc., Kenya, Uganda and Tanzania, haven shared integrative institutions before, and to certain extent still do, could form a nucleus for a larger grouping of African states.

The concept of community or group feeling is closely related to nationalism, regionalism, and can even be extended to the tribe, village, town, district, province, city, religion and groups of migrants within

6

a given social entity. The Jewish community in America is not only concerned with American Jews, but also with the state of Israel and its politics. Thus, community feeling can transcend geographical and national boundaries. In 1970 for instance, the United Women of Tanzania

> "played a leading role in organizing a protest against the Portuguese-led invasion of Guinea, Tanzania's West African sister nation. ...Some women even volunteered to go to Guinea and take up arms, had it been necessary."[17]

Numerous examples could be cited where an African country, or a group of African countries have aided another African country or group of countries, but these have occurred only at exigent times and there have been no permanent, institutionalized relationships to prevent, for an instance, "The Expulsion of West African Aliens."[18] This has led Alex Quaison-Sackey to ask: "Who is an alien?"[19] and to assert that

> "All West Africans are citizens of West Africa. They were even before the promulgation of ECOWAS. From Mauritania to Nigeria, the people criss-cross linguistically and culturally. Thus, Nigerians have relations in Benin who have relations in Ghana, who have relatives in the Ivory Coast, who have relatives in Liberia, who have relatives in Sierra Leone and so on."[20]

Quaison-Sackey's pan-African sentiments and considerations, however, have not prevented Ghanians from being expelled from Nigeria, Indians expelled out of Uganda, Guineans out of Sierra Leone, and the problems of

7

refugees in Somalia, Ethiopia, Kenya and other African countries.

Although we are mainly concerned here with larger geographical, social, and political entities, micro communities, such as the Indian and Lebanese communities in East and West Africa, and the white minority community in South Africa, could become potent drawbacks to effective social integration. If these small communities can benefit from African disunity, as the South African regime does, they will resist all moves for African unity under popular African leadership.

With respect to larger political entities, West, East, Central, South, and North Africa are not automatically compatible entities; and this becomes most telling in view of the regional organizations that have been formed and are slowing entrenching themselves. The Arab League, ECOWAS, Manor-River Union, the Front Line States and slogans such as "Think East Africa",[21] are a few examples that are seriously reinforcing regional or nationalistic group feelings. The question here is whether these various groupings, after entrenching or institutionalizing themselves, would be willing to transfer their loyalties to a larger African organization.

Within these regional settings, there are differences not only in colonial history, stages of economic and political ideological developments, but also differences in external alliances, fiscal currencies, racial composition, religious and ethnic alliances. There are class and educational differences within each African nation. African Urban centers are comparatively well endowed with good educational institutions, transportation systems, electricity and other modern facilities. Generally, while the urban centers have 'abundant' educational institutions, the hinterlands which need rapid development are often 'neglected' in light of the meager, underdeveloped resources of most African countries. Within each African nation, there are problems with respect to the diffusion of educational institutions and other educative facilities such as newspapers, telephone, theater and television.

The masses of the people in most African nations are illiterates and are politically and ideologically unsophisticated, poor, and in general, unequipped to critically explicate the myriad social, economic, and political zeitgeist of Africa and its relations to the world at large.

There are transportation and other infrastructure problems between and within most African countries. These delay and often times frustrate the delivery of people, goods and services, and ideas from one location to the next. Bad roads consume a lot of time, some of which could be used towards other productive activities. Bad roads shorten the life of vehicles such as cars, buses, taxies, trucks and lorries and damage goods that they may be transporting.

There is starvation in Africa.[22] When in 1960 seventeen African countries attained political independence, there were rising expectations that economic, social and cultural developments would follow. The economic situation in most African countries, after more than twenty years of independence, has not radically improved; in fact there are indications that there have been further underdevelopment in some countries, at least to the extent of Africans dying of starvation. Most of the Africans who die of starvation

9

are illiterate peasants, women, and children. Besides these, there are those peasants who eat once a day and live in the worst type of housing by anybody's standards. It is a well known fact about African countries that the urban areas are crowded by unskilled youth and adults who no longer wish to return to rural areas and to agricultural production. This overcrowding of Africa's urban areas has put additional strain on the meager resources of African nations. Starvation is no longer reserved for villagers; peasants in urban areas and the surrounding environs have also become candidates for shanty houses, malnutrition and starvation.

Economists and other scholars who write on African economic development see no immediate panacea for Africa's economic problems. Within the last twenty-odd years, Africa's agricultural production has deteriorated rather than improved. A few African countries have been able to feed their populations, but these are exceptions. For a large number of African countries, however, their economic problems might continue to get worse if they do not take drastic measures.

Soil erosion and desertification have plagued Africa and these have been cited as some of the major reasons for the retardation in Africa's agricultural production. The conversion of the once arable lands into deserts, heavy tropical rains that deplete the soil and the use of nontechnical farming methods are also reasons for the lack in food production.

Outmoded agricultural techniques, such as the use of hoes and machetes, the burning of bushes, forests and grass are no longer efficient to produce enough food for Africa's growing population, a good number of whom are aspiring city-dwellers. The absence of modern

agricultural technologies that could be used in large
scale farming, so as to produce abundance of diversified foodstuffs, for sale as well as for home consumption, continue to contribute to food shortages in
Africa.

Economic development theorists such as Samir
Armin[23] and Walter Rodney[24] have posited additional
reasons as to the why of Africa's undevelopment. These
theorists view that Africa, as is the case with most
developing countries in Asia and Latin America, is at
the periphery in the context of the world economy,
while Western Europe and North America form the core.
The core countries have been able to produce abundance
of food and attain high levels of technical know-how
for internal consumption as well as for exportation.
The core countries, assert the underdevelopment
theorists, have been able to develop their economies
because of their capacity to exploit the so-called
Third World countries.

In his study of the Upper Guinea Coast, Walter
Rodney provides convincing data to illustrate how
Europe had extracted economic surplus from Africa since
the 1500's[25] and this relationship has continued to the
present; European countries would sell their technical
products to Balkanized African nations at exorbitant
prices and buy African agricultural commodities
cheaply. Some economists have recommended comparative
advantage as a strategy for Third World development;
this strategy would enhance individual countries's
capabilities to maximize their economic position if
they were to specialize in commodities they can effi-
ciently produce with respect to their inputs such as
capital and labor. But as African countries are not
united, comparative advantage would merely heighten the

11

competition between African countries which produce the same commodities and with Latin American countries that do produce some of the same types of agricultural products that Africa does produce. Furthermore, Western technology has been able to produce synthetic foodstuffs that could effectively compete with African raw products. Without a pan-African economic program, Africa will remain poor.[26] Without a concerted effort on the part of African countries, they will collectively remain dependent on the West for food aid and thus, in other considerations as well, for you cannot bite the hand that feeds you.

There have been other reasons for Africa's underdevelopment aside from technical, economic and agricultural spheres. Those African leaders who have been perceptively development oriented have been exterminated by the enemies of African peoples, including some African intellectuals and military men. Kwame Nkrumah's program was development oriented, but his insistence on pan-Africanism won him many enemies within and without Africa. After the publication of his *Empiralism: The Last Stage of Capitalism*, that traced the interconnections between multinational corporations operating in Africa, he quickly fell out of favor. The aid Ghana had been receiving from the West quickly dropped. Shortly after this, Nknumah was deposed by his own military and police officials who claimed they could do better with the economy and corruption. Their claim has not been evident in more than twenty years. Amilcar Cabral, Patrice Lumumba, Oginga Odinga, Tom Boyah, Bildad Kaggia, Samori Toure, Malcolm X, Martin Luther King, Sekou Toure, Steve Biko, Dedan Kimathi, Michael Manley, J.M. Kariuki, Walter Rodney, and others radically motivated to change the conditions of African peoples have been either assassinated, deposed out of government, demoted, or publicly discredited in the media by the opponents of African development. Nyerere, for awhile, remained one of the key African leaders, but his programs were not threatening to the West because Tanzania made few radical improvements especially in the areas of food production, technological advancement and in the production of firearms or their accumulation, which a powerful country must have. Africans, more than any group of people must know the power of firearms.

One should never blame the West for all of Africa's problems. Corrupt African leadership, the tremendous transitions African countries are going through, traditional concepts of time, attitudes towards nature and work, etc. are all in concert and in part responsible for Africa's underdevelopment. "...Africa's marginality in the global arena can be reduced to three major weaknesses: technological underdevelopment, organizational incompetence and military weakness."[27]

African countries have not been able to radically change the educational systems that they inherited from their ex-colonial powers. Kaunda,[28] Nyerere,[29] Selassie,[30] and Nkrumah[31] have all written and spoken against the disastrous effects of western schooling in Africa but the programs they recommend have not yielded fruits or have not at all been implemented in toto.

Generally, western education in Africa was closely tied to capitalism, Christianity, slavery, and colonialism; none of these components can be dislodged from one or the other. In Africa, Christianity attracted first the outcasts, slaves, and others peripheral to the tribal society or community. The school and the church went hand in hand, so that when the African went to school, he also had to be a Christian. Thus, Forte Hare College in South Africa was a Christian school, Fourah Bay College in Sierra Leone was a Christian school, and many others that were both religious and educational, but rarely one without the other, and in some cases the religious aspects predominated. Thus, the African learned how to read and write with a new, Christianized name. The Creoles who were settled in Freetown, Sierra Leone, had European names and some were deeply Christian and anxious to educate their children and perpetuate Christianity to other Africans. Indeed, the Creoles were significant in the perpetuation of western education on the West Coast of Africa; some of them became teachers, while others became lawyers, medical doctors, surveyors, and other bureaucratic personnel needed to help rule the colonies.

The freetown of Eastern Africa was Freretown, a mission station of about ten miles away from the Coast; and again, it was a settlement for ex-slaves usually known as the Bombay Africans, for they had been first settled in India before being brought to the Mombasa Coast. These Bombay Africans became teachers and catechists and spread inland to teach their African brethren the new religion and education. Slaves who escaped from their Arab masters and other Africans who left their tribal confines were attracted to the Freretown mission station; they too became agents of Christianity and Western education. It was not until the completion of Kenya-Uganda railway that missionary activities penetrated the hinterland. In all, the African was 'converted' to Christianity, had his name changed to a Christian or European one, taught how to

14

read, write, and cipher, and was educated to despise
his own culture! He could not be a Christian, which
was the equivalent to being civilized, and still boast
of his culture and traditions such as maintaining his
traditional religion, polygamy and go through circumcision rites, especially that of women.

Under colonialism, writes Ali Mazrui,
"the warrior tradition in Africa was badly
damaged by two terrors which had come with
the white man, the terror of gun fire and
the terror of hellfire. ...the terror of
hellfire...came with Christianity. Death
for millions of Africans was now given a
new meaning. African ancestors were cut
down to size, denounced as insignificant
by the missionaries of the new religious
order."[32]

Other African authority figures were branded negative;
for instance, while Napolean was portrayed as a hero,
Samori Toure was denounced as blood thirsty. The Mullah of Somalia was referred to as 'mad' because he was
recalcitrant to succumb to foreign domination.[33]

Western education as was practiced in Africa, and
this remains largely true up to the present, reinforced
"...the African's disinclination toward certain kinds
of manual work due to traditional divisions of labor by
sex or social class."[34] Western education further
reinforced "the African's desire to imitate the white
man whom he saw largely in supervisory or office positions."[35]

As a result, the African began to view western
education "...as a means of escaping from the drudgery
of the farm,...and...to construe attempts to promote

vocational or non-academic studies as types of subtle discrimination designed to keep him in his place."[36]

Indeed, Western education has produced, whether intended or not, some capable African scholars and politicians and other modern men highly recognized in their fields of endeavors even at international standards. It has trained African personnel capable of working anywhere in the world; via colonialism, Christianity and capitalism, western medicine has been brought into Africa and has saved the lives of millions. Some Africans can now speak several European languages and can even write sophisticated poetry in at least one of them. The list of benefits Africa has obtained, directly and indirectly, from its relationship with the West, can be long, but there is that inevitable question: to whose comfort has this relationship been? George O. Cox was honest when he wrote:

> It will be ridiculous to deny that European capitalism and its effect on colonial Africa did not leave certain benefits, such as modern communication systems such as telegraphs, railway systems in some countries and the European languages. But it will be ridiculous to imagine that Africans and Asiatics did not communicate with each other or lacked schools and hospitals until the advent of Europeans. One can make such an assertion because it is consistent with the available data. Besides, the price that Africa had to pay for receiving what she did from the European counterparts was far more overwhelming in favor of Europe than Africa.[37]

Thus, there is still large scale illiteracy in Africa, large scale starvation, rampant infant mortality and other numerous manifestations of underdevelopment.

Notes

CHAPTER ONE

[1]Sheldon Weeks, Divergence in Educational Development: The Case of Kenya and Uganda (New York: Teachers College Press, 1967), p. 7.

[2]Edward H. Berman, "Tuskegee-In-Africa," The Journal of Negro Education. XLI (1972), pp. 99-112.

[3]Bryant W. Mumford, "Malangali School," Africa 3 (July 1930), pp. 265-290; see also his "Native Schools in Central Africa," Journal of the African Society, Vol. LLXI, No. Cl (October 1926), pp. 237-244.

[4]Wilson C. Williams and Jonathan Wise Pollier, "Pan-Africanism and the Dilemmas of National Development," Phylon, Vol. XXV, No. 1 (Spring 1964), p. 47.

[5]Gamel Abdel Nasser, The Philosophy of the Revolution (Buffalo, New York: Economic Books, Smith, Kaynes and Marshall Publishers, 1959), pp. 59-60.

[6]Ali A. Mazrui, Towards A Pax Africana (The University of Chicago Press, 1967), p. 46.

[7]Dunstan M. Wai, "Crisis in North-South Relations," Africa Report (March-April 1982), p. 22.

[8]Ibid.

[9]Ilan C. Fisher, Jr., "Rhodesia, A House Divided," National Geographic (May 1975), p. 642.

[10]Patricia Berko Wilde, "Radicals and Moderates in the OAU: Origins of Conflict and Basis for Co-existence," in Paul A. Tharp (ed.), Regional International Relations/Structure and Functions (N.Y.: St. Martin's Press, 1971), p. 37.

[11]Ibid.

[12]Abdul Rahman Mohamed Babu, African Socialism or Socialist Africa (Dar es Salaam: Tanzania Publishing House, 1981).

[13]Julius K. Nyerere, Freedom and Socialism (Dar es Salaam: Oxford University Press, 1968).

18

[14]Africa Report (March-April 1975), pp. 2-6.

[15]Leopold Sedar Senghor, On African Socialism (N.Y.: A. Praeger Publisher, 1964).

[16]Kenneth Kaunda, A Humanist in Africa: Letters to Colin M. Morris (London: Longmans, Green and Company Ltd., 1966).

[17]Joyce Ladner in Filomina Chioma Steady, The Black Woman Cross-culturally (Cambridge University Press, 1982), p. 111.

[18]Margaret Peil, "The Expulsion of West African Aliens," The Journal of Modern African Studies, Vol. 9, No. 2 (1971), pp. 205-229.

[19]Alex Quaison-Sackey, "Who is an Alien?" West Africa (February 21, 1983), p. 471.

[20]Ibid.

[21]Cited in Jane Martin (ed.), Global Studies: Africa (Guilford, Conn. 1985), p. 129.

[22]See the Author's article: "Starvation in Africa: A Challenge to African Leaders," Heritage News Magazine (August-September 1984), p. 8.

[23]Samir Amin, Imperialism and Underdevelopment (New York: Monthly Review Press, 1977); see also his Neo-Colonialism in West Africa (New York: Monthly Review Press, 1973).

[24]Walter Rodney, How Europe Underdeveloped Africa (Washington, D.C.: Howard University Press, 1974).

[25]---------- History of the Upper Guinea Coast 1545-1800 (New York: Monthly Review Press, 1980).

[26]Reginald H. Green and Ann Seidman, Unity or Poverty? The Economics of Pan-Africanism (Baltimore, Maryland: Penguin Books, 1968).

[27]Ali A. Mazrui, The African Condition (Cambridge University Press, 1980), p. 118.

[28]Kenneth Kaunda, A Letter to my Children (London: Longman Group, Ltd., 1973).

[29]Nyerere, op. cit., pp. 267-290.

[30]Haile Selassie, "Towards African Unity," The Journal of Modern African Studies, 11, 3 (1963), pp. 281-291.

[31]Kwame Nkrumah, Africa Must Unite (New York: International Publishers, 1970).

[32]Mazrui, op. cit., p. 123.

[33]Douglas, Jardine, The Mad Mullah of Somaliland (New York: Negro Universities Press, 1969).

[34]John W. Hanson, Hallucination in African Education (East Lansing, Michigan: Michigan State University), p. 33.

[35]Ibid.

[36]Ibid.

[37]George O. Cox, Education for the Black Race (New York: African Heritage Publishers, 1974), p. 27.

CHAPTER TWO

THE PROCESS OF TRADITIONAL EDUCATION IN AFRICA

The process of traditional education in Africa was intimately integrated with the social, cultural, artistic, religious, and recreational life of the tribal or ethnic group. That is, 'schooling' and 'education', or the learning of skills, social and cultural values and norms were not separated from the other spheres of life. As in any other society, the education of the African child started at birth and continued into manhood or adulthood. The education that was given to the African youth fitted him into his group and the roles he was expected to play in society had all been learned by the time of adulthood. Girls were socialized to effectively learn the roles of motherhood, wife, and other sex-appropriate skills. Boys were socialized to be hunters, herders, agriculturists, blacksmiths, etc. depending on how the particular ethnic, tribal group, clan or family derived its livelihood.

However, because there were no permanent school walls as in the case of the western countries, some European writers on African education tended, blinded

by their own cultural paradigms, to view that traditional African educational process was mainly informal.
Some early European writers on Africa in general even
went to the extent of saying that Africa, especially
South of the Sahara, had no culture, history or civilization. Murray (1967), for instance, states that
> "...outside Egypt there is nowhere in-
> digenous history. African history has al-
> ways been 'foreign' history."[1]

Laurie (1907), in his Historical Survey of Pre-
Christian Education,[2] did not even include Africa south
of the Sahara in his scheme of analysis or exposition;
he started with Egyptians and ended with the Romans.
He equated education with civilization and culture as
he knew them and, by implication, Africa south of the
Sahara was primitive.

Boas (1938) defines
> "primitive as those people whose ac-
> tivities are little diversified, whose
> forms of life are simple and uniform, and
> the contents and form of whose culture are
> meager and intellectually inconsistent.
> Their inventions, social order, intellec-
> tual and emotional life should be poorly
> developed."[3]

Boas goes on to justify a civilized culture by using
technical developments and the wealth of inventions as
yardsticks. The types of technology he singles out as
making a culture civilized are those which go beyond
merely satisfying daily basic needs; thus, Eskimo techniques are primitive since they do not greatly reduce
the Eskimo's daily physical preoccupation with
livelihood. One sees that Boas is favoring West
European culture as a measure of civilization.

22

However, the academic tradition of putting Europe at the pinnacle of civilizations has now largely been addressed and refuted by both Western and non-Western scholars and other men of ideas.

Brickman (1963) goes beyond Laurie's, Murray's and Boas' conceptions of civilizations and primitiveness by continuing with the Egyptian origins of African education to state, at least, that "African education dates back to ancient times in Egypt, to the establishment of Muslim mosques in the centuries following the death of Mohammed, to the University of Timbuktu in the sixteenth century, to the Dutch on the Gold Coast and in South Africa during the seventeenth century, and to the missionary schools in the nineteenth century."[4] Brickman goes on to concentrate on the May 1961 Addis Ababa Conference of African ministers of Education, UNESCO representatives and other observers concerned about the development of education in Africa. What is apparently missing in Brickman's survey is the education provided the African youth even before the coming of Islamic religion into Africa, especially south of the Sahara. Even with the case of Egyptian civilization, historians have begun to ascertain that Africa south of the Sahara affected North Africa considerably. Diop (1978) has used archeological evidences to substantiate that Kush, or Africa south of the Sahara, influenced Egyptian civilization rather than the other way around and that the empires of Ghana, Mali, Songhai, etc. attest to the cultural unity of Africa.[5] Of course, to completely determine which region influenced which, and to what extent, are some of the problems in African history and need further investigation.

Nonetheless, Watkins (1943), Ociti (1973), Scanlon (1964), Mbiti (1967), Boateng (1983) and others have described traditional systems of African education prior to the coming of Islam and Christianity, using several African countries, societies, or tribes. Scanlon states that "the education of the African before the coming of the Europeans was an education that prepared him for his responsibilities as an adult in his home, his village, and his tribe".[6] His tribe was his community that was held cohesive by rules and regulations, values and social sanctions, approvals, rewards and punishments, etc. into which he was inducted. He was taught social etiquettes, agricultural methods and others that would ensure the smooth running of the social entity of which he was an integral part. He observed and imitated his father's craft and learned practical skills which he performed according to his capacities and effectively as he matured into manhood and was now head of his own family unit. The education of girls was differentiated from that of the boys in accordance to the roles each sex was expected and socialized to play for the remainder of their adult lives.

Watkins (1943) has described traditional process of education in West Africa; she calls the traditional African educational institution the "Bush" school, for the Poro and Bondo societies conducted their training of boys and girls respectively outside of the village or town.[6] The training given the youth prepared them for military, family, agricultural, and cultural purposes. Mental and moral training are also undertaken. Each youth in the tribe must attend this training before he could be considered a worthy member of the society. The length of the training differs from tribe to tribe, but it usually takes several years before a boy is passed from adolescence into adulthood. The traditional system of education used is what westerners today call 'Mastery learning'[7] in that failure was virtually nonexistent; every effort was made, encouragements given, incentives provided so as to make sure that even the most coward goes through, say, the circumcision process. Group instruction, group assignments, apprenticeship and age groupings to experience a particular significant event were the most common methods employed to instruct the young. Private instruction by one's brother or sister, or one of the parents was also provided. Repetition, imitation, internalization and practice were the main methods used for learning, so that by adulthood, the African was a full member of the community into which he was born.

Smith (1940) has described the uses of folk-tales as educative devices in traditional African societies.[8] Stories are used not only to amuse and express feelings, but also to teach appropriate forms of behavior and morality. Children learn by listening to their elders, imitating or 'emulating' them. These stories are usually handed down from one generation to the next; their main concern is to induct the youth into the moral, philosophical, and cultural values of the community. In West Africa, there were griots, who were 'walking' dictionaries or historians, who memorized the history, legends of a whole people and can recite them and teach their apprentices or audiences, publicly or privately; direct instruction was also employed.

One of the major avenues through which the African youth received his or her education was, and it still is today in some quarters, during several grades or initiation ceremonies. For the Tiriki group in Kenya, East Africa, Basil Davidson has provided the following description:

"Until you are ten or so you are counted
as a 'small boy' with minimal social
duties such as herding the cattle. Then
you will expect, with some trepidation, to
undergo initiation to manhood by a process
of schooling which lasts about six months
and is punctuated by ritual
'examinations'. Selected groups of boys
are entered for this schooling once every
four or five years. ...All the initiates
of a hut eat, sleep, sing, dance, bathe,
do handicrafts, etc. ...but only when
commanded to do so by their counselor, who
will be a man under about twenty-five.
...circumcision gives it a ritual embodi-
ment within the first month or so, after
which social training continues as before
until the schooling period is complete.
Then come ceremonies at which elders teach
and exhort, the accent now being on
obedience to rules which have been
learned. The Tiriki social charter is
thus explained and then enshrined at the
center of the man's life."[9]

Throughout Africa, initiation rites and the
various rituals involved in the passage from childhood
to manhood were cultural devices to inculcate the
spirit of the community in the youth. As western
schools Americanized or Europeanized so also did these
traditional African schools Africanized. For the case
of the Tiriki again, Davidson continues that during the
initiation:

"There is inculcated a sense of respect
for elders, of brotherhood among members

of the age set in question, and of skill
in practical matters such as the use of
arms. The parallel may be wildly remote
in context and content, but one is ir-
resistibly reminded of the English public
schools. Even visiting Tiriki mums are
said to be like their English counterparts, alarmed for their offspring but
jealously proud of their progress."[10]

Camara Laye (1954) in his excellent autobiographi-
cal novel The Dark Child describes his circumcision experiences in Guinea, West Africa:

"The teaching we received in the bush, far
from all prying eyes, had nothing very
mysterious about it; nothing, I think,
that was not fit for ears other than our
own. These lessons, the same as had been
taught to all who had preceded us, con-
fined themselves to outlining what a man's
conduct should be: we were to be absolutely straightforward, to cultivate all
the virtues that go to make an honest man,
to fulfill our duties toward God, toward
our parents, our superiors and our neighbors. We must tell nothing of what we
learned, either to women or to the
uninitiated; neither were we to reveal any
of the secret rites of circumcision. That
is the custom. Women, too, are not allowed to tell anything about the rites of
excision."[11]

Ociti (1973) has also described the education of
African youth under the traditional system, stressing
that the process starts from the time of the unborn

27

child and refutes writers who have construed that "...since the Africans knew no reading or writing, they therefore had no systems of education and so no contents and methods to pass on to the young."[12] For the scholars who think Africa was Tabla Rasa with respect to educational institutions and processes, "...education...meant western civilizations; take away western civilization, and you have no education."[13]

On the contrary, the educational systems that existed in Africa prior to the West European taught the African child to avoid affairs that the community scorned. The African child was educated to know, internalize and practice roles appropriate to his sex and age. In the early years of childhood, the child's education is largely in the hands of the biological mother,[14] and the community assumes great role as he approaches adolescence. He received language training from the mother, the extended family and the tribe at large. The peer group, or age-set also becomes significant as the youth approaches the stage of circumcision. At this stage orature, comprising of myths, legends, folksongs and folktales, proverbs, dances, etc. are all in line to prepare the youth for adulthood.[15] Thus, "before the advent of the Europeans African indigenous education...was quite adequate in so far as it met the requirements of the society at that time."[16] And "like any good system of education, it had its objectives, scope and methods which clearly reflected the ways of life or cultural patterns of the clan or chieftian."[17] Traditional African systems of education were and are still so effective that their "...total rejection...will leave African societies in a vacuum that can only be filled with confusion, loss of

identity, and a total break in intergenerational communication."[18]   Boateng (1983) claims that "the essential goal of traditional education is still admirable
and challenging."[19]

Traditional African education, like any system of
education, had and still has its own weaknesses and
strengths.   In the modern context, however, and in
light of Africa's moves for rapid economic, political,
technical and cultural developments, traditional
African education falls far too short.   Traditional
education was tribalistic and therefore exclusive of
others who did not belong to the tribe or particular
ethnic group. If it were not so, the various tribes in
Africa might have been integrated into large communities or political groups. If traditional systems
of education were not tribalistic, the various tribal
wars in Africa would have been less.   Granted, there
are many other reasons that gave rise, and still do, to
tribal antagonisms, but the educational process, content and conduct are not immune and cannot be discarded
out of the variables or reasons that cause ethnic or
tribal antagonisms.

Traditional education educated men to be men and
women to be women. This functioned well "...at a time
when a man was a man and women were won by those who
deserve them,..."[20] but in the context of modern
Africa, where all human resources must be mobilized for
rapid political and technical development, African
traditional systems of education fail immensely.

Traditional systems of education did not produce
scientists as we know scientists today and did not
produce great military men, at least not great enough
to counter the onslaught of the British, French, German, Portuguese armies and the South African Trekers.

29

"This history of Africa's military weakness has continued to haunt African leaders and thinkers."[21] And,
as President Sekou Touri once put it: "It was because
of the inferiority of Africa's means of self-defense
that it was subjected to foreign domination."[22]

There are many other weaknesses in traditional
African education that could be pointed out, but, is
not sufficient to say that these weaknesses are
reflected in the present undeveloped condition of
Africa? Peasants still use traditional methods of
farming, healing and traveling. Infant mortality,
starvation, peripheriality of African women in
politics-that-makes-a-difference, etc. are still rampant in Africa. Certainly, much of Africa's problems
could be attributed to colonialism, capitalism, neo-
colonialism and thus, Western exploitation of Africa's
raw materials and other commodities but, must Africa's
problems be blamed solely on Europeans? And, in fact,
is it not Africa's failings that in the first place
subjected her to her current peripheriality in world
politics, economics and mechanization?

The weaknesses in traditional African education
were explicitly revealed with the advent of Christianity and the European formal school system. "Tribal
education was not an education for change;"[23] it
demanded conformity, but not individuality, creativity
or individual uniqueness. It taught strict obedience
to the elders' rules and authority, which were not always necessarily founded, so that when the missionaries
brought their schools into Africa, it became a 'refuge'
for those Africans who wanted to be different from
other members of the tribal group.[24] The old system
"...assumed that human nature was constant; that there
was no Revolution to upset the status quo of the old

order."[25] To this old order's amazement, western
schools in Africa became the places to go to earn
diplomas and degrees, and therefore social prestige,
fine clothes, cars, houses, economic and political
power. Traditional educational systems still exist
among the African peasants, but western schools confer
much more, especially onto those who complete the
universities, whether they are employed or not. The
hope that they will one day be employed or under-
employed and maybe frustrated in their employment is
still more comforting than to be unschooled and without
the paper certificate from a western school, prestigious or not. And many university teachers know this
very well and "...can attest that the vast majority of
African students today are first and foremost job
seekers who aspire to well-paid, high status,
materially comfortable occupations"[26] their degrees,
political alliances and ideological conformity can get
them. It has become the ineluctable case "...that one
who possesses a diploma, any diploma, can bargain,
whereas those without certificates have no cards to
play."[27] And in the case of Africa, that means the
majority who cannot play the cards.

NOTES

CHAPTER TWO

[1]A. Victor Murray, The School in the Bush: A Critical Study of the Theory and Practice of Native Education in Africa (London: Frank Cass and Co., Ltd., 1967), p. 14.

[2]Simon Somerville Laurie, Historical Survey of Pre-Christian Education (London and New York: Longmans, Green, and Co., 1904).

[3]Franz Boas, The Mind of Primitive Man (New York: The Free Press, 1938), p. 180.

[4]William W. Brickman, "Tendencies in African Education," The Educational Forum, Vol. XXVII, No. 4 (May 1963), p. 399.

[5]Anta Cheikh Diop, The Cultural Unity of Black Africa (New York: Third World Press, 1978).

[6]David Scanlon, Traditions of African Education (New York: Teacher's College, Columbia University, 1964), p. 3. See also Mark Hanna Watkins, "The West African 'Bush' Schools," The American Journal of Sociology, Vol. XLVII, No. 6 (May 1943), pp. 666-675.

[7]James H. Block, "Teaching, Teachers, and Mastery Learning," Today's Education (November-December 1973), p. 35.

[8]Edwin W. Smith, "The Function of Folk-Tales," Journal of the African Royal Society, Vol. XXXIX, No. CLIV (January 1940), pp. 64-83.

[9]Basil Davidson, The African Genius: An Introduction to African Social and Cultural History (The Atlantic Monthly Press, 1969), pp. 84-85.

[10]Ibid., p. 85.

[11]Camara Laye, The Dark Child (New York: Farrar, Straus and Girous, 1954), pp. 128-129.

[12]J. P. Ociti, African Indigenous Education (Nairobi, Kenya: East African Literature Bureau, 1973), p. 105.

[13]Ibid.

[14]Ibid., p. 56.

[15]Ibid., pp. 63-79.

[16]Ibid., p. 91.

[17]Ibid.

[18]Felix Boateng, "African Traditional Education: A Method of Disseminating Cultural Values," Journal of Black Studies, 3 (1983), pp. 335-336.

[19]Ibid., p. 336.

[20]Cyprian Ekwensi, The Passport of Mallam Ilia (Cambridge University Press, 1966), p. 13.

[21]Ali A. Mazrui, The African Condition (Cambridge University Press, 1980), p. 123.

[22]Ibid.

[23]Ociti, Op. Cit., p. 107.

[24]Chinua Achebe, Things Fall Apart (Heinemann Educational Books Ltd., 1958).

[25]Ociti, Op. Cit., p. 95.

[26]Richard L. Sklar, "Political Science and National Integration - A Radical Approach." The Journal of Modern African Studies, Vol. 5, No. 1 (May 1967), p. 11.

[27]J. R. Hooker, Henry Sylvester Williams - Imperial Pan-Africanist (London: Rex Collins, 1975), p. 21.

CHAPTER THREE
WESTERN EDUCATION IN AFRICA

Writers on colonial education in Africa have tended to distinguish between German, British, French, Phelps-Stokes Commission's Report for 1923 and 1925.[1] The Germans are said to have emphasized vocational training and practical work, knowledge of German language and civilizations and at the initial stages depended heavily on German missionaries.[2] The British encouraged African initiatives, voluntary efforts, used missionaries and put emphasis on agriculture and native 'industrial' development.[3] The French are known to have emphasized the 'universal' use of their French language, agriculture and vocational training for the African masses, while secondary and university levels were to be as academically strong as the metropolitan educational institutions.[4] The Belgian government concentrated on primary education and relied heavily on the missionaries in educating the African Congolese.[5] "The Congo requires a special school system, carefully adapted to the social environment."[6] The African environment was appalling to the Belgian European, and thus the native African teacher, after imbibing European cultural mannerisms, would be a valuable figure in teaching his own brethren whom he knows very well.[7] The educational adaptation philosophy recommended in the Phelps-Stokes Reports also encouraged "adapting education to the African setting."[8]

While it is a valuable academic exercise to make subtle distinctions between the various colonial educational policies in Africa, this chapter concentrates on the general, or the pan-African impact of Western education on Africans. It must therefore be of import to state that the colonialists and missionaries recommended and constructed their systems of education in Africa from their own vantage point of view and no attempt was made to assess the views of the Africans whom the educational institutions were going to affect, for whose interests, presumably, the institutions were being built. It is also important to recognize that some European powers recommended vocational education because they needed skilled African workers to produce for the metropolitan countries; the missionaries needed Christianized African teachers to impart western religions to the African natives, and thus their emphasis on teacher training. It all seems to fall into place with respect to the notion in the 1920's that African nations be guided by their colonial masters to whom they had been entrusted by the mandates of the League of Nations. The European's own sense of his cultural superiority in comparison to that of the African compelled him to dictate the type of education the African should receive. In this context, the impacts of western education on Africans, especially black African peoples, are overwhelmingly similar irrespective of the various colonial policies that were pursued by each of the European colonialists. They were all alien governments desirous of exploiting African resources and spreading their religion and culture; they were all intent on 'civilizing' the African who was perceived as primitive and even uneducable.[9] All the colonial masters emphasized the teaching of their metropolitan languages, history and cultural heroes, and all had negative attitudes towards the African with respect to the latter's perceived culture, civilizations and mental capacity.[10] It is further significant to note that missionary education, educational adaptation, and colonial government's involvement in African education were not distinct in any significant degree, but were part and parcel of the same colonial intent to dominate African peoples ideologically, politically, religiously, economically and psychologically.

European Missionaries in African Education

The Portuguese were the first Europeans known to have established strategic ports on the West African Coast [and the last external colonial power to be out of Africa] and then to other African regions such as East and Central Africa in the late fourteen-hundreds. It was not, however, until the eighteen hundreds that Europeans started penetrating Africa; and by this time, the Portuguese were no longer the only interested European nationals. France had, in the twelfth century, established trading relations with some parts of Northern and Western Africa, but had not erected any permanent settlements as the Portuguese had done.[11] By the 1490's, the Portuguese had established forts in

Mozambique and were interested in joining it with Angola. For an example,

> In 1560 Society of Jesus representatives
> arrived in the East African port of
> Sofala, which was rapidly expanding into
> an important commercial emporium. From
> their coastal base the missionaries fanned
> out into the interior of Mozambique until
> they encountered the Monomotapa empire.
> In 1652, the same year the Dutch arrived
> at the Cape, the King of the Monomapatas
> himself was baptized, these early gains by
> the Portuguese Catholics did not take deep
> root.[12]

By the 1840's the Portuguese were in competition with other Europeans for African converts. In 1844, for instance, Johann Krapf, a German-trained missionary, had established himself at Mombasa after he had been rejected by the Gala tribe whom he found hostile to Christian missionaries. In Mombasa, too, the Arabs were not tolerant to European Christians; they did not want their slaves to find haven in the mission stations.

The missionaries attracted first the outcasts and slaves of the African society;[13] these were then trained to evangelize amongst the reluctant Africans. Porter (1963), Temu (1972), Tasie (1978) describe missionary endeavors in three different regions in Africa that had used outcasts and ex-slaves to perpetuate Christianity. Porter deals with the Creoles in Sierra Leone who had been freed slaves in England, Nova Scotia, and the recalcitrant Maroons of Jamaica, West Indies. Upon their return to Sierra Leone, they took active interest in education. Other recaptured slaves, mainly Nigerians, were added to the small Freetown settlement. But "most of the Negro settlers, with perhaps the exception of the Maroons, had lost their African cultural heritage and had developed new habits to meet the complex situations of the Western World."[14] The Yorubas and other Nigerians who had been captured before reaching the Americas remained Muslims and were reluctant to be Christianized. The educated Creoles, however, became the clerks, teachers and/or preachers and worked for the colonial governments in Nigeria, Gambia, Ghana and as far as the Congo. The Creoles dominated in the legal professions of law, medicine, teaching, preaching and occupied important positions in the colonial administrations and private practice; they soon became representatives of the prestigious status groups in Freetown and beyond. Fourah Bay College, now the University College of Sierra Leone, established in 1827 by the Christ Missionary Society (CMS), was the vehicle used by the Creoles for academic and social upward mobility.

Almost all the 134 degrees awarded by Fourah Bay College between 1878, shortly after its affiliation with Durham University, and 1949 went to Creoles, an important factor in the perpetuation of their economic and political dominance. Outside Freetown, missionaries concentrated their efforts on the Pagan Mende people rather than working among the much more Islamized tribes farther North. In 1938, 80 percent of the missionary schools were among the Mende; not surprisingly this group dominated the police, civil service, and liberal professions in the Protectorate

(the area outside the capital of
Freetown), just as the Creoles dominated
the Freetown area.[15]

The 'Freetown' of Eastern Africa was Freretown, a
mission station about ten miles away from Mombasa. The
Africans who were resettled here were called Bombay
Africans for they had first been resettled in Bombay,
India, and later brought to the Freretown Mission Station near Mombasa. "The second group of settlers to
join the mission station were misfits and exiles from
their own tribal society in the interior...they were
social outcasts..."[16] Freretown Mission Station grew
as more slaves ran away from their Arab masters to seek
refuge. The first act that was done to the refugee
from the interior or the recaptured slave was to bap-
tize him.

> This was the condition the missionaries
> made for residence in their mission sta-
> tions. Baptism for the freed slaves or
> the Africans was not an indication of con-
> version on their part. Most Africans
> agreed to be baptized because they were
> attracted by the material comforts and
> wealth of the missions.[17]

Some Bombay Africans, however, had been long converted to Christianity, and like the Creoles in Western
Africa, they were employed as teachers and catechists
by the mission station. In India, they had

> ...first been trained as Christians. But
> to make them and their families self-
> supporting, the CMS gave them training in
> industrial skills. While some were
> trained as catechists, evangelists and

teachers, others were trained as carpen-
ters, masons and bricklayers; the women
were taught needlework and weaving.[18]

In due course, Freretown became an educational center
for teachers and preachers who became 'missionaries' in
the hinterlands. The missionaries further expanded
their stations and fanned out into the interior especially at the completion of Kenya-Uganda Railroad in
1901. By the nineteen-twenties, there was already much
competition between the various Christian sects who
'battled' over African converts.

The Africans were surprised by the multiplicity of different sects...they could
not understand the cause for antagonism
and rancor between the different sects and
societies. In African eyes they were the
gospel and the difference in doctrine between the missions seemed meaningless and
mystifying.[19]

The competition between the various mission sects for
African converts reached a climax in the nineteen-
twenties and it was soon apparent that some form of
collaboration was necessary. Thus, the Alliance High
School, for instance, was named after the alliance of
the CMS, United Methodist Missionary Society, the
Church of Scotland Mission, etc. for the education of
Africans.[20]

When a mission begins work in a new district in Africa it begins with a school...
The primary object of the education given
is to enable each person to learn for himself and to understand the record, the
character and the teaching of Jesus and

the chief doctrines of historical Christianity.[21]

The school was the nucleus of Christianity and the
emphasis on imparting Western religion undermined
traditional African religions. The Christian converts
in the Niger region, for instance, denounced traditional forms of worship.[22] Some of the converts became
rebellious towards traditional paradigm of viewing the
world and against tribal authority figures. Other converts publicly professed Christianity, but practiced
their African religions privately and at traditional
ceremonies. In Kenya, the converted Africans remained
Christian but continued to practice key traditions that
were denounced by European Christianity.

In East and West Africa alike, Christianity was
first embraced by the runaway slaves and/or outcasted
Africans, and in the case of Ghana, by the mulattos and
the sons of traders and therefore by persons who were
"peripheral to the African traditional society..."[23]
and this included "...the children of African traders,
who were intimately involved with emergent coastal
economy."[24] In Uganda, a large number of the "members
of the royal court"[25] were baptized in 1884;

> The ready acceptance by the Buganda of
> Christianity was due at least partly to
> factors other than Kabaka's political cal-
> culation. One of these was that in
> Buganda, there was 'no firmly entrenched
> ancestry worship to provide a stumbling
> block to the new religions.'[26]

Where Christians faced 'stumbling blocks' such as
an entrenched Arabic presence and a strong traditional

religious group, western education didn't penetrate until the early nineteen-sixties when the African nationalists began to provide mass education.

The African youth educated in the mission schools received religious, agricultural, and 'academic' education, although the former predominated. The language of the missionaries was the most often used as the mode of instruction. There was an "insistence on manual labor"[27] and there was also "strict regimentation"[28] especially in the boarding schools.

> Boarding schools, particularly at the post-primary level, were meant to insure a setting in which students could be inducted into the Christian fellowship without fear of contaminating indigenous influences...nothing was left to chances. Each day's activities were minutely programmed, even including the little 'free' time during which students could indulge only in approved activities.[29]

Tasie (1972) provides a time-table for the Delta Schools in the late eighteen-hundreds (see Table 1). The missionaries concentrated on elementary and teacher education.

> Teaching was oral by the missionary in charge. Gradually literacy was taught to enable the people to read the gospels. Bush schools were opened, led progressively by catechists, catechist-teachers, and then teachers, with little or no training.[30]

42

TABLE 1

A TYPICAL SCHOOL WEEK TIME-TABLE

IN THE DELTA SCHOOLS, 1874

		10-10:40	10:40-11:30	11:30-12	12-1	1-2
Monday	I	Bible Lesson	English Grammar Analysis	Reading		Arithmetic
	II	Collective Lesson	Reading & Spelling	Tables		Languages & Object
Tuesday	I	Dr Watt's Scripture History	Drawing & Geometry	Church Catechism		Writing (Copybook)
	II	Dr Watt's First Catechism	Reading & Spelling	Writing		Lesson & Number
Wednesday	I	Bible Lesson	Historical Reading	Mental Arithmetic	R E C E S S	Geography
	II	Collective Lesson	Reading & Spelling	Writing		Language & Object
Thursday	I	Dr Watt's Scripture History	English Grammar & Parsing	Tables		Arithmetic
	II	Dr Watt's First Catechism	Reading & Spelling	Drawing		Lesson & Number
Friday	I	Explanatory Church Catechism	Reproduction	Reading		Theoretical & Practical
	II	Commandments The Lord's Prayer	Reading & Spelling	Tables		Music

Source of Table 1 G. D. M. Tasie, Christian Missionary Enterprise on the Niger Delta 1864-1918, Leiden: S. J. Brill, 1978, p.241.

The missionaries often learned and translated the major native languages through which, in the initial stages of the encounter, they must try to communicate. The missionary trained teacher was referred to as the teacher-evangelist,[31] or as the "pupil-teacher."[32]

> Pupils were trained specifically for religious propagation. In such a setting the missionary teacher kept school in his premises, and most of the pupils lived with him and formed part of his family.[33]

Table 2 is an example of the time kept by missionary educators in Uganda, East Africa, and the content of their curriculum.[34] The pupil teacher learned on the job while the missionary took the place of the teacher-educator; it was he (the missionary teacher-educator) who had the command of the English or the metropolitan language and was prepared to see the pupil-teacher succeed in imparting new ideas, a new religion, and the concommitant new values and skills to the pupils who were curious and ready to learn. The teacher-educator observed the pupil-teacher on the job and in this way he was in touch with life-classroom problems. In turn, the teacher-educator provided an example, and "example is doubtless an excellent factor in training."[35]

Meanwhile, the African teacher educated by missionaries occupied a valuable social and cultural position; he was usually perceived to be more intelligent than the rest of the natives, and armed with the ability to speak the metropolitan language and his tribal language, and possibly other languages in his locality, he was an intermediary between the European and the African natives. To the Africans he was the source of new ideas, new patterns of livelihood, and one of the few who had 'steady' income, and as such

TABLE 2

KAJUNA CMS STATION: TIME TABLE 1902

Time of Day	Activity
8:00 - 9:00 9:00 - 9:30 9:30 - 10:30	Topclass: Arithmetic Prayers and Class for Children Writing for all classes - pupil-teachers take part
10:30 - 11:30	Special class for pupil-teachers and pastor
11:00 - 1:00 1:30 - 2:00 2:00 - 3:00	Attending to the sick and other matters Special class for teachers and the pastor Pastor takes a general class

Source of Table 2 Asavia Wandira, "Teacher Education for Mass Education in Africa," Teachers College Record (Fall, 1978), p. 78.

45

commanded high prestige, at least in the African community. To the Europeans, the Christianized African
teacher was a necessity; he was needed to administer to
his brethren who were perceived to have more thrust in
their own kind who knew them better. Thus, he could be
used effectively not only as a teacher, evangelist,
catechist, but also as a translator and letter-reader
for the natives; he was therefore a salient agent in
the 'modernization' or 'westernization' of the other
Africans not so opportuned as to have been 'schooled'
or trained. Pontian Walakira describes such a teacher-
catechist in Uganda, East Africa:

> In lieu of the priest there was the
> catechist and his family. The catechist,
> besides being married, and by married I
> mean married in a Catholic Church, was ex-
> pected not only to be more literate than
> the average folks, but also to lead an ex-
> emplary Christian life. The catechist's
> functions, like those of a priest, carried
> with them certain responsibilities and
> status, not to mention influence. The
> catechist, like the chiefs in the system
> of indirect rule, was the person in direct
> and immediate communication with the
> majority of the people.[36]

The African teacher was perhaps the first native
colonial agent in Africa. He was paid to transmit
western cultural values and ideas to his brethren and
was one of the first to be armed with an 'intimate'
knowledge of both the African and the European worlds.
It is not a coincidence therefore that most of the
African nationalist politicians in the nineteen-sixties

had been educators before joining politics.[37] And because there were "similarities which characterized the
educational and evangelical efforts of numerous mission
groups in Africa"[38] there was "uniformity of African
reactions to missionaries attempts at education and
conversion."[39]

> This was the case despite the differing
> national and cultural heritages of the
> missionaries involved, the prevalent
> denominational and political rivalries,
> the various modes of church governance,
> and the different educational oppor-
> tunities offered by the various missions.
> Nor did it matter what type of institution
> the students found themselves in; the
> reactions by those in teacher-training in-
> stitutions, academic secondary schools,
> and seminaries are quite similar.[40]

Colonial Governments' Involvement In African Education

The colonial governments were hardly involved in
the education of the African, which was dominated by
missionaries, until in the early nineteen-twenties.
"By 1910 it was apparent that it would be impossible
for missions to staff and finance the rapidly expanding
educational system..."[41] However, it was not until
after World War I that the colonial governments began
to have determined inputs into African education. The
1923 and 1924 Phelps-Stokes Commissions on education in
Africa Reports for West, East, Central and South Africa
both urged collaboration between the colonial governments and missionary groups for the education of the

47

African.[42]   Both Commissions noted the lack of coordination between the governments and the missions and
saw too much emphasis being placed on book learning;
industrial education, fashioned after that of Tuskegee
Institute and its philosophy of educational adaptation
was commended.   Some of the missions, however, were
reluctant in soliciting grants-in-aid from the colonial
governments for the "...mission experience in West
Africa and elsewhere shows that governments making
grants to mission schools give little and want much."[43]

Nonetheless, from the nineteen-twenties and all
through the nineteen-fifties the colonial governments
and the missionaries worked side by side; the missions
dominating in elementary and teacher education, while
the colonial governments concentrated on liberal and
technical education, for they needed educated Africans
as clerks to fill minor bureaucratic positions within
the colonial framework.   Other interested parties, opting that the African be trained to be an efficient
worker, also had inputs into how the African was to be
educated or trained.   Jessie Jones, the prime author of
the two Phelps-Stokes Commissions' Reports on African
education, observed in the case of East Africa that

> ...the attitude of the missionaries has
> been determined by their religious ideas
> to the native people and to win them to a
> Christian way of life. The government of-
> ficials have naturally thought of the
> colonial administration and have felt the
> necessity for clerical help and such
> skilled workers as are needed for the sur-
> veying of roads and other means of
> transportation. Settlers and traders have
> been concerned for the various needs of

their special occupations. The traders
have joined the government in a demand for
clerks. The settlers' demand has been
primarily for laborers to till the soil
and to carry on the varied activities of
the farm. These diversities of views have
been further intensified by the attitude
taken toward the native people.[44]

The attitude toward the African natives was based
on the ethnocentric belief that Africans were not as
mentally capable as the European settlers. The autochthonous Africans were viewed and treated as inferior
beings physically, socially, culturally and also intellectually. In his nineteen-thirties' studies of the
mental capacity of the African, for instance, Gordon
states that he consistently found the mental capacity
of the African inferior to that of the European[45] and
that this "...consistent inferiority was not only in
brain capacity as estimated by head measurements and in
certain physical attributes, but also in reaction to
mental tests used by the enquiry, although it's not intended that mental tests suitable to the East African
have yet been arrived at."[46] Nonetheless, the tests
were carried out and their results were utilized by
even the highly educated European colonialists who often referred to the child-like ability of the
African.[47] Gordon, wittingly or not, had inherited the
western pseudo-scientific tradition of phrenology which
had been "...first set down by Franz Gall of Vienna
(1757-1828)."[48] The British scientists took over this
tradition and conducted several studies in order to
justify that Africans were not at par with Europeans
and thus to rationalize their actions against the
colonized Africans. "Of course, not everybody in the

field in Britain agreed with these rather pessimistic views of the intellectual potentiality of the black man."[49] Several scholars, including some missionaries, provided contrary data and argument to assert that the African was as intellectually capable as the European,[50] but "the racist scientists were not without their counter-arguments."[51] Thus, Gordon's studies, using the phrenological paradigm simply fell into the category of western racist literature and pseudo-scientific methodology.

Plausibly deriving their views from the western tradition of seeing the African as intellectually, morally, and spiritually deficient, the Phelps-Stokes Commissions clarified educational methods and processes that they saw appropriate for the natives and agreeable to the European settlers in East and South Africa, the colonial government, the missions, and other interested local agencies such as the merchants and agriculturists. Thus, religion, character training and development, health, agricultural and industrial skills, family life and recreation, etc., occupied the minds of the advocates of educational adaptation as appropos curriculum for the Africans' condition which was mainly rural and agricultural in contrast to the largely industrialized Europe and North America. In the view of educational adaptation "education must...leave the African in his natural environment, not uproot him, and the school must not stand in complete contrast to his accustomed life."[52]

Several schools were built around the concept of educational adaptation and some of these schools have been described by Mumford (1926),[53] George (1966),[54] Weatherhead (1914),[55] Scanlon (1964),[56] Jones (1925),[57] Berman (1972),[58] and Yates (1976, 1978).[59] There were a lot of controversies that surrounded the concept of educational adaptation and most of the schools that were based on the concept failed in their attempts to institute a perceived appropriate type of education for the African natives who were from the nineteen-twenties suspicious of any sort of education that was not mostly literary and equivalent to the metropolitan standards. "...education with a rural bias as advocated by the Commission was unacceptable to Africans who now saw that in literary education lay the road to success."[60] In reaction against the implementation of educational adaptation, Azikiwe wrote "How shall we educate the African"[61] in which he suggested that Africans be educated industrially and technically as well as liberally.

The desire for more western education on the part of Africans grew faster after World War One and Two; the large scale economic depression in the 1930's, the effects of the first and second world wars, in which the colonial powers were involved, had taken their toll on the economies of the metropolitan countries and this in turn had effects and retarded the development of westernized African education. However, during the two world wars many African soldiers had fought overseas and had come in contact with new ideas, clearer perspectives about their European colonizers, and had met various groups of people, including lower class Europeans, European women prostitutes,[62] some European intellectuals who did not approve of colonialism and the exploitation of man by man, and other colonized people who were struggling to liberate their lands. Africans then equated education with the liberation of their own countries.[63] That is, the more European

schooling they had, the better they would be in a position to free and govern themselves.

The European colonialists had felt Africans'
desires for more western schools and were by the
nineteen-thirties and forties opting for "mass" education in Africa; the British colonialists, for instance,
opted for the establishment of unitary schools of
higher education,[64] and other European countries followed suit by establishing schools of higher education
in their respective colonies. Technical education had
not been advanced on a large scale even though Fourah
Bay College (1827), Fort Hare (1915), Makerere (1922),
Gordon Memorial College (1924), Achimota (1927), Higher
College, Yaba (1934), and William Ponte (1957) were
providing liberal and technical education on national
as well as on regional basis; these schools, however,
were too few in comparison to the African demands for
more European education, for then and now, in European
education, Africans obtain social mobility and therefore comfortable material life.

The effects of the two world wars on the African
soldiers were numerous; they attained political consciousness and the motivation to liberate their own
lands. Furthermore, they saw the European in his
homeland where some were street sweepers, radicals,
prostitutes and some who were not terribly intelligent.
The soldiers, then, were qualified to judge the
European and to refute his claim of superiority.

The establishment of the United Nations and its
UNESCO organ also removed some of the direct and odious
aspects of the colonialists' domination of some African
countries such as Tanganyika and its cultural affairs
now had an "unbiased" interest group; American interests in African education grew as well. Thus, the

colonial powers were no longer the sole arbiters of Africa's educational policies. In 1957, Ghana attained the status of political independence and by this time African nationalist movements had already begun and a renewed faith in education as an effective tool for the rapid development of Africa was well on its way.

The Reception and Reactions of Africans to Western Education at the Initial Stage of Contact

The missionaries, as has already been stated, laid the foundations for the metropolitan countries to penetrate and balkanize Africa. Nkrumah, in 1957, recognized the great influence European missionaries had on the education of the Africans.[65] Julius Nyerere has also had praise for those "...devoted missionaries and their colleagues, the lay teachers..."[66] who undoubtedly contributed to African education and Africans' enlightenment; some of them even died in Africa.

Although missionary and colonial governments' emphasis in African education differ in terms of curriculum content, they are complementary in many ways including their alienness to the African context. Missionaries propagated their various national languages, national heroes and their ideas and their national governments backed them in these efforts and others.

> ...in countries which had what westerners
> regarded as a high religious culture (like
> Hinduism, Buddhism and Islam), the Chris-
> tian effort was careful and circumspect,
> fearing a backlash from militant religious
> 'Zealots.' But Black Africans were not
> regarded as having at best 'folk' or

'tribal' religions. The missionaries could challenge these without impunities, and the imperial power let them do it, confident that there would be no significant backlash from 'tribal' zealots.[67]

But since the 'tribal' zealots were different, specific African regions, kingdoms, and tribes responded differently to missionary and colonial education at the initial stages of contact between Europeans and Africans with special notation on the dominant idiosyncrasies of the tribal group, kingdom or region. For instance, the presence of European settlers in Kenya meant a different emphasis on certain aspects of European education than those attended to in, say, Uganda. Because of the presence of European farmers and industrialists in Kenya, educational adaptation was directly implemented to produce dedicated workers, not radicalized political aspirants. Furthermore, the British practice of indirect-rule in Nigeria, Ghana, Tanganyika, Sierra Leone, etc. could not, without radical modifications, be implemented in Kenya which had a large European settlement that was politically aspirant. Unlike other countries in Africa, Sierra Leone had a unique colonial educational history; the first university South of the Sahara was built in Sierra Leone and was a recipient of groups of freed slaves who had been 'Christianized' and Europeanized and took vivacious interest in western education as soon as they were settled.[68] They transmitted a thirst for western education to their children and, as teachers, to other Africans as well. Liberia received groups of blacks from the United States who were, having lived in North America for long periods of time, culturally distinct from the African natives; the

Americo-Liberians were the first recipients of western education and their children and their subsequent generations of Americo-Liberians continue to dominate in the educational sphere. For Ghana, Foster has revealed that western education was first embraced by the children of the coastal traders, merchants and mulattos.[69] The early schools were built on the coast and the castles provided education to "...the children born to the European traders and their Ghanian wives..."[70] In the case of Tanganyika under German occupation "the sons of chiefs and headmen received priority."[71] In Kenya and Uganda, the case over who received western education and what type was different;[72] the Kabaka's compound and sons and relations were favored and received education for leadership. In Kenya "it was not until after the first world war, the Kikuyu in any numbers began to accept Christianity, and then it was mainly because they wanted schooling."[73] During World War I many African soldiers "had been called up and had come into contact with new ideas...and generally to prove to those who considered it axiomatic that Africans were inferior to whites in intelligence, that they were wrong."[74] Furthermore, the conflict over the circumcision of African women, which was denounced by the missionaries as incompatible with Christianity compelled some Kikuyu Africans, including teachers, to establish independent Africanized western schools that were Christian and at the same time maintained and practiced some key African traditions, the circumcision of women being one of them. European persistence that African peoples wholeheartedly embrace western Christianity, culture, take up European names and marriage patterns was a way of saying that Africans had no culture of their own. Billingsley aptly puts it this way:

55

> To say that a people have no culture is to say that they have no common history which has shaped them and taught them. And to deny the history of a people is to deny their humanity.[75]

The continued development of Africanized schools in Kenya manifests the humanity of the Africans and their determination to retain some of their cultural idiosyncrasies that have made and taught them. Furthermore, it manifests that the composition of the colonial society mattered with respect to how that community responded to western educational systems. While there was much conflict in Kenya between Europeans and Africans, and between Christianity and some salient African cultural idiosyncrasies such as circumcision of women, dancing, polygamy and other ritualisms, the Toro Africans in Uganda had by and large minimized such conflicts and African Christians had effectively participated in perpetuating Christianity. In addition, the Uganda government had in 1900 made an agreement with European colonizers to restrict landownership to Africans; thus, European settlements were not as highly advanced as in Kenya. The subsequent of this was that "...landlords, the chiefs and industrious peasants, had a source of wealth that made possible the payment of school fees for the education of their children."[76] 'Class' then rather than race seems to be more of a determinant in Uganda than in Kenya in terms of whose children attended school and the type of school. In Kenya major differences existed in economics and types of schools attended by the European settlers and the African especially at the initial stages of contact.

As in Uganda, the class system in Ethiopia was more of a determining factor with respect to whose children received education and the extent of that education. Ethiopian educational history differs from other African countries:

"Education for the children of aristocracy was, as might be expected, more important. Nearly all the great men send their children to convents to learn reading and to repeat the psalms from memory."[77]

Priests and teachers, who were often one and the same, taught their students with cordiality; students followed several stages until they were able "...to compose a whole series of poems every day."[78] Undoubtedly, the Ethiopian orthodox church played the major role in the education of a select segment of the feudal society.[79] There was no mass education and even "...the nobles were usually illiterate and obliged to employ youths educated in the church to look after their correspondence."[80]

By the 1840's a few foreign educated Ethiopians were in government service usually as interpreters. They had received their education individually and not on government expense. "It was...the great modernizing Emperor Menelik who sent ...students abroad at government expense."[81] Emperor Menelik advocated that modern schools be built and foreign teachers hired, but was opposed by the church which had dominated Ethiopian education. Menelik felt that modern or western education would make Ethiopia an equal to developed modernized nations. "The first modern school...was opened by the Emperor in October, 1908."[82] After the Emperor's initiative in establishing western types of schools, "various missionary societies"[83] then began to be active in establishing schools of their own. Emperor Selassie continued in Menelik's direction in terms of encouraging and establishing modern schools, even though comparatively, Ethiopia remains to be one of the most illiterate countries in Africa.

However, Ethiopia's educational history remains different from other African countries where western education was brought without the consent of the African leadership. Even though the Ethiopian church leaders opposed western education at the initial stages, the oppositions were not strong or farsighted and convincing enough to prevent Menelik and Selassie from establishing western schools. Missionary schools were not as many as state schools as was the case in most African countries.

> Missionary education in Ethiopia, unlike that in many other parts of Africa, was restricted to the primary level...the country's sole missionary secondary school had 778 pupils, in contrast to the 7,927 in government secondary schools. In 1962- 63 there were 199 missionary schools, with an enrollment of 30,029 pupils, as against 701 government schools with an enrollment of 212,002.[84]

The same cannot be said for Nigeria, where "...for an example, the missions controlled 99% of the schools and enrolled 97% of the pupils in the country in 1942."[85] With this well established Ethiopian tradition of state schools, it is not surprising that in 1963, Selassie delivered a significant speech in which he expressed his views against foreign education and advocated the establishment of an all-African university.[86]

African reactions and reception of western education went through several stages. The coastal areas where Europeans first built their forts were the first to receive western schools. The capitals of most of the independent African nations were also located on these same coasts. As Europeans began to move inland in the late 1800's, the hinterlands too began to be recipients of western schools. Large cities and industrial or provincial administrative headquarters, other than the capital cities, too began to have schools but always after the point of initial contact has had schools and other modern conveniences such as hospitals, electricity, newspaper, radio stations and television. African reactions toward western education moved, generally, from indifference to curiosity and then "...finally widespread acceptance."[87] African elders were hostile towards European education in the initial stages of contact "...which tended to limit education to station boarding schools for unwanted children and freed slaves."[88] Missionaries often recaptured or 'repurchased' children and adults from slavery into mission schools; they were also successful in attracting some Africans who were by then escaping from the disintegrating, and yet highly confocal African tribal societies. The attraction to books, the written word, the economic and political benefits associated with the man of learning, and possibly recalcitrance in one's desire to be different from and be respected by the community all in concert contributed to Africans' desire for more European education and schools at the latter stages of contact between Europeans and Africans. For other reasons such as to enhance rapid economic development, to integrate and enlighten African societies, to propagate the ideology of African leaders, etc., the 1960's African nationalist politicians implemented mass education in their respective countries.

Western schools are now 'fully' entrenched in Africa and it was mostly after World War II that Africans began to see fully "...that the path of the future was through western education."[89]

Although there are those differences touched on above with respect to African reactions and the various stages that western education took to penetrate and entrench itself in Africa, there are overwhelming similarities as well in the ways the alien school systems affected African societies. Furthermore, even though European colonial educational policies can in general be differently categorized, they do not lend themselves to clear-cut distinctions for several reasons. European countries were themselves similar in their economic and technical development; they brought alien school systems, which are culture bound, into the context of Africa; they came from cultures that had similar religions and beliefs; therefore, in Africans' acceptance of Christianity "there was a meeting of two religions and at the same time a meeting of two cultures."[90] In addition, West European school systems are more similar in structure than they are different, and they came into contact with African systems of education that were also similar. Lastly, irrespective of the "great variations of conditions, attributes and behavior"[91] Negroes or African peoples are seen by the European "throughout the world...as a group, a category, set apart from other peoples..."[92] and it has been increasingly coming into vogue that "Black people have a common history, a common set of relations with the white world, and a common destiny."[93] The European's insistence on putting African peoples into a specific category, a set apart within the macro world gave them the 'courage' to treat African peoples similarly negatively. Thus, European school systems might be different in terms of curriculum content, school organization in the sense of one being central- ized and the other discentralized, one employing in- direct methods, while the other direct approach, etc., but in the final analysis they all came to Africa to conquer, 'civilize' and to make Africans more like the European colonizers themselves in terms of language, marriage patterns, religion, dress, political institu- tions and legal systems.

A Look at the French and British Colonial and Educational Policies-Practice in Africa

Generally, the French, who colonized the most part of Africa, are recorded to have implemented the assimilationist approach in their colonial and educa- tional policies, while the British utilized the accom- modationist strategy.[94] But the concepts of assimila- tion and accommodation are ambiguous, especially when applied to the complex situation of cultural contact between two social and cultural entities that are ever changing. "...assimilation requires Africans to aban- don traditional modes of interaction and analysis, and hence to accommodate to the European mode."[95] The question of what is being assimilated and to what ex- tent that assimilation is taking place comes to mind. For instance, French assimilation policies were not so complete in Algeria for upon Napolean's visit to that country in 1860, he declared that France and Algeria were two different countries and that each must "develop along its own lines"[96] and left the choice for Algerians to be citizens of France, a choice that was

hardly taken up especially by the Islamized Algerians.[97]   This led to the adoption, by mainland
France, of the doctrine of association.[98]   In this
respect, Algerians were not assimilated in the sense of
total absorption into French culture irrespective of
the presence of French cultural institutions such as
schools, churches, boulevards and the French language;
Algerians merely accommodated some of the French institutions they found culturally and politically compatible with the Algerian Zeitgeist.   In the process,
French institutions were not left unaffected by
Algeria's refusal to be part of France, for the policy
of association was subsequently adopted by the French
leadership.   Accommodation seem to be the real
phenomenon when two cultures contact, especially when
both cultures are 'equally' strong.   With the case of
Black Africans, and especially Senegalese, who were
'easily' defeated by the Europeans, Mumford states that
the students at William Ponty school in Senegal were

> French in all but the colour of their
> skin.   They read intelligently and are
> eager to discuss, not only the best known
> writings in French literature, but even
> the works of the lesser-known French
> philosophers. The graduate of the William
> Ponty school is so fine a product that the
> education there given seems a complete
> vindication of French colonial theory and
> practice in Africa.[99]

Thus, French colonial theory and practice educated the
African with little or no modifications, except where
there were strong Islamic influences and large scale
resistance, in the metropolitan curriculum. As soon as
the Black African child entered school he was taught in

62

French by French teachers or by African teachers who
had been prepared on the same curriculum as the French
teachers. As Mumford's observations indicate, French
literature and literary heroes were the ones introduced
to the African as the exemplum of literary excellence;
it was French history and French philosophy that were
taught to Africans. The similarities in the curriculum
of the metropole to that of the colonies stem from the
centralized system of French education and their belief
in extending their ideology of equality that was institutionalized after the French Revolution of the
1790's. The political leaders of that revolution had
specific directives as to the conduct of French
republican education;[100] French schools were not to
deviate from those directions.

Charton (1949) states that French policy under assimilation theory was aimed to educate Africans to become citizens of the metropole and in order to accomplish this feat it was necessary to have Black
Africans go through the same school system, take the
same tests, the same degrees, and thereby minimize the
sharp cultural differences between the French and the
African, and as a result

> Africans learn to French. And this is
> true. The whole system, from the bush
> school to the Lycee has its aim French
> life, French culture, and French citizen-
> ship.[101]

By the 1890's, as has been pointed out in the case
of Algeria, France's colonial policy had been changed
from Assimilation to Association. "Education in as-
sociationist theory sought to combine lessons in French
morality and western technical expertise with as many
references as possible to indigenous culture."[102] It

must, however, be pointed out that the many references that were to be made to indigenous culture were not necessarily positive. A case could be made for this with respect to Ahmed Sekou Toure, the first president of the Republic of Guinea. One could argue that Sekou Toure received three types of education as a youth. In traditional African education he was taught that his great-grandfather, Samori Toure, was a great man and an empire builder. In the Islamic or Koranic school he must have been taught that his great-grandfather, who took the name Alimamy to identify with previous Islamic Mandigo leaders such as Mansa KanKan Musa, Askia Mohammed, Suni Ali Ber, was an Islam and had propagated Islamic religion to Mandigoes and other Africans. In the French colonial school, however, Sekou Toure was taught French civilization, history and about French heroes such as Bonaparte. At this school, Sekou Toure refused to accept European history as was being taught; he saw a marked partiality toward French history and distortions made in the presentation of African history. In the French colonial school, Sekou Toure was one of the brightest and was a voracious reader. He saw that while Bonaparte was being hailed as a hero, his great-grandfather, Alimamy Samori Toure, was being denounced as blood thirsty because he was recalcitrant towards the French in their attempts to colonize Guinea. "Sekou Toure reasoned that if Bonaparte was a hero to the French people, so also must Samori be to the Mandika people, and if Samori was blood thirsty, Bonaparte was even more so."[103]

Sekou Toure's refusal to accept how African and European histories were being taught in the French colonial school brought him into conflict with the school authorities, and this caused him the opportunity

64

to attend Ecole Primarie Superiure, an academically
oriented middle school which would have prepared him to
probably attend William Ponty in Senegal or its equivalent in France. Sekou Toure's elementary school head-
master wrote in the former's school records that Toure
"was an intelligent boy but a danger to France."[104] He
was therefore recommended to study in a technical
school in Conakry where he again came into conflict
with the school authorities and after leading a
foodstrike was expelled from school. Sekou Toure was
never made a Black French man, as Mumford states about
the students in William Ponty school.

Sekou Toure's conflicts with the French colonial
school authorities illustrate that French culture was
the one taught with sympathy whether it was under the
policy of assimilation or association.

The French government's centralized administrative
approach utilized other agencies that were interested
in educating Africans during both policies of assimilation and association. The Catholic Church, for instance, carried out religious education that was not
antagonistic to the French government's ideological
stance on colonialism. The religious schools received
government financial support and were therefore subject
to government supervision and had to abide to the
centralized government standards.

> If France proclaimed as one of her major
> reasons for being in Africa the extension
> of 'civilization,' this could most easily
> be done by those who were themselves part
> of French culture and could extend French
> 'civilization.' National missionaries...
> would have a greater sympathy for the
> political and economic objectives of

France. And while missionaries carried
the 'word of God,' French colonial officials preferred to have the 'word' spoken
in French. Colonial officers in French-
speaking Africa might be personally an-
ticlerical, but ordinarily this did not
blind them to the fact that the French
missionaries were serving France as well
as their religion.[105]

While France's colonial policies in Africa were
centralized in the French government, Britain's was
basically decentralized. That is, while the French
employed direct colonial rule and gave direct instruction in French culture, the British employed indirect
rule, which required adjustments in their implementation in the African context. This is undoubtedly an
oversimplification of the complexities involved in cultural contacts between two different groups of people,
even though most writers on African education have consistently made similar observations.

For the British "formal schooling is not perceived
as a right guaranteed by central government, but rather
as a privilege to be acquired, or a duty to be individually performed."[106] The result of this policy
was that, unlike in the French African colonies where
French Catholics were the only religious denomination
to provide religious education, many more various
religious groups participated in educating Africans in
the British African colonies. These various Christian
denominations in English Africa were often in competition with each other due not only to their varying
ideologies but also in their competition for African
converts and interests in land accumulation. Temu
(1972) states that in Eastern Africa, the various

66

denominations were so much in competition with each
other that the colonial government imposed a three mile
distance between any two different denominations and to
increase this to ten miles if the competition and conflict did not abate.[107] It was not until the nineteen-
twenties that the various sects combined their efforts
to establish the Alliance High School for the education
of Africans from various tribes.[108] By this time, some
Kenyan Africans had formed organizations interested in
providing education for themselves that were not
European missionary or government dominated. These
schools established by Africans were tolerated by the
British government which held that different educational systems under African initiatives were acceptable. This policy was aimed to remove some of the
blatant aspects of British colonial indirect-rule. As
Bertram states:

> Great importance is attached to the educa-
> tive effect of indirect-rule. We have to
> make the native a good African. We should
> not achieve this by destroying his in-
> stitutions and traditions and superimpos-
> ing our alien rule.[109]

The British, therefore, utilized some traditional
African institutions such as the chieftency to administer their colonies. Indirect-rule policy had
first been implemented by Lugard who had served as a
military man in India, and as an administrator in
Uganda and Nigeria he had made use of local chiefs who
already had much influence amongst their people. To
have removed such chiefs would have resulted in large
scale disapproval from the subjects. "The chiefs were
kept happy by retaining the spoils and honour of office, while the colonial regime avoided some of the

odium which attaches to an imposed alien power."[110]
Sir Donald Cameron had worked under Lugard in Nigeria
before he was made governor of Tanganyika which was
then a mandated state under the auspices of the League
of Nations. In Nigeria, "Christian missionaries were
encouraged to open churches and schools in the pagan
areas...while they were discouraged from operating in
the emirates of the Far North."[111] The British
colonial government took upon itself to establish
secular schools in the North that did not compete with
Islamic religion which was popularly practiced in
Northern Nigeria; but as more schools were established
in the South than in the North, an educational gap sub-
sequented between the two regions and therefore between
the two dominant ethnic groups that inhabited the two
regions respectively.[112]

In Tanganyika "Cameron immediately set about introducing a system of indirect-rule, which he called
Local Native Administration,"[113] or as viewed negatively by the European settlers in Eastern Africa, for
it appeared to give much room for local African input -
the West Coast policy. The basic theme in indirect-
rule is to administer Africans as long as possible
through their own institutions and to make sure they
were not radically uprooted from their traditions, with
the aim of their eventual liberation when they mature.
It could be viewed as a paternalistic doctrine that im-
plied that Africans were 'children' and needed guidance
until they were politically mature to govern themselves.[114] Cameron himself recalls that "in 1936 the
Colonial Office Advisory Committee formulated an interesting scheme for the 'Education of African
Communities' designed to make the school in the village
the 'spiritual' centre in improving the conditions in

which the general mass of people live, by a coordination of effort proceeding from the people themselves
and all that is helpful in their own indigenous institutions and customs, as well as the government, the
missions, and other outside sources of inspiration."[115]
The chiefs, through the Native Administration, managed
the schools and the pupils were permitted to maintain
some of their traditional customs such as clothing and
"...their curriculum...permitted them to be readily ab-
sorbed into the life of the tribe when their school
course was completed."[116]

Such schools resulted in British Africa due to
Britain's acceptance of the philosophy of educational
adaptation which was an importation from the Southern
states of the United States of America.[117] The political experience by the British in India, which had its
independence in 1947, could have signalled to the
British the effects of the spread of mass education to
colonial subjects. In the English, as well as in the
French colonies, different types of education were
restricted to different groups of people, especially in
Eastern and Southern Africa where there are large scale
European settlements, and where much more monies were
spent on European education in comparison to the
African natives. Not unlike in Great Britain, the sons
of chiefs received the education for leadership. Furley and Watson (1966), for instance, state that Tabora
School in Tanganyika was built specifically for the
sons of African chiefs; the students received six years
of course work in native government and returned to be
indirect agents for the colonial administration as
paramount chiefs.[118] Government Bo secondary school in
Sierra Leone performed tasks similar to Tabora School

in Tanganyika. In a sense these schools could be compared to their British counterparts such as Eton and
Crossgates that educated members of the future English
ruling classes.[119] The other schools designed for the
African masses were adapted "to the African milieu"[120]
and developed"...a system of rural schools in which
agriculture and practical farming were stressed."[121]

> In both the British and French ter-
> ritories...the division between the educa-
> tion for village children who would leave
> school after a few years and the education
> for those who were selected for formal
> academic training was sharp. For the lat-
> ter, close supervision was maintained
> through the device of examinations given
> at the end of the secondary-school
> course.[122]

This does not mean that the British, or the
French, were oblivious to the importance of higher
education. Kerr (1968) gives a first hand account of
the establishment of Fort Hare which began work in native education in 1915, and was designed to be a school
of higher learning, for the 'non-European' population
and was to be a Christian College.[123] The South
African State, since 1948, has had the uppermost hand
in the 'education' of the various ethnic groups in the
country, which had previously been the main preoccupation of the missionaries. The South African
government's apartheid doctrine has been directly
translated into educational policies. Thus, there are
Bantu and white minority educational systems.[124]
"Before the Bantu education policy, African pupils followed the same secondary programs as white pupils."[125]
Before the Bantu education policies were implemented,

South African missionaries had taken serious efforts in educating the African natives, but they were soon viewed as creating expectations of equality between the African natives and the European settlers. Dr. Verwoerd, who was in 1953 Minister of Native Affairs, reasoned that "if the native in South Africa today in any kind of school in existence is being taught to expect that he will lead his adult life under a policy of equal rights, he is making a big mistake."[126]

In Eastern Africa, Makarere College was by the nineteen-forties, providing higher education for African students from Kenya, Tanganyika, Zanzibar, the Rhodesias and those in Uganda. Fourah Bay College, the present University College of Sierra Leone, was until nineteen-forty-five, the only institution of higher learning in British West Africa where a university degree could be obtained. The earliest graduates of this university were mostly Creoles, a good number of whom became teachers, evangelists, lawyers, colonial administrators, etc., in other parts of West Africa, mainly in Nigeria and the former Gold Coast.[127] As in the case of Fort Hare, Kerr (1968) states that most of the graduates of the South African native college in 1936 became teachers.

In 1945 the Asquith Commission recommended that in the British African territories should be established university colleges that would have special relationships with the University of London similar to Fourah Bay College which had maintained relations with the University of Durham.[128] Okafor (1971) states that the University of Ibadan, started in 1948, could then be considered a full-fledged university and had academic standards equal to metropolitan universities; most of the other Nigerian universities were started in the 1960's.[129]

In the field of higher education, the French concentrated their efforts on the University Institute of Dakar, which was created in 1948 and placed under the supervision of the University of Paris and the University of Bordeaux. The Institute was to serve as an academic center for students from all of French Africa. As late as 1953, however, the Grand Council heard a motion to abolish the institute and send all African students to France for their college education.[130]

The nineteen-fifties found all the colonial powers providing higher education to their colonial subjects. "Aided by the development funds of the various colonies, by the United Nations, and by technical assistance from many countries, African education began to move forward at a rate rarely before equated in the history of education."[131]

The 1960's can be called the years of the proliferation of African universities. It became conspicuously important for each independent African nation to have its own university. Teacher training colleges multiplied and African countries began to accept foreign teachers in large numbers. Education became all too often equated with development and the concept of 'mass education' came into vogue. African politics came to be intensely involved with education; the nationalist politicians began to scrutinize the functions of their universities with respect to the contributions they must make toward health, social, cultural, economic and national developments; national and

72

pan-African integration all became areas that African education must affect.

While African nations were building their own national universities, African countries became further balkanized with the entrenchment of those nationalistic universities. The French had the University College at Dakar that recruited students from other French African countries and thus integrating the French speaking Africans by educating them in one regional school. Makerere College in Uganda had recruited students from the English speaking East African countries as Fourah Bay College had done for much of English speaking West Africa. But when Kenya, Tanzania, Ivory Coast, etc., had their own national universities in the 1960's, the integration of various African students in one centrally located, regional college became less and less; these students could now attend their own national universities and thereby have minimal contact with Africans from other African countries. Emphasis came to be placed on national development, while lip service was paid to larger African student integration. This has been the case since the 1960's; educationally, Africa has been more balkanized after independence than during European colonialism under which regional educational institutions had recruited students from various African countries under the same colonial power. Selassie's 1963 speech about building an all-African university did not, and has not materialized; each African nation has become an island unto itself in the area of education, educational institutions, student body, staff and faculty, and other school personnel.

If African countries are to unite, they must institute common educational institutions that recruit staff, students, and other school personnel from

various African countries. For pan-Africanism to become a reality, pan-African educational institutions
must be institutionalized. The integration of African
students, staff and faculty from various African
countries in all of Africa's schools is only one aspect
of pan-African education; another aspect of pan-African
education deals with the content, curriculum, and practice of education in Africa that are conducive to
larger African integration. Chapter four describes
Educational Adaptation as an aspect of colonial education but also as the root of pan-African education.

Notes

CHAPTER THREE

[1]David Scanlon (ed.), Traditions of African Education (New York, Bureau of Publications: Teachers College, Columbia University, 1964).

[2]Ibid., p. 28.

[3]Ibid., pp. 91-94.

[4]Ibid., p. 118.

[5]Ibid., p. 141.

[6]Ibid., p. 142.

[7]Ibid., p. 145.

[8]Ibid., p. 52.

[9]Charles Lyons, "The Educable African," in M. Battle and Charles H. Lyons (eds.), Essays in the History of African Education (New York: Teachers College Press, Columbia University, 1970), pp. 1-31.

[10]Ibid., see also Gordon D. Morgan, "The Performance of East African Students on an Experimental Battery Test," The Journal of Negro Education, Vol. XXVIII, No. 4 (Fall 1969), pp. 378-383, and H.L. Gordon, "The Mental Capacity of the African," Journal of the African Society, Vol. XXXIII, No. LXXXII (July 1934), pp. 226-242.

[11]W. Bryant Mumford, Africans Learn to be French (New York: Negro Universities Press, 1970), p. 18.

[12]Edward H. Berman (ed.), African Reactions to Missionary Education (New York: Teachers College Press, 1975), pp. 1-2.

[13]Chinua Achebe, Things Fall Apart (Heinemann Educational Books Ltd., 1958).

[14]Arthur T. Porter, Creoledom: A Study of the Development of Freetown Society (London: Oxford University Press, 1963), p. 11.

[15]Berman, Op. Cit., pp. 40-41.

[16]A.J. Temu, British Protestant Missions (London: Longman, 1972), p. 14.

[17]Ibid., p. 15.

[18]Ibid., p. 64.

[19]Ibid., p. 103.

[20]J. Stephen Smith, The History of Alliance High School (Heinemann Educational Books 1973).

[21]Quoted in Temu, Op. Cit., p. 140.

[22]G.O.M. Tasie, Christian Missionary Enterprise in the Niger Delta, 1864-1918 (Leiden: E.J. Brill, 1978), p. 43.

[23]Phillip Foster, Education and Social Change in Ghana (The University of Chicago Press, 1965), p. 45.

[24]Ibid.

[25]Berman, Op. Cit., p. 135.

[26]Ibid., p. 136.

[27]Ibid., p. 207.

[28]Ibid.

[29]Ibid., pp. 206-207.

[30]J. Stephen Smith, Op. Cit., p. 9.

[31]A.F. Ogunsola, "Teacher Education Program in Nigeria," West African Journal of Education, Vol. XIX, No. 2 (June 1975), p. 229.

[32]Asavia Wandira, "Teacher Education for Mass Education in Africa," Teachers College Record, Vol. 81, No. 1 (Fall 1979), p. 78.

[33]Ogunsola, Op. Cit., p. 229.

[34]Wandira, Op. Cit., p. 78.

[35]Quoted in W.E.F. Ward, Fraiser of Trinity and Achimota (New York: Bantam Books, 1963), p. 20.

[36]Berman, Op. Cit., pp. 138-139.

[37]David B. Abernathy, "Teachers in Politics: The Southern Nigerian Case," in Joseph Fisher (ed.), The Social Sciences and the Comparative Study of Educational Systems (Scranton, Pennsylvania: International Textbook Company, 1970), Chapter 10.

[38]Berman, Op. Cit., p. 210.

[39]Ibid., pp. 210-211.

[40]Ibid., p. 211.

[41]David Scanlon (ed.), Church, State and Education in Africa (New York: Teachers College Press, 1966), p. 15.

[42]Thomas Jesse Jones, Education in East Africa: A Study of East, Central and South Africa (New York: Negro Universities Press, 1925).

[43]Ward, Op. Cit., p. 29.

[44]Jones, Op. Cit., p. 7.

[45]H.L. Gordon, "The Mental Capacity of the African," Journal of the African Society, Vol. XXXIII, No. LXXXII (July 1934), pp. 226-242.

[46]Ibid., p. 235.

[47]Lyons, Op. Cit., p. 1-31.

[48]Ibid., p. 5.

[49]Ibid., p. 9.

[50]Ibid., pp. 9-10.

[51]Ibid., p. 11.

[52]O.W. Furley and T. Watson, "Education in Tanganyika Between the Wars: Attempts to Blend Two Cultures," The South Atlantic Quarterly, Vol. LXV, No. 4 (Autumn 1966), p. 476.

[53]Bryant W. Mumford, "Malangali School, "Africa", Vol. 3 (July 1930), pp. 265-290; see also his "Native Schools in Central Africa", Journal of the African Society, Vol. XXVI, No. CI (October 1926), pp. 237-244.

[54]Betty George, Educational Developments in The Congo (Leopoldville) (Washington, D.C.:   U.S. Government Printing Press, 1966).

[55]H.W. Weatherhead, "The Educational Value of Industrial Work as Illustrated in Kings School, Burdo, Uganda", International Review of Missions, No. 3 (April 1914), pp. 343-348.

[56]Scanlon, Traditions of African Education.   (Teachers College Press, 1964).

[57]Jones, Op. Cit.

[58]Edward H. Berman, "Tuskegee-In-Africa", The Journal of Negro Education, Vol. XLI, No. XX (1972), pp. 99-112.

[59]Barbara Yates, "The Triumph and Failure of Vocational Education in Zaire, 1879-1908", Comparative Education Review, Vol. 20 (1976), pp. 193-208, and her "Shifting Goals of Industrial Education in the Congo, 1878-1908", The African Studies Review, Vol. 21, No. 1 (1978), pp. 33-48.

[60]Smith, Op. Cit., p. 12.

[61]Nnamdi Azikiwe, "How Shall We Educate the African?" Journal of the African Society, Vol. 33 (April 1934), pp. 143-151.

[62]Bildad Kaggia, Roots of Freedom, 1921-1962 (Nairobi, Kenya: East African Publishing House, 1975), pp. 44-45.

[63]James Ngugi, Weep Not, Child, (London: Heinemann Educational Books, 1964).

[64]L.J. Lewis, "Education in Africa," The Yearbook of Education (London: Evans Brothers, 1949), p. 369.

[65]Christian Council, Prelude to Ghana: The Churches' Part (Edinburgh: Edinburgh House Press, 1957), p. 1.

[66]Allen J. Cottneid (ed.), Church and Education in Tanzania (Nairobi, Kenya: East African Publishing House, 1976), p. 101.

[67]Mazrui, Op. Cit., p. 51.

[68]Porter, Op. Cit.

[69]Foster, Op. Cit., p. 45.

[70]Nicholas O. Anim, "Ghana," in David Scanlon (ed.), Church, State and Education in Africa (New York: Teachers College Press, 1966), p. 168.

[71]T. Watson, "Education in German East Africa," Makerere Institute of Social Research (1968/69), p. 90.

[72]M.L. Pirouet, "A Comparison of the Response of Three Societies to Christianity (Tero, Teso, KiKuyu)," Makerere Institute of Social Research (1968/69), p. 45.

[73]Ibid.

[74]Ibid.

[75]Andrew Billingsley, Black Families in White America (Englewood Cliffs, New Jersey: Prentice-Hall, Inc., 1968), p. 37.

[76]Sheldon Weeks, Divergence in Educational Developments: The Case of Kenya and Uganda (New York: Teachers College Press, 1967), p. 3.

[77]Richard Pankhurst, "Ethiopia," in Scanlon Church, State, Op. Cit., p. 29.

[78]Ibid., p. 33.

[79]Ibid., p. 34.

[80]Ibid., p. 36.

[81]Ibid., p. 43.

[82]Ibid., p. 45.

[83]Ibid., p. 57.

[84]Ibid.

[85]Ibid.

[86]Haile Selassie, "Towards African Unity," The Journal of Modern African Studies, 1, 3 (1963), pp. 281-291.

[87]Barbara A. Yates, "African Reactions to Education: The Congolese Case," Comparative Education Review, Vol. XV, No. 2 (June 1971), p. 158.

[88]Ibid., p. 159.

[89]Bennett, Op. Cit., p. 183.

[90]Anim, Op. Cit., p. 184.

[91]Billingsley, Op. Cit., p. 6.

[92]Ibid.

[93]Ibid., p. 11.

[94]Remi Clignet, "Inadequacies of the Notion of Assimilation in African Education," The Journal of Modern
African Studies, 8, 3 (1970), p. 426.

[95]Ibid.

[96]Bennett, Op. Cit., p. 129.

[97]Ibid., p. 130.

[98]Ibid., p. 128.

[99]William Bryant Mumford, Africans Learn to be French
(New York: Negro Universities Press, 1970), p. 47.

[100]A. Charton, "French Tropical and Equatorial Africa,"
The Year Book of Education (London: Evans and
Brothers, 1949), pp. 366-379.

[101]Ibid., p. 369.

[102]Sekou Toure, Panaf Great Lives, (London: Panaf
Books, 1978).

[103]Ibid., p. 30.

[104]Ibid.

[105]Scanlon (1966), Op. Cit., p. 12.

[106]Clignet, Op. Cit., p. 430.

[107]Temu, Op. Cit., pp. 102-103.

[108]Smith, Op. Cit.

[109]Anton Bertram, The Colonial Service (Cambridge
University Press, 1930), p. 82.

[110]A.J. Hughes, East Africa: The Search for Unity Kenya, Tanganyika, Uganda, and Zanzibar (Penguin Books Ltd., 1963), p. 30.

[111]David B. Abernathy, "Nigeria," in Scanlon (ed.), Op. Cit., p. 204.

[112]Ibid., p. 206.

[113]Hughes, Op. Cit., p. 51.

[114]J.R. Hooker, Op. Cit., pp. 10-11.

[115]Donald Cameron, My Tanganyika Services and Some Nigerian (London: George Allen & Unwin Ltd., 1939), p. 130. Emphasis mine.

[116]Ibid., p. 131.

[117]Edward H. Berman, "Tuskegee-In-Africa," The Journal of Negro Education, Vol. XLI (1972), pp. 99-122.

[118]Furley and Watson, Op. Cit., pp. 471-490.

[119]Ibid., p. 484.

[120]Scanlon, Op. Cit., p. 8.

[121]Ibid.

[122]Ibid., p. 9.

[123]Alexander Kerr, Forte Hare 1915-1948: The Evolution of an African College (London: C. Hurst and Co., 1968).

[124]A.P. Hunter, "Republic of South Africa," in Scanlon (ed.), Op. Cit., pp. 247-306.

[125]Ibid., p. 282.

[126]Ibid., p. 291.

[127]Porter, Op. Cit., p. 57.

[128]Godfrey N. Brown, "The Development of Universities in Anglo-Phone Africa," West African Journal of Education, Vol. XV, No. 1 (February 1971), p. 42.

[129]Nduka Okafor, The Development of Universities in Nigeria (London: Longman, 1971), pp. 4-5.

[130]Scanlon, Op. Cit., p. 11.

[131]Ibid.

CHAPTER FOUR
EDUCATIONAL ADAPTATION:
THE EUROPEAN COLONIAL FASHION OF PAN-AFRICAN EDUCATION

Educational adaptation, on the surface, seems to be an easily understood concept, but upon closer examination, it could prove a complex phenomenon. At the outset, educational adaptation conveys that educational institutions, as they should, must adapt to the social, cultural, political, and economic zeitgeist of the people they serve. Such a stance can hardly be refuted only if it were the people themselves who are the prime-movers of the philosophy or concept. In the case of Africa, however, it was the colonialist who recommended the type of education Africans and African peoples in the Diaspora should receive. If African peoples are colonial people, as they still are in the significant economic and political cases, it follows that their colonial masters would not educate them to challenge that colonial-colonized relationship. European colonizers were interested in dedicated workers, evangelists, teachers, surveyors, foresters, domestic servants, and other workers to build roads and produce agricultural foodstuffs such as cocoa, tea, coffee, etc., and other tropical crops, but they did not want a set of radicalized Africans who would challenge European hegemony. If Africans are to be rulers of themselves, this stage should come slowly and not violently.

As in the case of the 1984-85 Berlin Conference that Balkanized Africa, no African was the prime-mover of the concept of educational adaptation for Africa. The one African who was used as a token black, Dr. Aggrey of Ghana, was even discriminated against on board ship to Ghana to build Achimota School.[1] He was discriminated against by the very Europeans who were going to build schools in Africa for Africans' interests and by implication, the supposedly selflessness of the European colonizers.

This chapter will concentrate on educational adaptation as conceived by Europeans for Africans; pan-African education under African leadership is discussed in Chapter Nine. Educational adaptation is discussed in this chapter as a pan-African educational system conceived by European colonizers which is quite different from that advocated by African nationalists, and especially the pan-African nationalists such as Nnamdi Azikiwe, Haile Selassie, Kwame Nkrumah, Kenneth Kaunda, Julius Nyerere, Edward Blyden, Case-Hayford, and Ahmed Sekou Toure.

As pan-African politics is the extension of Indigene[2] and Negritude[3] literature, which recognized "...the close relationship between ideology and literary creativity,"[4] so also is pan-African education under African leadership an extension of the philosophy of educational adaptation. Pan-African education could be said to have been first advocated by David Walker in

84

1829;[5] but Mr. Walker was killed and his platform suppressed by European-Americans.

In other colonies where blacks were being oppressed, political upheavals could not be contained as easily as in the case of David Walker. The more the French, for instance, were bent on assimilating Africans, the more the Africans were bent on rejecting the cultural, political, economic, and intellectual domination by the French man. This rejection of France's domination was intellectually challenged in Haitian literature especially as a result of the American occupation of Haiti in 1915 and the return of Jean Price Mars and his founding of the indigene school.[6] The indigene school exposed the hostilities of French administration and culture and hailed the past glories of Africa.[7] The indigene school laid the foundation for Negritude literature that was headed by Aime Cesaire, Leopold Senghor, Rene Maran, Leon Damas, and other French African and West Indian writers.

The English colonial Africans too rejected British economic, cultural and political domination. The British colonials rejection of British domination culminated itself in the political movement for pan-Africanism.[8]

Even though the French are said to be more outright in their attempts to make a French man out of the African, the English colonies were also not without their own Black English men. The late Richard Wright met one such Black English man during his voyage to Africa.[9] K.A. Busia of Ghana, an Oxford sociology graduate, claims to be an English man. In his own words, he states:

> I am a westerner, I was educated in the
> West. Oxford has made me what I am today.

I have had eleven years contact with it
and consider it my second home, most of my
friends are here....[10]

In Eastern Africa, the African who tries to be
European is generally referred to as a Black Muzungu.
Okot P'Bitek has, in his Song of Lawino, dramatized the
aping predicament of the educated African male in his
relations with his 'unschooled' wife.[11] Nyerere so admired Shakespeare's "Julius Ceasar" that he didn't only
translate the play into Swahilli, but also adopted the
name Julius; Obote so admired John Milton's "Pilgrim's
Progress" that he adopted John Milton's last name to
call himself Milton Obote. In French Africa, Senghor
is salient with respect to his mastery of the French
language and his lengthy stays in the metropole.
Indeed, both French and English colonialists were able
to indoctrinate a few Africans to be assimilated into
the metropolitan cultures. Okot P'Bitek[12] and
Chenweizu[13] have literally called this set of educated
Africans 'Apes' in their imitations of the outward
European mannerisms, often superficially. In America,
Franklin Frazier has called such an educated set of
Blacks as the Black Bourgeoisie,[14] especially in their
attempts to employ fantasy of denial which is the
process of attempting to remove themselves away from
their less educated brethren and thus appear to be
oblivious to the problems of the black masses, but at
the same time accepting a place assigned to them in
their relation to the white man.[15]

This small segment of educated Blacks was not too
much of a problem for it could be easily contained and
even worked for the colonial masters in strategic
bureaucratic positions. And since these educated
Africans were not a problem for the colonial masters,

educational adaptation was not for them or their kinds to come, but for the masses of Africans who could not be so contained or predicted. But what of the African masses who did not share the leisures and comforts of the colonizing nations? What was to be done to them? How are they to be educated? These were some of the exigent questions that the United States had to answer as soon as slavery was officially abolished in 1865.

Thus, after "two centuries of bondage"[16] the Negroes were finally 'freed' in the United States, and this meant they could move about 'freely' and could settle in any state of the union of their choice. The newly formed United States, however, was not psychologically, educationally and physically ready to deal with such a large number of freed Africans.

> There were no national, regional, or other large-scale plans for dealing with the ex-slaves. How could they be integrated into the life of the embattered republic as free men? Uncertainty abounded... The Freedman's Bureau, probably the first na-tional social welfare administration, during six short years with severely limited funds, administrative imagination and courage, and in the face of apathy in the North and hostility in the South, strove to feed poor whites, and to estab-lish hospitals and schools.[17]

Even though there was a large number of poor whites alongside the newly freed slaves, the white segment was not considered as much of a problem. "They were poor, but gentlemen - at least they were white."[18] For the newly freed Africans, however, something exigent needed to be done. Some prominent American founding fathers, including Thomas Jefferson and George Washington, had advocated that blacks be sent to a tropical region to which they can naturally acclimatize. Although Benjamin Franklin owned one or two slaves, he was against the large importation of African slaves in the United States on racial grounds. He saw America as basically the purer white nation because Russia, Italy, France, and Sweden could be considered as inhibited by mostly people of non-white complexion. He asked:

> Why should we in the Sight of Superior beings, darken its people? Why increase the Sons of Africa, by planting them in America, where we have so fair an Opportunity, by excluding all Blacks and Tawneys, of excluding the lovely white and red? But perhaps I am partial to the complexion of my country, for such Kind of Partiality is natural to Mankind.[19]

In addition, Franklin saw "almost every slave being by Nature a Thief"[20] and negligent, and to be "negligent is natural to the man who is not to be benefited by his Own Care or Diligence."[21] These attitudes of the American leadership had already been ingrained in the American population by the time of emancipation. The Negro was popularly seen as not diligent, thrifty, clean, dutiful, trustworthy, but viewed as dirty and lazy, etc., and must therefore be thought those qualities he naturally lacked. It is not surprising therefore that

> The students of Hampton, of both sexes, were first taught how to take care of their bodies and how to conduct themselves. A high standard of cleanliness and neatness was established and rigidly

enforced. Then came instruction in some craft, the women being taught domestic duties.[22]

The Europeans emphasized these aspects in Black education because they viewed that these were the qualities most deficient in the African Negro. At the cultural level, educational adaptation meant the educating of African descents in the U.S. and Africans on the continent in a way that will not uproot them mentally and physically from their accustomed rural life. To the colonialists, Africans and African peoples were morally, intellectually and industrially inferior to the European, and must therefore be instructed in religion, work habits and on an 'appropriate' academic study that would ensure the development of the other productive qualities lacking in them.

Booker T. Washington, the founder of Tuskegee Institute, institutionalized and embodied the concept of educational adaptation. He had attended Hampton Institute, founded by General Armstrong shortly after the emancipation of American slaves in 1865 and the subsequent establishment of the Freedman's Bureau that supported Hampton and other Black educational institutions. He had great admiration for Armstrong's educational philosophy of handwork, promptness, and cleanliness. Armstrong had been influenced by his father who had been a missionary in Hawaii and while a youth he had "...had a lingering salvationist faith in the power of proper schooling..."[23] Armstrong's father had not believed in the integration of the native Hawaiians with the European missionaries.

During the Civil War, Samuel Chapman Armstrong had been put in charge of a Black regiment and had attended

Williams College where he studied European theories of industrial education[24] mainly geared to the working classes in Britain. Since the majority of the newly freed slaves were undoubtedly of the working or peasant class, industrial education then was viewed as the most appropriate type of education the ex-slaves should receive. Armstrong "professed that his goal at Hampton Institute was to civilize the blacks, to imbue them with 'general deportment... habits of living and labor... and right ideas of life and duty."[25] Furthermore, "he advised the blacks that if they devoted themselves to labor, they would grow in character and purpose."[26]

The founder of Hampton emphasized the education of the 'head and Heart;' the heart was to be Christianized. He introduced military training that would produce in the male students respect for law and order, punctuality and discipline. "At Hampton, the Three R's were Religion, Respect for Rules and Responsibility."[27]

Washington relates in his autobiography that his test for admittance to Hampton Institute consisted of sweeping a room clean enough to have illustrated diligence.[28] In 1881, Washington 'established' Tuskegee Institute in which his mentor's philosophy of education formed the core. At Tuskegee, "industrial education was prized over academic, at least industrial education should come first because the education of blacks in Arts was out of the reach of most of his race."[29] The economic position of the blacks made it virtually impossible for them to pursue Liberal Arts education which was overly expensive, and since most of them lived in rural areas, there they must work and obtain economic subsistence. This position was supported by industrialists, Northern philanthropic organizations, cooperations, and religious groups; their emphasis was on the education of blacks to work in the rural areas where they must adapt. Some semi-skilled blacks were also needed to work in towns and cities where black women could also be employed as domestic servants. The education blacks received under educational adaptation prepared them for work, not for political agitations, or civic leadership.

Thrasher (1969) includes in his work one of Booker T. Washington's "...Sunday evening talks..."[30] in which he stressed that happiness can be obtained through work and nature. By 1913 Washington had been convinced that Africans on the continent and those in the southern states of U.S.A. were in similar social and political conditions[31] and that "American blacks, like their African Brethren were living in a naturally ordered world..."[32] and such order must not be radically or violently changed.

One of the groups that sympathized with Washington's ideas was the American Missionary Association which had started Hampton Institute. Individual northern philanthropists also contributed financially and by the 1900's more than 1,000 students had enrolled in Tuskegee Institute from more than 25 states and territories.[33] The institute permeated its immediate surroundings by sending teachers into the country-sides and holding farmers' conferences periodically to teach them how to better their crops. "These gatherings became teaching opportunities where farmers were exhorted to better themselves gradually."[34] Washington was not going to advocate a radical political education of the blacks who were surrounded by whites who previously had them in slavery. Indeed,

When the white citizens of Alabama,
charged with the responsibility of selecting a person to head a school for Negroes,
approached the principal of Hampton Institute, he had one name to recommend:
Booker T. Washington. There was opposition to such a school, but Washington
eliminated most of the opposition by as-
suring the whites that the education he
was offering would not lure Negroes from
the farms or spoil them for service in the
white community. He soon had their
support; having made peace with the whites
of Alabama, he was able to tap the
resources of northern philanthropy.[35]

The education that was given under educational
adaptation did not educate, except inadvertently, for
political leadership. The product of educational adaptation was first and foremost a worker who did not
agitate for political participation at the leadership
level. Women were educated mainly in the domestic
sciences and could fulfill other 'feminine' roles such
as nursing, teaching, being a clean and good wife, and
participated in religious and other social and community activities. Furthermore, educational adaptation
philosophy could be categorized as one advocating the
education of the working classes. Blacks were, and
still are in many regions, states and cities in the
United States, working class people or ethnic group.
Coming out of slavery, or Up from Slavery, as Booker T.
Washington's biography is entitled, they were not expected to 'rush' into the political or public sphere.
Washington,

In his celebrated address at the Cotton
States Exposition in Atlanta in 1895, he
placated white supremacists by renouncing
social equality and by urging Negroes to
make friends with the whites and to pursue
careers in 'agriculture, mechanics, in
commerce, in domestic service, and in the
professions'. He called for the intelligent management of farms, ownership of
land, habits of thrift, patience, and per-
severance, and the cultivation of high
morals and good manners.[36]
These were some of the major qualities that whites
viewed Negroes in general lacked, and thus, Negro
education must instill these qualities in the Africans
on the continent and those in the diaspora.

By the beginning of the new century,
Washington was one of the most powerful
men in the United States. Great
philanthropists and industrialists such as
Andrew Carnegie and John D. Rockefeller
listened to him courteously and were influenced by his advice. Presidents such
as Theodore Roosevelt and William Howard
Taft depended on him for suggestions
regarding the resolution of problems in-
volving race. Southern whites in high
places knew that a good word in their behalf by Washington would open doors previously closed to them. If most whites
and many Negroes regarded Washington as
one of the great and gifted leaders of
their time, some Negroes entertained

93

doubts about the validity of his position and the effectiveness of his leadership.[37] Nonetheless, Tuskegee Institute had already had strong interest groups and could not be obliterated. It trained rural teachers and its impact was felt not only in the southern states of U.S.A. but also in Europe and Africa. In Africa, it was regarded as a positive salient example of what a black man could accomplish. Edward Blyden in Liberia was impressed by Tuskegee Institute.[38] The European colonial governments in Africa regarded Tuskegee and the philosophy of educational adaptation as an appropriate system for their colonial subjects who must be educated to live in peace with their colonial masters regardless of their positions as subjects, producers of raw materials for the metropole; and perceived as an intellectually incapacitated people who must be gradually brought up to a position of self-rule. For the Europeans, educational adaptation at Tuskegee could be used as a pertinent tool to train Africans as working class peasants were being educated notably in Great Britain.

Sinclair (1976) likens Washington's educational philosophy for the education of Blacks in America to that which was used in the Charity Schools in England in the late 1800's.[39] These Charity schools were basically interested in the poor in terms of educating them to abate their poverty by giving them industrial education and adequate literary skills. The education they received was not an education for leadership; it was to ameliorate their working class conditions. The lower class members were regarded as intellectually and behaviorally inferior to those attending Eton, Grossgates or Oxford. By 1840 teacher training colleges were

being built to prepare teachers from lower class backgrounds to teach in schools overwhelmingly attended by
students from lower class backgrounds. This was also
the time when the 'hand and eye' theory was in vogue.
"According to the 'hand and eye' theory...the brain
center connected with hand was developed between the
first and fourteenth year."[40] It was therefore imperative not to "neglect...handwork during these
years..."[41] which "might therefore lead to an enduring
underdevelopment of craft skills..."[42]

This European attitude towards their lower class
members as intellectually and behaviorally inferior was
applied to African peoples as a whole and the African's
capacity to learn beyond a certain level was questioned. The lower classes in Europe were construed to
be slower in their intellectual capacities and were
equated to the African natives, especially those with
pure Negro blood and characteristics. In 1865 "the
Reverend Elias Shrenk of the Basil Mission at Chris-
tiansborg Castle felt himself under attack on May 4"[43]
by some prominent members of the British Anthropologi-
cal Society who questioned him about the educability of
the African natives beyond a certain level. Shrenk
equated the lower classes in Britain to Africans with
respect to their "...great slowness in thinking facult-
ings."[44] Shrenk went on to equate the thinking
faculties of African natives to those of European
children by stating: "Here at home, when they are 17,
youths lose sometimes their energy, and you know the
reason of it; but that is much more the case among
Africans, for where there is no moral power, there is
no resistance."[45]

The European missionaries embarked upon the supposedly moral power of their religion with respect to

95

its capacity to elevate and strengthen the African natives; the colonial administrators depended on the pseudo-scientific results of phrenology and determined that the African should receive a special type of education equivalent to that given to European youth from the working classes. Since age 17 seemed to be about the time African natives began to lose their smartness and energy for further learning, similar to the British lower class youth, the methods and philosophy guiding the teaching of the British under-class was implemented in British African colonies.

Thus the philosophy of educational adaptation advocated and practiced for the southern Negroes of the United States of American was compatible to the British colonial masters' philosophy concerned with the educability of their African subjects. Missionaries as well as British government agents "...believed that the African differed from the European in his level of industriousness;"[46] industrial education then was what the African should receive. In concert with the colonial office in London, educational adaptation advocated in the southern states of North America found its way into Africa, especially in those areas under British rule. The Hampton-Tuskegee models gave birth to schools in East, West and Southern Africa.[47]

King (1971) establishes in his well-documented treatise, Pan-Africanism and Education: A Study of Race Philanthropy and Education in the Southern States and East Africa, that the philosophy of educational adaptation was an attempt on the part of American Philanthropic organizations, the London Colonial Office, and the European settlers in the East and Southern Africa to retard the political and social aspirations of the subject people, aspirations which were being advanced by Dubois and members of his school of thought. Lindsay and Harris (1976) state that "...the appropriateness of the Tuskegee industrial educational model was suitable for Kenyan white colonial settlers, the missionaries, the colonial government, as it was for white southern society."[48] It must be recalled that Washington had assured the southern whites of the United States of America that the education that he was giving to the American Negroes would not lure them away from the farms, nor would they challenge European hegemony. If this had worked so well in America, why not transplant it into Africa? It was in the interest of the colonial powers in Africa, as it was in the interest of southern whites in America, "...to relish a philosophy of education and life that stood for Black acquiescence and obedience to the status quo."[49] Students from Tuskegee were sent to Belgian Congo, South Africa, British East Africa, Togo[50] and Liberia.[51]

Northern industrialist philanthropists Rockefeller, Carnegie, Rosewald, Slater, Peabody, and Baldwin, agreed to support the expansion of Negro education at the collegiate and secondary level. It must, however, be built on a pattern that prepared Blacks for their limited roles in society at this stage in their development. This meant for Blacks to avoid social questions, learn to live moral lives, live simply, learn to work and not allow themselves to be educated out of their environment.[52]

Berman (1972) points out that a model of Tuskegee Institute was transplanted into Liberia and that this was done to apply the system of education of the Blacks in the American South to those in Liberia. "...the people in Africa are dependent and black, like those in

97

the southern United States; ergo, the same policy that works so well there should work in Africa."[53]

The Jeanes industrial teacher in Kenya, a product of the philosophy of educational adaptation, taught recreational, health, industrial, and agricultural skills, and his wife was trained in child care and household management skills. The behavior of the Jeanes industrial teacher, his clean home, church and educational activities were to serve as exemplum for the African natives. The Jeanes teacher was viewed as a positive cultural agent for the African natives and was not expected to be a cantankerously political activist. He was, as his American counterpart, to teach the virtues of labor and racial harmony. Educational adaptation philosophy concentrated on the training of African teachers, minor office clerks and other civil servants. To educate American blacks and Africans similarly was good because "racial unity and compromise...would be enhanced through such means."[54]

The enhancement of racial unity in Africa through educational institutions, educational practice and curriculum content is pan-African education; and here then lies the roots of pan-African education, but which was started in the United States of America under the concept of educational adaptation. One of the philanthropic funds that was to perpetuate the philosophy of adapting African education to African countries was the Phelps-Stokes fund which "...had pan-African education at the heart of its work from the very beginning,"[55] and that is to say "the education of Negroes, both in Africa and the United States."[56] Under educational adaptation, African peoples were to be taught to live in peace with their colonizers in Africa and in the United States.

However, Pan-African education promoted by European and American colonialists under the rubric of educational adaptation was rejected by Dubois and other genuine pan-African nationalists as a scheme to mis-educate African peoples. David Walker's Appeal to the Colored Citizens of the World, published in 1829, could be seen as a pioneer for the 1960's pan-African nationalists interested in the relevant education of African peoples. Nnamdi Azikiwe, Caseley-Hayford, Edward Blyden, Haile Selassie, Julius Nyerere, Kenneth Kaunda, Kwame Nkrumah and other African nationalist rejected the premises of educational adaptation especially in its attempts to educate African peoples uniformly and supposedly inferiority. Some Africans rebelled against educational adaptation by saying:

> No longer must Africans be taught to believe that the meek are blessed to inherit the earth when it is too plain that the strong in mind and body are inheriting every inch of the earth's surface. ...The renascent African must believe that for him to survive the struggle of existence, he must now repeat with verve: 'Blessed are the mentally emancipated Africans, for they shall enjoy life more abundantly in Africa.' [57]

Educational adaptation had been particularly set aside for African peoples who were, and are still, viewed as a group of people unlike any other group of people, and extremely different, especially from the European by whom he was enslaved and colonized. Educational adaptation then, was a colonial educational scheme to educate African peoples as workers, meek domestic servants and for other occupations commensurate to their perceived intellectual abilities; its significance for African peoples lies in its attempts to promote unity between Africans. It was repugnant to Pan-African leaders such as Dubois and Nnamdi Azikiwe because of its premise which was based on African people's racial inferiority and their questionable ability for educability. It is not surprising therefore that African nationalists before and during the 1960's were the most vocal in opposing European colonial educational paradigms in Africa including Bantu educational schemes set aside for the natives of Southern Africa.

Notes

CHAPTER FOUR

[1]W.E.F. Ward, _Fraiser of Trinity and Achimota_ (ACCRA, Ghana; Ghana University Press, 1965), p. 29.

[2]Jean Price Mars established the Indigene School of Thought upon his return to Haiti in the 1930's; the object was to praise Africa's glorious past and to denounce French colonialism and all its forms of oppression of African peoples.

[3] Aime Cesaire and Leopold Senghor have been the most acclaimed with respect to their Negritudis ideology, philosophy, or African attitudes towards life.

[4]Selwyn R. Cudjoe, _Resistance and Caribbean Literature_ (Athens, Ohio: Ohio University Press, 1980), p. 126.

[5]Charles M. Wiltse (ed.), _David Walker's Appeal to the Colored Citizens of the World...._ (New York: Hill and Wang, 1965).

[6]Cudjoe, Op. Cit., p. 120.

[7]_Ibid._, pp. 122-123.

[8]Owen Charles Mathurin, _Henry Sylvester Williams and the Origins of the Pan-African Movement, 1869-1911_ (Westport, Connecticut: Greenwood Press, 1976).

[9]Richard Wright, _Black Power: A Record of Reactions in a Land of Pathos_ (Westport, Conn: Greenwood Press Publishers, 1974), pp. 13-17, 228.

[10]Quoted in Bob Fitch and Mary Oppenheiman, _Ghana: End of an Illusion_ (New York: Monthly Review Press, 1966), p. 62, 64.

[11]Okot P'Bitek, _Song of Lawino and Song of Ocol_ (London: Heinemann, 1984), pp. 34-36.

[12]--------, _Africa's Cultural Revolution_ (Nairobi, Kenya: MacMillan Books for Africa, 1973), p. 5.

[13]Chenweizu, "Towards a Liberated African Culture", _East Africa Journal_ (September 1972), p. 20.

[14]Franklin Frazier, Black Bourgeoisie (New York: The Free Press, 1957).

[15]Oliver C. Cox, Introduction to Nathan Hare's, The Black Anglo-Saxons (New York: Marzani and Munsell Publishers, Inc. 1965), p. 8.

[16]Andrew Billingsley, Black Families in White America (Englewood Cliffs, New Jersey: Prentice-Hall, 1968), pp. 69-70.

[17]Ibid.

[18]Giles B. Jackson and Davis Webster, Industrial History of the Negro Race in the United States (New York: Books for Libraries Press, 1971), p. 383.

[19]Thomas Fleming (ed.), Benjamin Franklin: A Biography in His Own Words (New York: Newsweek Book Division, 1972), pp. 105-106.

[20]Ibid., p. 101.

[21]Ibid.

[22]Jackson and Webster, Op. Cit., p. 381.

[23]Donald Spivey, Schooling for the New Slavery: Black Industrial Education, 1868-1915 (Westpoint, Connecticut: Greenwood Press, 1978), p. 11.

[24]Ibid., p. 17.

[25]Ibid., p. 19.

[26]Ibid.

[27]Ibid., p. 28.

[28]Booker T. Washington, Up From Slavery (Bantam Books, 1963), pp. 35-36.

[29]Spivey, Op. Cit., p. 51.

[30]Max Bennett Thrasher, Tuskegee: Its Story and Its Work (New York: Negro University Press, 1969), p. 87.

[31]Booker T. Washington, "David Livingstone and the Negro", International Review of Missions, Vol. 2 (1913), pp. 224-235.

[32]Spivey, Op. Cit., p. 112.

[33]Thrasher, Op. Cit., p. 53.

[34]Ibid., pp. 172-173.

[35]John Hope Franklin, "Introduction" in Three Negro Classics (New York: Avon Books, 1965), p. x.

[36]Ibid., p. xi.

[37]Ibid.

[38]Ibid.

[39]M.E. Sinclair, "Education, Relevance and the Community: A First Look at the History of Attempts to Introduce Productive Work into Primary School Curriculum", in Kenneth King (ed.), Education and Community in Africa (University of Edinburgh: Center of African Studies, 1976, pp. 45-80.

[40]Ibid., p. 49.

[41]Ibid.

[42]Ibid.

[43]Charles Lyons and Vincent M. Battle (eds.), Essays in the History of African Education (Center for Education in Africa, Column University, 19XX), p. 21.

[44]Ibid., p. 22.

[45]Ibid., p. 18.

[46]Ibid.

[47]Edward H. Berman, "Tuskegee-in-Africa", The Journal of Negro Education, Vol. XLI, No. 2 (Spring 1972), pp. 99-112.

[48]Beverly Lindsay and J. John Harris, "A Review of Pan-Africanism and Education", The African Review, Vol. 6, No. 2 (1976), p. 265.

[49]Spivey, Op. Cit., p. 111.

[50]Berman, Op. Cit., p. 99.

[51]Ibid., p. 106.

[52]Ibid., pp. 103-104.

[53]Lindsay and Harris, Op. Cit., p. 226.

[54]Kenneth King, <u>Pan-Africanism: A Study of Race Philanthropy and Education in the Southern States of America and East Africa</u> (London: Oxford University Press, 1971), p. 3.

[55]Ibid.

[56]Ibid.

[57]Nnamdi Azikiwe, <u>Renascent Africa</u>, Frank Cass & Co., Ltd., 1968, p. 81.

CHAPTER FIVE
SOME CRITICISMS OF WESTERN EDUCATION IN AFRICA

1. The earliest missionary schools in Africa were boarding schools; these recruited students from their African environment to one that set them apart from their own people not likewise 'privileged.' The students were required to wear a uniform and to speak mainly in the language of the colonial master. Often, to speak in their tribal languages brought upon them punishments, scorn and disapprovals. Speaking and dressing like their colonial masters, they were thus set apart as new breeds of 'Africans'. And because the school culture was not a progressive continuation of African culture, a cultural gap developed between those who were 'schooled' and those who were not. Okot P'Bitek has effectively dramatized some of the cultural differences between the 'educated' African male and his 'illiterate' African wife, and the general attitude of the former towards the latter:

> Husband, now you despise me
> Now you treat me with spite

And say I have inherited the stupidity
   of my aunt;
Son of the Chief,
Now you compare me
With the rubbish in the rubbish pit,
You say you no longer want me
Because I am like the things left behind
In the deserted homestead.
You insult me
You laugh at me
You say I do not know the letter A
Because 1 have not been to school
And I have not been baptized

My clansmen, I cry
Listen to my voice:
The insults of my man
Are painful beyond bearing.

My husband abuses me together with
   my parents;
He says terrible things about my mother
And I am so ashamed!

He abuses me in English
And he is so arrogant.

He says I am rubbish,
He no longer wants me!
In cruel jokes, he laughs at me,
He says I am primitive
Because I cannot play the guitar,
He says my eyes are dead
And I cannot read,

He says my ears are blocked
And cannot hear a single foreign word,
That I cannot count the coins.

2.   One of the first acts that was done to the
African student in the missionary school was to change
his name; he or she was then baptized and attempts were
made to Christianize him.   Nkrumah was named Francis
and for a while thought of going into priesthood.[2]
Some Africans admired European names and changed or
added the European names to their African ones.   Thus,
Julius Nyerere took Ceasar's first name, while Milton
Obote took John Milton's last name.   'What is there in
a name?' some might ask; but this could be answered
with some questions: why change African names in the
first place?   Are Africans not proud of their African
names?   What we know for certain is that names are important in that they substantiate one's cultural identity and roots.   Black Americans know this very well,
because when they lost their African names, they found
it much more difficult to trace back their exact ethnic
or tribal origins.   Most Black Americans came from West
Africa, but some did come from Mozambique as well.
Kunta Kinte, who steadfastly retained his name, was one
of the keys that Alex Hailey used to search for his
historical roots in Gambia, West Africa.   How much more
had most Black Americans retained their names?
3.   Western education in Africa sharpened
religious-regional ethnic differences based on which
ethnic group first came into contact with Western
schools.   Western education reached Africa hand in hand
with colonial administrators, capitalism and western
religion; the schools were first established on the
coasts, the first point of contact, and gradually found

their way into the interior among Africans considered as pagans. To take the case of Nigeria, for example,

> The missionaries were discouraged and often excluded from Muslim areas in the North by direct governmental policy and the British administration. On the other hand, the missionaries were allowed free play among those who were considered 'pagans'. One result was that the difference between the Hausa in the North and the Ibo in the East was in time no longer simply that one group was Hausa and the other was Ibo. There arose the additional distinction that the Hausa were mainly Muslim and the Ibo mainly Christian. And there was the third distinction that because the Ibo had been more exposed to missionary activity and had therefore gone to missionary schools, they had learned more of the Western educational and verbal skills than the Hausa had done. In terms of those Western skills, the Hausa gradually began to look as they were 'backward' or 'pre-modern'. What this in turn amounts to is a deepening of ethnic consciousness as a result of the impact of Islam among the Hausa and Christianity among the Ibo.[3]

This "...ethnic differentiation in the recruitment into the schools and in the orientations and motivations acquired by students"[4] continue to plague Africa. Those Africans on the coast and who first engaged in market economy with the European continue to dominate in this sector as well as in the educational sphere, for they had the first contact with the European and could afford to 'buy' western education for their children who do not have to leave the city in pursuant of educational institutions; the children of the Northerners, until recently, had to travel long distances to urban areas where the most prestigious educational institutions had been established, and here they face problems of housing, rent and other inconveniences reminiscent of the types European students suffered in the medieval times, where there were numerous letters from students to parents asking for money "to secure...fundamental necessity of student life."[5]

4.   In addition to the sharpening of ethnic differences, western education in Africa "created rigidly stratified societies"[6] in which "groups of intermediate status, such as Creoles, Mulattoes or Asian immigrant communities"[7] remain progressively and recalcitrantly dominant and hand down their economic, occupational and social status positions to their children, relatives and friends, making it extremely difficult for the newcomers to the scene of schooling to make a headway into the school culture, and especially at the university levels. The fact remains that African societies, under colonialism, became "...much more stratified than almost all of the traditional societies of Africa had been before."[8] And western schools are significant institutions that contributed and continue to further stratify African societies, both between and within individual ethnic groups.

5.   Western education has not integrated Africa. In fact it has been used to disintegrate Africa on class as well as on racial lines. With respect to race, the Bantu educational system, from elementary to the university level education in South Africa, offers

a prime example; with respect to class,[9] western education in Africa offers those with college degrees not only economic benefits, political prestige, social as well as psychological security, but also an exaggerated sense of apartness from those not so educated. Those parents who are wealthy buy for their children expensive diplomas from European, American and prestigious African universities, while the masses of 'illiterate' Africans become objects of scorn, shame, ignorance, disease, malnutrition, starvation, and possibly self-hate; the educated African uses his or her diploma, knowingly or unknowingly, to intimidate the uneducated African to, say, vote for him or respect him, at least.

6.   Western education and capitalism in Africa brought Africans into the folds of the world's market economy, international capitalism and consumerism, etc., but to which the majority of the less educated Africans remain peripheral politically and economically; within Africa, this has led to the educated Africans exploiting the 'uneducated' from the standpoint of the better educated Africans consuming much more of Africa's natural resources than the masses of the 'uneducated' Africans.   Okot P'Bitek was undoubtedly angered over such a phenomenon when he stated: "I feel like shouting a revolutionary slogan: uneducated people of Africa unite," and defined "African socialism...as a government of the people by the educated for the educated."[11]

7.   Western schools in Africa "...stressed white values at the expense of directly or indirectly African ones but - partially through design and partially through lack of knowledge and of teaching materials - unfitted Africans for life in their own country."[12]   It

is no wonder therefore that a large segment of the educated Africans live in urban centers which do not
reflect the true nature or developmental state of the
larger Africa, or live in the metropoles in which their
educational attainments have prepared them to live and
feel comfortable.

8.   In colonial western education "emphasis was
on verbal skills which led to a kind of rote learning
hostile to original thinking, and this plagues African
education to this day."[13]   As in traditional African
education, colonial education did not encourage
creativity and deviance in students thought patterns;
it encouraged and rewarded obedience to teacher's
authority and severely punished deviants.   Teachers
gave notes, students memorized and gave back to the
teacher what he had given them.   The teacher too had
taken these notes during his college training days, and
he merely transmits the knowledge as he had received
it.   Because there was and there is still a lack in the
availability of diverse reading materials and other
educative resources, there is a great dependence on
textbooks and teachers for knowledge, and in turn student dependence on memorization of restricted 'facts',
especially if students want to enhance their chances
for upward social mobility.

9.   "Perhaps no aspect of culture is more important in shaping the future of Africa than education,"[14]
but western education in Africa has not been able to
synthesize "the old and the new, the universal and the
uniquely African"[15] so that Africans have not been able
"to live as confident members of the world community."[16] "The African elite, by virtue of the education he has received, has become a Europeanized African
whose cultural values have been misplaced, in terms of

111

African culture, at least."[17] And because his cultural values have been misplaced, he spends a great deal of time not knowing how to genuinely develop Africa. He is not confident in his knowledge base which is a conglomeration of western, eastern and some African ideas which are often incompatible because of the incompatibility of the different societies that produced them. Should the educated African adopt Marxism in a highly religious African society, or should he employ capitalism in a group oriented society, or African socialism in a society that is now aspirantly materialistic? Because the educated African has been inducted superficially into each of this paradigms, he is not confident to definitely apply one without the trappings of the others, and thus there is intellectual, political, emotional, and economic inertia in Africa.

10.   Western education in Africa was much more Euro-centric than Afro-centric. It did not, for instance, teach Africans about the harsh conditions of their brethren in the West Indies and those in the United States of America. To this day some educated Africans subjectively believe that the Black American's inability to take advantage of, say, educational facilities, the economic and political spheres are due to his own failings, rather than that of the mainstream society. Some Africans still have 'no' sympathy towards Black Americans, some of whom were even sold by African chiefs, some tribal authorities, and coastal African capitalists who would rather have bottles of rum, a couple of trinkets, or ammunitions to fight other tribes, than fight against slavery itself. Some African chiefs did indeed fight against the sale of

their brethren, but these were too far powerless to 'terminate' the trade in human flesh.

11. As Africans on the continent were 'miseducated' with respect to the conditions of the Africans in the Diaspora, so also were those in the diaspora miseducated with respect to the Africans on the continent, at least up to the 1960's. With respect to the miseducation of the Black American, Billingsley explains:

> Negroes, under the tutelage of white Americans, have long viewed their African background with a sense of shame. To be called an African when I was growing up in Alabama was much worse than being called a nigger. And, to be called a "black African" was a sign of extreme derision. Later, when I was a student in a Negro college, we were more sophisticated, but we were no less ambivalent about our heritage. The two or three African students on campus were isolated. They were viewed and treated with great disdain, while the two or three white students were the objects of adulation. The African students represented the deep, dark past, while the Caucasians represented the great white hope of the future. In spite of vast changes which have occurred in the world since World War II, with respect to Africa and its place in the world, large numbers of Negroes still feel just a twinge of inferiority associated with their African heritage. How could it be

otherwise, considering the sources of our
knowledge about ourselves and our past?[18]

12. Western education in Africa, and the education of African peoples in the western paradigm (as
Billingsley's observations indicate) tended to concentrate on the negative aspects of African history and
civilizations, but taught the 'juicy' aspects of
European civilizations and culture. Sekou Toure, for
instance, was so angered by the way African heroes were
being denounced by the French colonial educational system that he challenged the school system by asserting
that if Samori Toure was being portrayed as blood
thirsty, Bonaparte was even more so.[19] The Mullah of
Somalia has been recorded as 'mad' because he recalcitrantly opposed the Europeans in their attempts to
subjugate Somalian people by negating their lands.[20]

13. Western education in Africa negated the
African youths not only from their African heroes, but
also from their agrarian background. At school, they
were punished by being sent to dig the school gardens,
pick up rubbish and debris from the school compound, or
brush the football field; these taught African students
that farming or working with hands is a form of punish-
ment, reserved for those who break rules, rather than
as a necessity in a predominantly agrarian society.
Furthermore, the teachers were always dressed as westerners, in ties, and had smooth hands that manifested
the life of leisure; the African student therefore
equated western education with a future life of
leisure.[21] In addition, European colonial administrators, who were often objects of imitation and
superficial emulation, were first and foremost office
workers; the African student therefore saw himself as a
future office worker in a modernized town or city.

14.   Western education in Africa was not for the education of the masses; it concentrated on a small minority who were 'uprooted' from their culture and sent back to teach their African brethren about the superiority of their new master, and the inferiority of the African.   It was the case of "...miseducated individuals graduating, then proceeding to teach and miseducate others."[22]   The mis-educated African minority had been 'schooled' out of their environment and had been taught 'irrelevant' mannerisms, knowledge and skills so far as the genuine development of Africa and African peoples was and is concerned.   Certainly, lawyers, teachers, nurses, dentists, architects, medical doctors, etc., are needed in Africa, but far more needed are Africanized African teachers, nurses, lawyers, dentists, architects, and medical doctors.   An African doctor, for instance, with a concentration in tropical diseases, their prevention and cure, an African teacher inducted into the Afro-centric rather than the Euro-centric paradigm, the African lawyer with an Afro-centric, pan-African outlook, sympathy and empathy, etc., are far more needed in Africa than their Europeanized copies, and far more needed in African universities than they are in western countries which are already highly advanced by anyone's standards.

15.   The process of western education in Africa can be seen as a period of pain and deprivation, especially for the recalcitrant youth in general and the children from the poor-working and the non-working classes.   "Life generally was not at once active, fun and creative"[23] as was abundantly possible in traditional Africa.   These children now had to travel daily long distances to school, experience hunger and study

in crowded rooms or houses with bad lighting conditions, lack of additional reading materials and other
educative modes of learning. They often have to study
for longer hours, in comparison to their western or
westernized counterparts, due to the foreign language,
and because of the teaching and examination modes that
encourage memorization of long passages and
'impossible' formulas, which often fade away after the
examination. The attitude acquired after this long
period of pain and deprivation includes the feeling
that one is now entitled to an adult life of relaxation
and comfort; because one has studied so hard and for so
long, at the end of schooling, one doesn't 'have-to'
study any longer for having supposedly attained the
highest or some recognizable degree of learning by
reading 'numerous' books and passing numerous tests.
The harder and longer it takes to acquire an education,
the more comfort and social authority is expected at
the end of schooling. And there seem to be some truth
in this even from the point of view of the African
parents themselves. The pains and deprivations experienced in the process of schooling are viewed and
internalized as ineluctable because to be comfortable
in the future, one must delay, and not indulge in immediate gratifications. The school fees, provisions
and other school paraphernalia that parents provide are
viewed as investments into the future, for parents too
have come to believe what the African student believes
- the end of schooling has to be a period of relaxation, comfort, and assured employment by the government.

16. Western education in Africa was valued more
for its utilitarian aspects. As in western societies,
it could be used to retain one's inherited social

status and also for the social mobility of those from working classes. Western learning in Africa was, and it still is not an end in itself; reading for the genuine love of books and ideas is quite minimal because Africa is still more of an oral society than a reading one. Those who submit themselves to the pains and deprivations in the process of attaining education are viewed as distinct and negated from the masses; and they use their distinctiveness to gather around them social prestige; sometimes they are too far removed from the masses and are often arrogant in their relations to the 'uneducated' African, even those who are wealthy.

17.   Western education in Africa introduced various grades and types of tests into the African social millieu.   While there was minimal failure in traditional African education, there is maximum failure in western education in Africa.   Western education tested and still tests African children many more times than traditional African education.   From class one through secondary and post secondary education, the African does not only have to pass academic tests, but also social, cultural, and values tests.   His conduct, mannerisms and ways of dressing are tested.   His behavior has to conform to the norms of the European who colonized him.   Sekou Toure was not recommended to attend an academically oriented school because his behavior and intellectual orientations were viewed as "danger to France."[24]   Kwame Nkrumah could not go to Achimota because his grades in his examinations were too low for the school to accept him.[25]   It seems ironic that these men, rejected by western colonial school systems, became great African political and intellectual leaders.

18. The issue of testing in the process of education is a problematic one; in the case of Africa, this is even more so. African societies were not socially stratified as western societies - the poor and wealthy, the slave and the master often interacted without much fuss. With the coming of western education and its ineluctable numerous tests, there were introduced into Africa many more variables on which the individual could be judged. The schools this writer attended in Sierra Leone, West Africa, could be used and could suffice as examples. Examinations were normally given at the end of each term or semester. Failure was publicly announced during assembly where all students and teachers are gathered for the purpose. The student walked up to embrace his failure in public; in the process he acquired a sense of worthlessness, shame and stupidity; the public knew that he failed. Those who pass are likewise publicly called, and they acquire, in the process of walking up to embrace their success, a sense of apartness from those who failed and those unschooled, the 'illiterate' ones in town. Those who pass consistently, acquire, by the end of secondary school, a feeling of superiority to those who failed, and the illiterates. Those who fail are often given the privilege to repeat, that is, to be with those who have been promoted; frequent repetition gives the sense of stupidity and within a few years the whole school knew who was who. Those who cannot bear the shame normally drop out and these are the ones 'crowding' the cities; assured of themselves not to be so humiliated again, they refuse to go back to school or to the farm. Schooling for this group has been nothing but pain, and they are angry and frustrated, and rightly so, for they have been tested by an alien institution whose values

are not primordial in the African society as they know it; and the school has not been radically changed to accommodate them or significant African idiosyncrasies. Those who passed consistently are now the 'rulers' of Africa, and what they've done to improve Africa is there for everyone to see. However, we know that starvation, malnutrition, poor housing and poor sanitation are rampant in Africa more than ever before, and may be more so than in any other country in the world.

19. Western education in Africa has been and it still is male dominated, especially at the post elementary, secondary and at the university levels. Some African cultural traditions attribute to this male dominance, such as the feeling that the educated African woman would be less of a wife. Furthermore, whenever the African female gets pregnant, this most often terminates her schooling. However, as it is generally known, no society, and especially Africa, is going to develop[26] while the African woman, the mother of the tribes and nation is kept 'uneducated' either by design or the lack of it.

20. Western education in Africa introduced and has entrenched French, German, English, Portuguese, Afrikaans in addition to the already polyglotness of the continent.[27] English and French have the majority of Africa, but Swahili in East Africa and Creole in West Africa have a large number of speakers; Arabic is widely spoken in Africa; but the most prestigious languages are the western languages. They are the ones that get one the jobs, political positions, and allow one to keep abreast with contemporary and historical world events. It is true that a good part of African history is in Arabic, but really, is it not the western languages that have entrenched themselves in Africa,

119

that are laden with scientific terminologies? Africa's
borrowed institutional and political concepts of
Democracy, Republicanism, Capitalism, Neo-colonialism,
one-man-one-vote, formal education, marriage, Christianity, Liberty, Apartheid, etc., are all western
derived. East Europeans and Asians have perpetuated in
Africa concepts such as Scientific Socialism, Communism, exploitation of man by man, democratic
centralism, revolution, etc., but Russian and Chinese
languages have not infiltrated Africa. Even though a
large segment of Africa speaks Arabic, Arabic culture
itself is undergoing tremendous transformations having
come head on with western technology and ideas. What
is certain is that French, English, and Portuguese will
continue to be the-language-to-be-spoken for the
majority of Black Africa, and English and French will
continue to be the most popular western languages in
Black Africa; except of course if a super-pan-
Africanist-patriot, linguist, genius is to come to
devise a pan-African language which would be a syn-
thesis of the various Bantu, Semitic, Arabic, Swahili
and western languages currently spoken in Africa; and
this is not an impossibility, because for the revolutionary, genius, linguist, pan-African patriot, the
desire is to have Africa as one Africa by whatever
means necessary.

21. As a general summary of the impact of western
education in Africa, the following lengthy quotation
could suffice:

> In the education of natives the guiding
> principle (was) not always the need of the
> people but the interest of the Colonizing
> Power. The (colonial) government decided
> what (was) to be taught in schools; it

(was) considered natural that the language
of the conquering nation should have the
foremost place in the curriculum; the native language (was) ignored or its use
prohibited in education, and where its use
(was) permitted it (was) done in the
silent hope that finally the European language will become so predominant
throughout the population that the vernacular will sink into insignificance.
The indigenous cultures, most of the social and political institutions, (were)
not given a chance of developing,
but...doomed to extinction under the
weight of Western influences, and even
such as seem able to resist the threatening disruption are deliberately dissolved
to make room for a new order of things
which the European dictates and which is
in conformity with his intentions. When
the political fabric of a tribe has been
destroyed and the tribal ruler with his
own government has been replaced by a
white man or (his chosen) native official,
the people as a living organism is
uprooted, the population changes into a
shapeless mass with no life of its own; it
is dismembered and...become(s) a fit
material in the hands of the European official, who can now shape it according to
his own plans.

But European domination (was) not
absolute; the native (was) given a modest
- and in some colonies also a growing -

share in the administration of his country.[28]

What has happened to African peoples and their cultures under the impact of western educational institutions could also be attributed to the imposed western political, economic, legal, religious, etc., institutions. None of these institutions were sympathetic to African peoples or their ways of doing things; being subject peoples, everything they did or had were also subject to the approval or rejection by the colonial masters; most of what Africans did or had were disapproved or shaped in a way to benefit the European masters more.

22.   Undoubtedly, western education in Africa benefited and still does Africa and some Africans. African leaders such as Nkrumah, Nyerere, Kaunda, etc., have paid tribute to western missionary-colonial education of which they were products, but this didn't blind them to the disruptive effects as well. The beneficial aspects of western education in Africa are numerous, especially from the European point of view, and seem to be far too obvious to require detailed enumeration here. However, the reader also knows to what extent these benefits have helped the majority of the Africans. In a sense, Western education in Africa was, and it still is, like Joseph Conrad's Kutz and Lord Jim in The Heart of Darkness, in which the latter represented good, while the former evil.[29] It must, however, be pointed out that "Both flee Europe to hide in barbarous places, secret and inaccessible; both managed to establish absolute dominion over the natives; both are persecuted by an obscure conscience, which they try to elude; and finally, both rightly belong to the historic moment of pervasive

colonialism."[30] This was made clear in the 1960's when
the African nationalists paid respects due to western
education and domination in Africa, and proceeded to
reject and oust some of their most blatant, negative
aspects.   The African nationalists seemed to believe
that

> The future of the Negro throughout the
> whole Africa lies with the Negro himself.
> No education, however wise, no envision,
> however benevolent, can lead a race to
> full manhood.   The race itself must blaze
> the trail and must decide to follow it.[31]

With this belief, derived from a prolonged domination
by European nationals who basically promoted their own
interests and cultures, the African nationalists in the
1960's and early 1970's demanded independence and established schools and other institutions they felt were
more appropriate and relevant for Africa and African
peoples.

Notes

CHAPTER FIVE

[1]Okot P'Bitek, Song of Lawino and Song of Ocol (London: Heinemann Educational Books, 1984), pp. 13-15.

[2]Kwame Nkrumah, Ghana: Autobiography of Kwame Nkrumah (Thomas Nelson and Sons Ltd., 1957), p. 22.

[3]Ali A. Mazrui, The African Condition (Cambridge University Press, 1980), pp. 99-100.

[4]Remi Clignet, "Education and Ethnicity in Africa", in Pierre L. Vanden Berghe (ed.), Race and Ethnicity in Africa (East African Publishing House, 1970), p. 139.

[5]Charles Homer Haskings, The Rise of Universities (Ithaca, New York: Great Seal Books, 1963), p. 77.

[6]Pierre L. Vanden Berghe, Op. Cit., p. xv.

[7]Ibid., p. xvi.

[8]Ibid.

[9]Ali A. Mazrui, Political Values and the Educated Class in Africa (Berkeley and Los Angeles: University of California Press, 1978).

[10]Okot P'Bitek, Africa's Cultural Revolution (Nairobi, Kenya: MacMillan Books for Africa, 1973), p. 7.

[11]Ibid.

[12]Victor C. Ferkiss, Africa's Search for Identity (New York: George Braziller, Inc., 1966), p. 165.

[13]Ibid.

[14]Ibid., p. 167.

[15]Ibid.

[16]Ibid.

[17]George O. Cox, Education for the Black Race (New York: African Heritage Publishers, 1974), p. 52.

[18]Andrew Billingsley, Black Families in White America (Englewood Cliffs, New Jersey: Prentice-Hall, Inc., 1968), pp. 38-39.
[19]Panaf Great Lives, Sekou Toure (London: Panaf Books, 1978), p. 30.

[20]Douglas James Jardine, The Mad Mullah of Somaliland (New York: Negro Univ Press, 1969).

[21]Ali A. Mazrui, Political Values and the Educated Class in Africa (Berkeley and Los Angeles, California: University of California Press, 1978), p. 222.

[22]Charles H. Wesley and Thelma D. Perry, in their Introduction to Carter Godwin Woodson's, The Mis-Education of the Negro (Washington, D.C.: The Associated Publishers, 1969), p. vii.

[23]Mazrui, Op. Cit., p. 37.

[24]Panaf Great Lives, Sekou Toure, Op. Cit., p. 30.

[25]Nkrumah, Op. Cit., p. 23.

[26]Malcolm X, cited in Robert Staples, The Black Woman in America: Sex, Marriage and the Family (Chicago: Nelson Hall Publishers, 1973), p. 209.

[27]Neville Denny, "Languages and Education in Africa", in John Spencer (ed.), Language in Africa (Cambridge University Press, 1963).

[28]Diedrich Westermann, Africa and Christianity (New York, New York: AMS Press, 1977), pp. 40-41.

[29]Joseph Conrad, The Heart of Darkness (Bletchley, Open University 1974).

[30]Alberto Moravia, "Congo on my Mind", The New York Times Magazine (Part 2, October 7, 1984), p. 70.

[31]Diedrich Westermann, The Africa of Today and Tomorrow (London: Dawsons Pall Mall, 1969), p. 165.

CHAPTER SIX
SOME COMPARISONS OF AFRICAN NATIONALISTS ON
AFRICAN EDUCATION TO AMERICAN NATIONALISTS ON
AMERICAN EDUCATION

We have already alluded, in chapter three, to the
Kenyan African nationalists breaking away from the
colonial missionary educational system which had made
the circumcision of women an improper practice for
African Christians irrespective of the fact that circumcision ceremonies involved other significant African
traditions such as the carrying out of traditional
African education, the emphasis and instilling of group
or age set cohesion, and the attainment of ethnic or
mature identity. The colonial missionary denunciation
of these African cultural practices compelled the
Kenyan African nationalists and teachers, who were bent
on retaining some significant aspects of their African
cultures, to establish their own schools, independent
from missionary and government manipulation, for the
education of their brethren in ways they found appropriate. The African nationalists and teachers had
come to value western education and religion, but they

were going to carry them out in ways they found appropriate for their own concerns and had refused to be dictated to. It was much later on that the missions capitulated and established Alliance High School that recruited students from various tribes and denominations.[1]

Educated Africans on the West Coast such as Nnamdi Azikiwe, James Africanus Horton, Edward Blyden and Casely Hayford had all been interested in African education. They had all along wanted African education to be responsive to African history, culture, economics, intellectual, political and social conditions. They had all wanted Africans to be trained within Africa and African education to be true to Africa's peculiar predicament.

The earliest known of these nationalists was Africanus Horton who was an Ibo born in Sierra Leone as a result of the resettlement of the recaptured slaves in Freetown. Although he was a trained medical doctor, he took great interest in African education and even went to the extent of suggesting to the colonial office that a West African University should be established.[2] He further detailed the courses of study and the teaching method to be employed in his proposed West African University:

> ...It is high time to abolish that system of Lancastrian Schoolboy learning...A professor should be appointed to one or two subjects and should give lectures on the results of extensive reading and research. Lectures should be given in the theory and practice of education, classics, mathematics, natural philosophy,

127

mensuration and bookkeeping, English language and literature, French, German, Hebrew, history in general, mineralogy, physiology, civil and commercial law, drawing and music; besides the various subjects which might be included under the term theology. But the study of physical sciences which are closely connected with our daily wants and conveniences, should form an essential part of the curriculum.[3]

Horton's African University would, of course, be Fourah Bay College and its professors would be classical scholars who would lecture on classical subjects in an African environment. It is however interesting to note that as early as 1868, he was preoccupied with an idea that was to occupy the minds of the later African nationalists such as Azikiwe and Selassie who recommended a similar university for the whole of Africa during and after the formation of the Organization of African Unity.[4]

Although Edward Blyden was not born in West Africa but in St. Thomas West Indies, he nonetheless contributed immensely to African Nationalist thought. He studied the classics of Western thinkers, the Koran, became a teacher, administrator, writer, and professor of Latin and Greek at Liberia College which he proposed should be moved into the interior of the country so that the indigenous Africans would too be incorporated and educated. He was instrumental in introducing the concept of "the African personality" and was a vehement opponent of the practice of sending Africans to Europe for education, where some of them literally die, and where also, in his opinion they learned to imitate European mannerisms and in the process devalue their own racial characteristics; they become, in a sense, inferior copies of the European and are no longer truly Africans. Thus, they become, in general, ineffective in Africa.

Through Blyden's readings of Arabic and European literature, he was convinced that Islam had more favorable attitudes towards the Negro than Christianity.[5] Malcolm X seemed to have experienced a similar predicament when he pilgrimaged to Mecca.[6] Lewis (1971) has, however, not taken too fastidious a stance when he revealed in his Race and Color in Islam, that Arabs, despite their great emphasis on Islam as a fundamental binding religion, discriminated against black African Muslims.[7] Furthermore, Lewis substantiates that Arab Muslims had Black African slaves from Eastern Africa in Iraq and Basra where they numbered up to

> ...Some tens of thousands....lived and worked in conditions of extreme misery. They rose in several successive rebellions, the most important of which lasted fifteen years, from 868 to 883, and for a while offered a serious threat to the Baghdad Caliphate. The leader of these black rebels was a white man.
>
> Even religious groups with what some would nowadays call radical and progressive ideals seem to have accepted the slavery of the black man as natural. Thus in the eleventh century we are told that the Carmathians established a kind of republic in Bahrain, abolished many of the prescriptions regarding persons and property which conventional Islam imposed

- and had a force of thirty thousand black slaves to do the rough work.

A common explanation of this status, among Muslim authors, is that the ancestor of the dark-skinned peoples was Ham, the son of Noah (according to Muslim legend) who was damned black for his sin. The curse of blackness, and with it that of slavery, passed to all the black peoples who are his descendants.[8]

Irrespective of this challenge to Blyden's scholarship, he had great impact on later African scholars and exhibited dedicated interest in African education and nationalism. As Horton had recommended to the Colonial Office opting for a West African University, so also did Blyden suggest to J.P. Hennessy who was in 1869 the governor of Sierra Leone and also to William Grant, a Legislative Council member of Sierra Leone.[9] Blyden believed, as Selassie believed in 1963, that the proper education of Africans within Africa was much more fruitful than education attained abroad,[10] where most likely their racial instincts would be marred.[11] "...if the people are ever to become fit or entrusted with the functions of self-government; if they are ever to become ripe for free and progressive institutions, it must be by a system of education adopted to the exigencies of the country and race; such a system as shall prepare the intelligent youth for the responsibilities which must desolve upon them; and without interfering with their native instincts, and throwing them altogether out of harmony and sympathy with their own countrymen..."[12]

Blyden's call for "The West African University"[13] is reminiscent of George Washington and others who were, in the 1800's, likewise concerned about the negating impact European education might have on the American youth who went to schools in European countries. Washington wanted a national university before he left office; shortly after his term of presidency, he wrote: "my solicitude for the establishment of a national university has been great and increasing; but as the sentiments of the legislature have not been in unison herewith, I had postponed the further consideration of the subject to a moment of more leisure...to see if I could devise some plan by which my wishes could be carried into effect."[14] Thomas Jefferson, Benjamin Rush, and James Monroe all favored the establishment of a national university in the late seventeen-hundreds until the late eighteen-hundreds. The Republican government was new and was under tests for there were Europeans who doubted whether the American system would work. During this crucial time, American leaders found it exigent to form citizens dedicated to the new regime and educational institutions were built to enhance the feat. Benjamin Rush advocated for the establishment of

> ...one federal university under the patronage of Congress, where the youth of all states may be melted...together into one mass of citizens after they have acquired the first principles of knowledge in the colleges of their respective states. Let the law of nature and nations, the common law of our country, the different systems of government, history and everything else connected with the advancement of Republican knowledge and

131

principles be taught by able professors in this university.[15]

Rush and Jefferson and their school of thought realized that a new society needed a new system of education that would enhance it. Jefferson, like Blyden in Africa, was against foreign education on the grounds that such an alien education could undermine the students' nationality or patriotism and could disrupt national cohesiveness. Implicitly, he believed that each nation has its unique national character that is different from each and every other nation.

> Cast your eye over America: Who are the men of most learning, of most eloquence, most beloved by their country and most trusted and promoted by them? They are those who have been educated among them, and whose manners, morals, and habits are perfectly homogeneous with those of the country...the consequences of foreign education are alarming to me as an American.[16]

Benjamin Rush was as Jefferson about the proper education of the American youth. "He must be taught to love his fellow creatures in every part of the world, but he must cherish with a more intense and peculiar affection, the citizens of Pennsylvania and of the United States."[17] Tyack (1966) states that "A pervasive fear of European contamination persuaded the Georgia legislature to pass a law in 1785 disbarring its residents from civic office for as many years as they had studied abroad (if sent overseas under the age of sixteen)."[18] George Washington advocated a federal university so that American youth would not need to go abroad for higher education and run the danger of "contracting

principles unfavorable to republican government."[19]   It
is with such comparative considerations that the cases
of Azikiwe, Hayford, and Blyden in Africa, can be jus-
tified with more clarity for these men were also of
foresight and influenced events in their times considerably as their American counterparts.

Although Blyden's West African University did not
come to fruition, his ideas about an educational institution that would take into account cultural and racial idiosyncracies of the African were not dead or in
moribund.   Hayford, in his 1911 narrative Ethiopia Unbound, picks up the same topic.   Hayford was a personal
friend of Blyden and both men believed in the proper
education of the African.   Like Blyden, Hayford
strongly believed that "The system existing in most
missionary and government schools tends distinctly to
separate those thus educated from their own race."[20]
And that "The African who comes to his brethren with a
red-hot civilization straight from Regent Circus, or
the Boulevards of Paris, and cries anathema to all
Black folk who would not adopt his views or mode of
life, is perhaps, not the man who is, or can be, of
much help in developing African life and African
idiosyncracies along the line of natural and healthy
development."[21]   Hayford took his ideas about African
education along the lines of his predecessors by recommending the establishment of a West African University
which would be a

> ...seat of learning so renowned and at-
> tractive that students from the United
> States, the West Indies, Sierra Leone, and
> Liberia, as well as from Lagos and the
> Gambia, would flock to it.   And they would

come to this Mecca--this alma mater of national conservancy not in top and broad
cloth, but in the sober garb in which the
Romans conquered the material world, and
in which we may conquer the spiritual
world.[22]

Like Blyden, Hayford wanted an African education that
would preserve Africans' Africanness, and their racial
instincts, and would prefer his national university to
be away from the coastal region which in his view has
been corrupted by western influences. He went on to
emphasize that African history, languages, etc., would
be taught in his proposed university with special emphasis on Hausa and Fanti and the part Ethiopia has
played in world history and civilizations.

Hayford's protagonist, Kwamankra, is an intellectual who has influenced "...the thoughts of the nations...due to some extent to the work of the Gold
Coast Nation and Ethiopian Review, promoted by
Kwamankra just before the close of the first ten years
of the century in the interest of the Gold Coast national conservancy; but as time went on it has
broadened out in sympathy to embrace the needs of the
entire race."[23] Hayford in this connection could have
been (foretelling) the advent of Nkrumah in Africa's
continental politics and could also be signalling the
coming of the New African who has been detribalized and
deregionalized. As Ashby (1964) correctly recognized,
"Horton, Blyden, and Hayford were ahead of their
time.[24]

Some of the 1960's African Nationalists on African Education

It was Nnamdi Azikiwe, an Ibo educated in Nigeria and the United States, who returned to the Gold Coast in nineteen-thirty-four and became the editor of the Morning Post. Three years later he returned to Nigeria where he became the first governor-general and was soon the president of Eastern Nigeria.

Azikiwe was not only a journalist and politician, but also had interests in African education. Okafor (1971) states of Azikiwe that his

> ...writings and speeches on educational matters were numerous. His earliest writings were directed toward the 'new' or 'Renascent' African. This African refuses to view his future passively. He is articulate. He is destined to usher forth the New Africa. The philosophy of the New African had five bases: (a) spiritual balance, (b) social regeneration, (c) economic determination, (d) mental emancipation, and (e) national resurgence. Education was specially discussed under the two latter headings.[25]

Azikiwe practically founded the University of Nigeria at Nsukka in 1955

> ...that had no need to be consistent with British traditions of University government nor to be constrained by British colonial policy...One of the aspirations of the founder of the new university was to break away from the British tradition

135

and to adopt some features of the American
Land Grant College.[26]
Although critics opined that the curriculum at Nsukka
lowered academic standards, the college pertinently
responded to the basic needs of the community it served
and it illustrated the founder's views against the
Ivory Tower image of Oxford, Cambridge, and the likes.
It was a bold challenge to the established European
academic tradition in Africa; it challenged not only
the concept of academic standards, but also that of
educational adaptation that had been recommended for
Africans in the 1920's by men like Jesse Jones, Chapman
Armstrong, and the imperialistic colonial governments,
philanthropic and missionary societies from the United
States of America, and the European settlers in East
and South Africa. At Nsukka, Africans adapted education to their needs as they saw them in contrast to
educational adaptation that saw Africa's needs from a
European paradigm or point of view which was
colonialist, imperialistic and derogatory towards
African peoples.

It can be seen that Hayford's emphasis on the new,
self-actualized educated African and the lack of an indigenous African university are echoed in Azikiwe's
writings on African education.

Black Africa has no university. Black
Africa has no intellectual centre where
the raw materials of African humanity may
be reshaped into leaders in all fields of
human endeavor. Why should African youth
depend upon Oxford, Cambridge, Harvard,
Yale, the Sorbonne, Berlin, Heidelberg,
for intellectual growth? These universities are mirrors which reflect their

> particular social idiosyncracies...give
> the Renascent African a University ...and
> this continent can become overnight a con-
> tinent of light.[27]

Although Blyden and Horton's curriculum would follow the classical educational tradition, they nonetheless demonstrate the preoccupation of these concerned
Africans with the proper education of the whole of
Africa. They at least believed that the establishment
of educational institutions based on African
idiosyncracies is a precondition for a new African civilization which would in turn be reflected in the curriculum, teaching methods and eventuate in Africans'
mental emancipation; they saw that continued
Europeanized education in Africa would lead to the
Europeanization of Africans. As Furley and Watson observed about European education in Africa

> ...the purpose of education is to
> Europeanize. Why disguise it? The
> European cannot decide what portions of
> European culture shall be followed by the
> African, so he will choose those for him-
> self.[28]

It is opportune to relate that Furley and Watson
were writing about Tanganyika which later united with
Zanzibar to form the present day Tanzania, the president of which has written "Education for Self-
Reliance." Nyerere became one of the few African
leaders who systematically stated his philosophy of
African education. He reiterated that the education
that was provided the African during colonialism was an
implantation from capitalist societies. Since he was
institutionalizing African socialism, the education
provided towards such a society must be contrary to the

imposed capitalist system.   In his own words,
>   ...the education system introduced into
>   Tanzania by the colonialists was modeled
>   on the British system, but with even
>   heavier emphasis on subservient attitudes
>   on white-collar skills...it was based on
>   the assumptions of a colonialist and
>   capitalist society. It emphasized and en-
>   couraged the individualistic instincts of
>   mankind, instead of his cooperative in-
>   stincts.   It led to the possession of in-
>   dividual material wealth being the major
>   criterion of social merit and worth.[29]

Nyerere goes on to outline the educational system appropriate for Tanzania with particular reference to the
retainment of viable African traditions and the attainment of his proposed African socialism--and in the
process of his exposition he reiterates one of the persistent criticisms of European education in Africa;
namely, that it negates the educated African from his
unschooled brethren in the rural areas and instills in
him the aspirations for white-collar occupations.

>   Mazrui (1978) points out one such criticism:
>   A major complaint against the educational
>   system which black Africa has inherited is
>   that it tends to promote an elite of
>   leisure rather than of labour. The syl-
>   labus is often geared toward the pursuits
>   of leisurely class, and the attitude at
>   the end tends to promote expectations of
>   white-collar work and minimal office
>   hours.[30]

This is so even though most Africans live on the land.
Hanson (1980) has reviewed research dealing with middle

and secondary school leavers in most of the African countries south of the Sahara. Although the school leavers' move to urban areas is not absolutely dependent on the education he has received, but due in part to the unmechanized farming methods and therefore low productivity in the rural areas, he states that "their dreams of urban employment die hard."[31] Table 3 illustrates the occupational inclination of secondary school students cited in Hanson, and it must be noted that all the occupations listed are those that must be held by an "educated" individual removed from actually working the land.

In the cultural sphere Ferron (1975) studied the preference for various subjects amongst secondary school children in Freetown and found that subjects such as African music, art, and handicrafts were not as popular as English grammar, English literature, and composition, because "probably more than anything else, these children want to become proficient in English, because in such proficiency they perceive that they have the key to their future success in life."[32] It is therefore the case that the African wants to "master the tools by which he had been colonized, the yardstick by which he looked deprived."[33] The colonialist's language, was by the 1960's in Africa, a powerful educational weapon which could be used for social mobility. Despite the nationalists' rejection of the political domination of Africa, West European languages were used to even argue for African independence. School children, all over Africa opted for mass instruction in their ex-master's language. Some African countries such as Kenya and Tanzania introduced Swahili as vernacular, Nigeria and other West African countries established "education in the Mother Tongue."[34] But frankly, anything short of the metropolitan language was regarded with some suspicion added to the fact that the students were now urged to be polyglots formally, in addition to the long length of time the study of multiple languages in school entailed. Adeyubobi (1977) found among Western Nigerian state students a high preference for English language as a subject taught in the schools; although the researcher was mainly concerned with differentiation based on sex, both boys and girls demonstrated a high preference for English language and English literature over history, geography, - and Yoruba was, among the boys at least, the last choice.[35] History was not the most popular choice among all the students because of the nature of its teaching[36] and Adeyubobi recommends that the subject be taught by specialist teachers who have been trained in the method of teaching history so as to promote critical thinking and better understanding of men and events.[37] Certainly, the critical teaching of African history in African schools cannot in anyway be over emphasized and the promotion of critical thinking and analysis of world events and men of ideas cannot be deemphasized either.

TABLE 3

OCCUPATIONAL INCLINATION OF SECONDARY SCHOOL STUDENTS

Occupation	Mean Score	% Inclined to Accept
1. Agricultural Officer	4.4	89.7
2. Modern Farmer	4.2	83.0
3. Agricultural Assistant	4.1	81.9
4. Large-Scale Farm Manager	3.9	75.7
5. Veterinary Officer	4.0	75.0
6. Research Assistant	3.9	70.4
. . . .		
9. Engineer	3.8	67.8
10. Medical Doctor	3.7	62.0

Source of Table 3:   Hanson (1980), p. 23.

What the above examples illustrate is that despite the loud criticisms of African nationalists against foreign education, before they took over their balkanized nations, Europe had already had strong cultural roots in Africa that could not be simply swept aside; the predominating influence of European curriculum in African schools and its effects on Africans, which culminates in their negation from their own traditions and cultures, can today be observed in African countries.   Of course, the literate, in a predominantly 'illiterate' society is bound to stand atop of those considered illiterate, and as Levine (1978) has observed, literacy creates "...in the individual an expanded awareness of environmental variation, alternative possibilities, and potentialities for

141

choice - an awareness that raises doubts about tradition and increases receptability to new forms of social participation."[38] But what good would the persistent negation of the African youth from his 'roots' be in the interest of Africans and Africa as a whole?

In another study dealing with cultural subjects Morgan (1969) concluded that the "...students in the school did not know much about their own culture."[39] Morgan had chosen cultural facts such as novels, African cultural agents, the names of tribes, etc., from various African countries and regions and the students were to draw analogies. The fifth item in the test was for students to choose the correct answer from (Morgan p. 382):

Shakespeare: Hamlet: Achebe: --

A) Mine Boy
B) Things Fall Apart
C) Harambee
D) Chief Luthuli

The students were to draw analogies for fifty-one such questions; the results of Morgan's study are presented in Table 4.

Recently, some writers have been wholly concerned about what African education and teacher education need to accomplish (Selassie, 1963, Mazrui, 1971; Tembo, 1978; Chinwezu, 1972; Brown, 1966; Wandira, 1970; Brickman, 1963, Jones, 1925). As early as 1925, Jesse Jones, the main author of the two Phelps-Stokes reports on education in Africa observed that African education

...proceded along lines too narrow and stereotyped to lay a sound foundation for African enlightenment. There was too much indigestible 'book-learning' and not enough training in self-help...A native

> youth was far more likely to know the
> names of Henry VIII's wives and the date
> of the Battle of Hastings than to have any
> inkling of the laws of plant nutri-
> tion...the principles of heredity on which
> the grading-up of flocks and herbs is
> based. He might know the names of the
> capital cities of Europe but be quite ig-
> norant of crafts such as carpentry or
> building or shoemaking.[40]

Jones and the Commission's concern was with the inap-
propriateness of Western education for African conditions although some African writers have criticized his
proposals that African countries adopt the Hampton-
Tuskegee model. Azikiwe (1934) states that educational
adaptation

> ...conceives the African as better adapted
> to industrial and agricultural pur-
> suits...In other words, so long as the
> African would be content at menial tasks,
> or would not seek complete social, politi-
> cal, and economic equality with the west-
> ern world, he is deemed to be a 'good'
> fellow.[41]

It can be recalled that Washington (1913) had recommended the Tuskegee model for African countries for he
viewed that the blacks in the southern states of North
America were in a similar economic and social position
as those in Africa and therefore the latter needed
similar education.[42] Furthermore, the educational concerns of Nyerere, Azikiwe, Blyden, Horton, etc., can
now be appreciatively understood in relation to their
denunciations of European influences in African educa-

tion, concerns which are not radically different from those of the American founding fathers.

TABLE 4

PERFORMANCE OF MAKERERE SCHOOL STUDENTS ON 51 ANALOGIES

Per Cent Right	Student Frequency
70-79	3
60-69	8
50-59	14
40-49	23
30-39	6
20-29	5
0-20	0

Source of Table 4: Morgan (1969), p. 382.

Until the nationalist movement in the 1960's, African educational ideas were largely 'supplied' from western countries. Britain had in the nineteen-forties and fifties attempted to implement mass education in her colonies to satisfy the rising demand by Africans for more education. In 1944, for instance, Britain's emphasis was on community development through regional universities and/or colleges that would maintain close collaboration with British universities; the other colonial powers such as France and Belgium all drew plans for the modernization or development of their dependencies.[43] At the end of World War II UN's UNESCO, the United States of America, and African ministers of education were all active participants and interest

144

groups in African education. Berman (1979) has done a thorough, but controversial study on United States' involvement in African education from nineteen-forty-five up to nineteen-seventy-five.[44] He isolates the involvement of major foundations such as Ford, Rockefeller, and Carnegie and relates these to major American educational institutions such as Columbia University and

> ...the Washington policy makers regarding the importance of the developing world for the United States...The first of the foundation programs in Africa involved the creation of lead universities in areas considered important to the United States.[45]

Those countries that were geographically, politically, and economically strategic were identified and were given support to establish universities that would train African personnel who would not be revolutionary but evolutionary and at the same time have positive attitudes and preference for American form of government. Nigeria, Zaire, and Ethiopia were identified and institutions in these countries were financially supported "...to enable a generation of Africans to accept the superiority of the Western-oriented, democratic-capitalist development model over its socialist counterpart."[46] This arrangement supported key African universities and brought sponsored African students to the participating American universities; in African universities emphasis was placed on social science research, teacher education and public administration programs. With respect to teacher education "the purpose of the program was to train African teacher-educators at Teachers College, to prepare Americans desirous of teaching in Africa at Teachers College and at the University of London's Institute of Education, and to allow Teachers College and by extension United States pedagogical principles and values to gain entry into the evolving network of teacher-training institutions in previously British Africa."[47] This is reminiscent of Dr. Frederic Fox's teaching methods and his exhibition of American values to his African students while he was a teacher in a Rhodesian African writing school. He gave a writing assignment to his students and one of them wrote this way:

> Our teacher, Dr. Fox, was more American
> than Christian, and more fox than either.
> He kept talking about 'America this...and
> America that...Nearly all his illustra-
> tions were from U.S.A., and he handed out
> a lot of propaganda. He was proud of his
> country that he got a big flag to hang on
> the wall of his room. None of us had
> flags in our rooms, except Harry Kwale.
> We had only photographs of our families.[48]

In the nineteen-sixties many African countries found it exigent to import American, British, and teachers from other western countries. Irrespective of Berman's implication that America's great interest in African education from nineteen-forty-five was a neo-colonialist move, Pifer (1979), Sutton (1979), and Stifel (1979), representing Carnegie, Ford, and Rock-efeller foundations respectively, have all criticized Berman's exposition as polemic and based on pre-conceived assumptions such as to think that American interests necessarily mean the subjugation of Africa interest.[49] It is nonetheless important to note that one of the major purposes of American Peace Corps in

146

Africa was to instill American ideas into the minds of Africans.[50] Explicitly, the Peace Corps themselves confess:

> communists could build a dam in Egypt as well as Americans can, or they could erect a good hospital in India or housing projects in Borneo or send a super highway across the Sahara. But with time, these things rot. Man's minds do not, and the ideas which are instilled into one generation grow larger in the next, even larger in the next.[51]

However, African interests in providing mass education for Africa had already started in the nineteen-fifties, and in nineteen-sixty-one between the fifteenth and twenty-fifth of May, an educational conference representing thirty-one African countries convened in Addis Ababa, Ethiopia; this was the first time that so many African ministers of education had met to discuss common educational problems; concerns about African education had been dealt with by Europeans on national and/or regional levels. The meeting of these ministers of education and some interested bodies brought to light some of Africa's common educational problems, and strategies to deal with them were surfaced. Brickman (1963) writing from extensive experience and interest in African education states that "The Addis Ababa report revealed that only 0.2 per cent of all Africans of university age were attending higher institutions of learning"[52] at the time of the 1961 Addis Ababa conference. Kilson (1961) provides data in Table 5 to show that Africa south of the Sahara, excluding the Union of South Africa, had too few universities and minimal enrollments to handle any major development project without outside aid.[53]

TABLE 5

UNIVERSITIES IN AFRICA 1960

State	Universities	Year Founded	No. Students	No. Staff
Algeria	University of Algiers	1879	6,027	308
Basutoland	University College of Pius XII	1945	170	37
Congo (ex-Belgian)	Lovanium University	1954	485	116
	State University, Elizabethville	1956	141	53
Egypt	University of Al-Azhar	970	3,798	—
	Cairo University	1980	27,000	1,380
	American University of Cairo	1919	732	65
	Alexandria University	1942	11,000	435
	Ain Shams University	1950	22,912	582
	University of Assiut	1957		
Ethiopia	University College of Arts and Sciences (Addis Ababa)	1950	426	96
Ghana	University College of Ghana	1948	671(61)	143
	Kumasi College of Technology	1951	800(61)	81

148

TABLE 5 Continued

State	Universities	Year Founded	No. Students	No. Staff
Kenya	Royal Technical College	1955	250	
Liberia	University of Liberia	1951	750	73
Libya	University of Libya	1956	728(61)	76
Malagasy	Institute of Higher Studies	1955	862(59)	-
Morocco	University of Tabat	1957	3,686	82
	Qaraouine University	859	2,086	-
Nigeria	University College, Ibadan	1948	1,136(61)	308
	University of Nigeria, Nsukka	1960	300(61)	15
	Nigerian College of Arts, Science, and Technology	1948	1,200	120
Senegal	University of Dakar	1957	1,398(61)	66
Sierra Leone	University College of Sierra Leone (formerly Fourah Bay College, Est. 1827)	1960	302	77

TABLE 5 Continued

State	Universities	Year Founded	No. Students	No. Staff
South Africa	(Total of 13 Universities)		33,884	3,072
Southern Rhodesia	University College of Rhodesia and Nyasaland	1955	232	63
Sudan	University of Khartoum (formerly Gordon Memorial College, Est. 1902)	1956	1,000	140
Tunisia	University of Tunisia (Incorporating the Institute of Higher Studies, Est. 1945)	1960	2,495(61)	-
	Zitouna University	-	881	-
Uganda	University College of East Africa (Makerere) (originally established as a secondary school in 1921)	1950	912(61)	170 (61)

Source of Table 5: Martin L. Kilson, "Trends in Higher Education," in Africa and the United States: Images and Realities, Boston: 8th National Conference, U.S. National Commission for UNESCO, 1961, pp. 63-64.

The education of women, adults, rural development, teacher education, the building of more elementary, secondary, laboratories, and teacher education institutions, the diffusion of technical and vocational education, the production of more suitable textbooks, etc., were some of the numerous topics that were brought to light during the Addis Ababa conference.

> The Addis Ababa Report indicates that one country would need to train 20,000 teachers in the next twenty years in order to achieve its goal of universal primary education by 1980. The teacher shortage is especially acute in the technical and agricultural fields in the secondary schools.[54]

Although Makerere, Fourah Bay College, Fort Hare, and other colleges had been preparing teachers, Africa needed more well-trained educators to man the newer schools that were aiming towards universal primary education: thirty per cent of which would receive secondary education, and twenty per cent of the secondary school graduates were projected to receive higher education.[55] These targets have not been met by most African countries and "in the meantime, some of the trained teachers are being attracted away to the commercial positions, and the foreign service, with the resultant gaps in teaching staffs in the schools of various countries."[56]

There have been persistent problems plaguing African education since this 1961 Addis Ababa Conference plausibly because of the fact that the projections were not based on research findings, but often on the opinions and enthusiasms of the ministers and other educational experts. However, it was obvious that

there was a shortage of qualified teachers as well as
an imbalance of educational opportunities between
elementary and secondary school enrollments, between
rural and urban areas and there was the inequality in
the access to formal and higher educational institutions, shortage of finance, difficulties in Africanizing the teaching force and school curriculum, and the
lack of a clear definition of what African educational
institutions can and should accomplish. The most
'academic' of these problems seem to relate to the concept of Africanizing the school curriculum.

There are arguments for and against an
Africanized curriculum. From the standpoint of modern ethnology and human relations, it would seem most logical, pedagogical, and diplomatic to stress the languages, the traditions, and the continent
which are closest to the African people.
On the other hand, there are many Africans
who fear that such a curriculum will, in
effect, isolate or segregate them from the
mainstream of European and world culture.[57]

On the practical side of the problems with African
education since 1961, Balogh (1962) has criticized the
Addis Ababa Conference's recommendations; his views are
that massive and rapid education would impede rather
than hasten African development. For instance, the
Conference recommended that each African nation use
five per cent of its national income towards education
which is to be doubled and tripled in the near future.[58] This sort of mass education would require
large scale industrialization so as to absorb school
graduates at various grade levels, but most African

152

countries are still agricultural and rural and we have
seen that education increases one's expectations beyond
the traditional ways of doing things.[59]

Several other conferences have been held about
African education under the leadership of UNESCO such
as the April 1962 African Ministers of Education Conference held in Paris which was also attended by representatives from most African countries and European observers from France, Belgium, Spain and the United
Kingdom.[60] On the whole, these subsequent conferences
have used the 1961 Addis Ababa Conference as a
springboard. However, the 1961 landmark conference illustrates a practical Pan-African movement in African
education. The Conference stressed the need for
African countries to coordinate their educational
policies, programs, research findings, and regional
educational projects; it remains the first conference
in which so many African ministers of education met to
discuss their educational problems and recommend
measures for mass education. The failure to accomplish
the targets that were set does not minimize the significance of the Conference in any consideration of
Pan-African education. Since that Conference, various
writers have written about African education and the
functions of an African University with a Pan-African
perspective.

Just to take a few examples, Wandira (1977) states
that

> The true African university cannot live
> within national boundaries only. It must
> accept a responsibility to pursue re-
> search, disseminate knowledge and take all
> other necessary action to emancipate the
> African continent from the prevailing

shackles of ignorance, artificial isola-
tion, colonialism and barriers due to language and cultural separation. The
university must equally re-discover Africa
and reinforce her image in the modern
world, thus identifying itself with and
promoting the ideals of the Organization
of African Unity, continental rapproche-
ment and international understanding.[61]

In 1963, the year that the Organization of African
Unity was formed, Selassie made a speech that carried
on the tradition of Africans' desire to have a common
university that would be responsive to the political,
cultural, social, and academic concerns of Africa.[62]
Edward Blyden, Africanus Horton, Casely Hayford, as
have been pointed out, were interested in a West
African University. Nnamdi Azikiwe carried his educational concerns further by including in his scheme of
an African University for all of Black Africa.
Selassie (1963) goes much further by recommending an
all-African University specifically for the realization, promotion, and maintenance of a United Africa.[63]
In his words,

> In no small measure, the handicaps under
> which we labour derive from the low educa-
> tional level attained by our peoples and
> from their lack of knowledge of their fel-
> low Africans. Education abroad is at best
> an unsatisfactory substitute for education
> at home. A massive effort must be
> launched in the educational and cultural
> field which will not only raise the level
> of literacy and provide a cadres of
> skilled and trained technicians requisite

to our growth and development but, as
well, acquaint us one with another...
Serious consideration should be given to
the establishment of an African University, sponsored by all African states
where future leaders of Africa will be
trained in an atmosphere of continental
brotherhood. In this African institution...African life would be emphasized
and study would be directed toward the ultimate goal of complete African unity.[64]

In retrospect, Selassie's concern is not radically different from that of Thomas Jefferson, who in 1785 was
against American students largely receiving their
education in Europe where they could contract
ideologies contrary to the Republican form of government. He states that in his view

...the medical class of students...is the
only one which need come to Europe. To
enumerate (all the reasons) would take a
volume. I will select a few. If he goes
to England he learns drinking, horse-
racing, and boxing. These are the
peculiarities of English education...he
acquires a fondness for European luxury
and dissipation and contempt for the
simplicity of his own country; he is fas-
cinated with the privileges of the
European aristocrats ...he contracts a
partiality for aristocracy or monarchy
...[65]

In a similar vein, Blyden and other African
nationalists have been cautious about the large influx

of African students into European institutions of higher learning.

Although Nkrumah was not against the sending of African students to the West, at least at the initial stages of Ghana's independence for he sent a lot of Ghanaians abroad especially to pursue technical education, however, he translated African unity to mean the dissolution of the balkanized predicament that the African countries inherited; he advocated the ease of movement of Africans from one African country into another with special privileges given to students.[66] He demonstrated his ideology of African unity by symbolically dissolving the boundary between Ghana and Togo[67] and was instrumental in establishing the Guinea-Ghana-Mali Union.[68] It was idiomatic with him to say that the independence of Ghana was meaningless in the face of other African countries still under colonialism, and for him, African unity was "an article of faith" and lastly that Africa must seek first a political kingdom and all else will follow. Even though his political kingdom has not been realized, he influenced the thoughts of many African leaders and scholars immensely.

Brown (1966) has made statements directly related to Pan-Africanism and how this should influence, or be reflected in African education; he complains that

> ...the pattern of education today tends still to be that of Europe, a Europe which practiced colonialism. We look forward to a free and united Africa whilst giving our children an essentially European-type education, which has contributed to the national divisions of Europe and has cut

156

the continent of Africa up as though it were a cake.[69]

Lightfoote-Wilson (1969) comes closest to the classroom teacher in his article "Teaching for National Development." Although he deals basically with the "nation" as opposed to a federated, confederated, or Africa in a union government, his nation, however, "implies a conjoined people" and he believes that teachers employing appropriate teaching methods can contribute in imparting the nation's values, norms, and ideologies to the students for "...teachers interact with the largest number of new comers to the newly evolving norms of a nation and they must conceive and exhibit the desired egalitarian and pluralistic norms if these norms are to become the 'realities' which are osmotically and deliberately transmitted to the students--the next generation."[70] Mazrui (1971) has also taken the nationalistic approach but has implications for African countries in general; he states that African education and teachers should contribute to national integration and that this is significant, for African countries are multi-racial, cultural, and multi-tribal.[71]

Finally, Wandira (1970) has consistently related the philosophy of Pan-Africanism to African teacher education. She believes that African

> ...education has a major role to play in
> the building of societies in Africa--that
> education is an instrument of change and
> development. It must follow that ques-
> tions of social and economic development,
> love and brotherhood of man, communication
> between peoples and continental identity
> which loom so large in minds of leaders in

157

Africa, must find their place in Africa's scheme of teacher education. In fact the discovery of what is African in education and then offering this to the rest of the world, the identification of solutions to Africa's educational problems--all these would become part of the profile of teacher education in Africa.[72]

Indeed, it is this predominant concern with education, teacher education, Pan-Africanism, and how the first two can contribute to the realization of the third that have given the impetus to the writing of this book.

The next chapter will deal with mass education and some of the problems in political, economic, and educational institutional arguments for Pan-Africanism; integration theories as presented by European and African theorists, political socialization and the contributions that educational institutions and teachers can make to enhance larger African unity are also examined.

Notes

CHAPTER SIX

[1]Stephen J. Smith, The History of Alliance High Schools (London: Heinemann Educational Books, 1973)

[2]James Africanus Horton, West African Countries and Peoples (Edinburgh University Press, 1969), p. 183.

[3]Ibid., pp. 183-184.

[4]Haile Selassie, "Towards African Unity", The Journal of Modern African Studies, Vol. 1, No. 3 (1963), pp. 281-291; see also Nnamdi Azikiwe, Renascent Africa (London: Frank Cass and Co. Ltd., 1968), pp. 134-140.

[5]Edward Wylmot Blyden, Christianity, Islam and the Negro Race (London: 1888).

[6]Alex Hailey, The Autobiography of Malcolm X (New York: Ballantine Books, 1973).

[7]Bernard Lewis, Race and Color in Islam (New York: Harper & Row Publishers, 1971).

[8]Ibid., pp. 66-67.

[9]Hollis R. Lynch (ed.), Black Spokesman: Selected Published Writings of Edward Wylmot Blyden (London: Frank Cass and Co. Ltd., 1971), pp. 223-225.

[10]Selassie, Op. Cit., pp. 281-291.

[11]Lynch (ed.), Op. Cit., p. 223.

[12]Ibid.

[13]Ibid.

[14]Quoted in Albert Castel, "The Founding Fathers and Vision of a National University", History of Education Quarterly, Vol. IV, No. 4 (December 1964), p. 287.

[15]Quoted in Hyman Kuritz, "Benjamin Rush: His Theory of Republican Education", History of Education Quarterly, Vol. VII, No. 4 (Winter 1967), p. 440.

[16]Quoted in David Tyack, "Forming the National Character", Harvard Educational Review, Vol. 36, No. 1 (1966), p. 32.

[17]Ibid., p. 34.

[18]Ibid., p. 32.

[19]Ibid.

[20]J.E. Casely Hayford, Ethiopia Unbound (London: Frank Cass and Co., 1969), p. 196.

[21]Ibid., p. 184.

[22]Ibid., pp. 96-97.

[23]Ibid., p. 207.

[24]Eric Ashby, African Universities and Western Tradition (Cambridge, Massachusetts: Harvard University Press, 1964), p. 15.

[25]Nduka Okafor, The Development of Universities in Nigeria (Longman, 1971), p. 42.

[26]Ibid.

[27]Nnamdi Azikiwe, Renascent Africa (Lagos, 1968), p. 144.

[28]O.W. Furley and T. Watson, "Education in Tanganyika Between the Wars: Attempts to Blend Two Cultures," The South Atlantic Journal, Vol. LXV, No. 4 (Autumn 1966), p. 486.

[29]Julius K. Nyerere, "Education for Self-Reliance," in Knud Eric Svendsen and Merese Teisen (eds.), Self-Reliant Tanzania (Dar es Salaam, 1969), pp. 220-221.

[30]Ali A. Mazrui, Political Values and the Educated Class in Africa (Los Angeles: University of California Press, 1978), p. 222.

[31]John W. Hanson, Is the School the Enemy of the Farm: The African Experience (East Lansing: Michigan State University, 1980), pp. 23-24.

[32]O.M. Ferron, "Curriculum Interests of Secondary School Children in Freetown," West African Journal of Education (February 1975), p. 14.

[33]Robert A Levine, "Western Schools in Non-Western Societies: Psychological Impact and Cultural Response," Teachers College Record, Vol. 79, No. 4 (May 1978), p. 749.

[34]Ayo Bamgbose (ed.), Mother Tongue Education: The West African Experience (London: Hodder and Stoughton, 1976).

[35]S.A. Adeyubobi, "An Investigation into the Subject Preference of Students in Western State of Nigeria Grammar Schools with Stress on Differentiated Interest Between Boys and Girls," West African Journal of Education, Vol. XX, No. 2 (June 1976), p. 262.

[36]Ibid., p. 259.

[37]Ibid., p. 266.

[38]Robert A. Levine, Op. Cit., p. 749.

[39]Gordon D. Morgan, "The Performance of East African Students on an Experimental Battery Test," The Journal of Negro Education, Vol. XXXVII, No. 4 (Fall 1969), p. 382.

[40]Thomas Jesse Jones, Education in East Africa: A Study of East, Central and South Africa (New York: Negro Universities Press, 1925), p. 40.

[41]Nnamdi Azikiwe, "How Shall We Educate the African?", Journal of the African Society, Vol. 33 (April 1934), p. 140.

[42]Booker T. Washington, "David Livingstone and the Negro," International Review of Missions, Vol. 2 (1913), pp. 224-235.

[43]L.J. Lewis, "Education in Africa," The Yearbook of Education (London: Evans Brothers, 1949), pp. 312-337.

[44]Edward H. Berman, "Foundations, United States Foreign Policy, and African Education, 1945-1975," Harvard Educational Review, Vol. 49, No. 2 (May 1979), pp. 146-179.

[45]Ibid., p. 155.

[46]Ibid., p. 154.

[47]Ibid., p. 166.

[48]Federick Fox, 14 Africans Vs. One American (New York: The MacMillan Co., 1961), pp. 164-165.

[49]"Responses to Edward H. Berman," Harvard Educational Review, Vol. 49, No. 2 (May 1979), pp. 180-184.

[50]Glenn D. Kittler, The Peace Corps (New York: Paperback Library, Inc., 1963), p. 122.

[51]Ibid.

[52]William Brickman, "Tendencies in African Education," The Educational Forum, Vol. XXVII, No. 4 (May 1963), p. 401.

[53]Martin L. Kilson, "Trends in Higher Education," in Africa and the United States: Images and Realities (Boston, Massachusetts: 8th National Conference, U.S. National Commission for UNESCO, 1961), pp. 63-64.

[54]Brickman, Op. Cit., p. 403.

[55]Ibid., p. 405.

[56]Ibid., p. 403.

[57]Ibid., p. 405.

[58]T. Balogh, "Catastrophe in Africa: UNESCO's Colonial Style Plan," The Times Educational Supplement (January 5, 1962), p. 8.

[59]Robert A. Levine, "Western Schools in Non-Western Societies: Psychological Impact and Cultural Response," Teachers College Record, Vol. 79, No. 4 (May 1978), pp. 749-755.

[60]Conference Reports, "Goals of Educational Developments in Africa," School and Society (October 20, 1962), pp. 379-381.

[61]Asavia Wandira, "The Special Tasks and Problems of the 'One-Country-One-University' Institution in Middle Africa," in Hendrik W. Van Der Merwe and David Welsh (eds.), The Future of the University in Southern Africa (Claremont, Cape, South Africa: David Philip, Publishers Ltd., 1977), p. 85.

[62]Haile Selassie, "Towards African Unity," The Journal of Modern African Studies, 1, 3 (1963), pp. 281-291.

[63] Ibid., p. 288.

[64] Ibid.

[65] Julian P. Boyd (ed.), The Papers of Thomas Jefferson, Vol. 8 (New Jersey: Princeton University Press, 1953), p. 636.

[66] Cited in Colin Legum, Pan-Africanism: A Short Political Guide (London: Pall Mall Press, 1962), p. 249.

[67] Immanuel Wallerstein, "Background to Paga-I," West Africa (July 29, 1961), p. 819, see also "End of an African Frontier," West Africa (July 8, 1961), p. 751.

[68] Claude E. Welch, Jr., Dream of Unity: Pan-Africanism and Political Unification in West Africa (Ithaca, New York: Cornell University Press, 1966), pp. 295-316.

[69] G.N. Brown, "Education for Responsibilty: The Teacher's Role," West African Journal of Education, Vol. 2 (June 1966), pp. 65-66.

[70] Thomasyne Lightfoot-Wilson, "Teaching for National Development," West African Journal of Education, Vol. XII, No. 3 (October 1969), pp. 145-146.

[71] Ali A. Mazrui, "The Educational Implications of National Goals and Political Values in Africa," Education in Eastern Africa, Vol. 2, No. 1 (1970), p. 38.

[72] Asavia Wandira, "Foundation Studies in Teacher Education in Africa," Education in Eastern Africa, Vol. 1, No. 1 (1970), p. 14.

CHAPTER SEVEN
MASS EDUCATION IN AFRICA AND SOME RELATED ARGUMENTS
FOR LARGER AFRICAN INTEGRATION

Although education has been emphasized in Africa
for many centuries, even before the advent of the
modern European educational institutions, the 1960's
presented, unprecedentedly, significant problems for
African leaders and educators. There was so much faith
placed in education that schools multiplied on the continent and they were charged with the duty to actively
participate in solving monumental problems, inadequacies, deficiencies, etc. that were perceived to
have held Africa down. Education was to provide
qualified manpower to propel economic development, social, technical, cultural, and political advancements.
Teachers were to be rapidly produced to man the
schools; women and adults were to receive education;
universal primary education was to be provided in each
African country; universities were to change their curricula so that they met national development plans; the
rural areas were to be attended to and in certain
countries they assumed priority. In addition to these

concerns about educational diffusion, there were also
questions about relevant education; that is, what
should be the purpose of African education? It was
clear that African education should contribute to
economic, social, cultural, and political developments
and also enhance national and Pan-African integration.
More teacher education institutions and more qualified
teachers were, however, needed to accomplish the
developmental plans; problems of staffing the educational institutions became concerns as well.

African Teacher Education

The story of African teacher education is intricately tied to the pioneer endeavors of the missionary
presence in Africa. During this initial encounter

> Teaching was oral by the missionary in
> charge. Gradually, literacy was taught to
> enable people to read the Gospels. Bush
> schools were opened, led progressively by
> Catechists, Catechist-teachers, and then
> teachers with little or no training.[1]

The missionaries concentrated on elementary education
and the training of elementary school teachers. The
colonial powers were hardly involved in teacher education until the 1920's and 1930's when collaboration between missions and governments was urged by the Phelps-
Stokes Commission from the United States of America.
Teachers during the missionary and colonial periods
were considered intellectuals in spite of their low
levels of education in comparison to contemporary
trends. In an illiterate environment, however, anyone
who could read and write was considered an academician.
Teachers were much more than teachers in the sense that

165

they also were interpreters, "letter readers,"[2] and writers, missionaries, intermediaries between the Western and the African Worlds. They were therefore accorded much respect and high status by the rest of the society. Teaching was a popular vocation because it was one of the only earlier and easier means by which Africans could enter the European world and at the same time be able to teach their brethren how to read, write, interpret news, and understand the Bible. It's no wonder then that most of the 1960's nationalist leaders were once classroom teachers. An epitome among the 1960's African nationalists is President Julius Nyerere of Tanzania who is often referred to as Mwalimu, the Swahili term for teacher. Kenneth Kuanda of Zambia, Kwame Nkrumah of Ghana, Arap Moi of Kenya, etc., were all teachers before they became leaders in their respective countries. Unlike the United States where the earliest nationalist leaders came from the military and the profession of law, the majority of the 1960's African leadership had been educators. African teachers should be proud to know that members of their profession have contributed immensely to advancements in African politics, academics, national as well as attempts at Pan-African integration.

In spite of the teaching background of most of the key nationalist leaders and their recognizance of the importance of teacher education, African teachers experienced low status during the 1960's. Teachers were no longer the only interpreters of news, the carriers of new ideas, or one of the only few groups who received 'steady' income. The 1960's opened up other positions, such as in the bureaucracy or private enterprise, which employed African high school or college graduates. These newer job opportunities offered better salaries and provided better chances for promotion. The general diffusion of literacy connoted that there were other sources of knowledge which the teacher at one time monopolized. Some political aspirants among the teaching profession opted out of the classroom to become ministers or representatives in their respective districts or countries. Abernathy (1970) provides data for the case of Southern Nigeria and other African countries in which most of the legislatures had been either school teachers or administrators as Tables 6, 7 and 8 demonstrate.

TABLE 6

TEACHERS IN NIGERIAN LEGISLATURES, PERCENT

	Headmaster or Principal	Teacher	Total
Eastern Region			
House of Assembly, 1952	24	15	39
House of Assembly, 1953	24	4	28
House of Assembly, 1957			28
House of Assembly, 1961			34
House of Representatives, 1951	30	15	45
House of Representatives, 1954	20	8	28
House of Representatives, 1959			36
Western Region			
House of Assembly, 1952	24	5	29
House of Assembly, 1956	27	6	33
House of Representatives, 1952	25	0	25
House of Representatives, 1954	17	3	20
House of Representatives, 1959			19

Source of Table 6, 7, 8: David B. Abernathy, "Teachers in Politics: The Southern Nigerian Case," in Joseph Fischer (ed.), The Social Sciences and the Comparative Study of Educational Systems, Scranton, Pennsylvania: International Textbook Company, 1970, p. 411.

TABLE 7

COMPOSITION OF FRENCH SPEAKING AFRICAN NATIONAL ASSEMBLIES BY OCCUPATION, 1962

Occupation	Cameroon #	Cameroon %	Chad #	Chad %	Central African Republic #	Central African Republic %	Congo(Br.) #	Congo(Br.) %	Dahomey #	Dahomey %	Gabon #	Gabon %	Guinea #	Guinea %
Education	20	21	6	9	15	30	19	33	18	30	24	37	10	23
Catechiste	2	2	-	-	-	-	-	-	-	-	1	1	-	-
Moniteur	5	5	2	3	7	14	7	12	-	-	11	17	-	-
Instituteur	8	8	4	6	4	8	6	10	17	28	8	12	10	23
Professor	-	-	-	-	-	-	1	2	-	-	-	-	-	-
Directeur c'ecole	3	3	-	-	1	2	3	5	1	2	4	6	-	-
Agent de l'enseignement	-	-	-	-	1	2	1	2	-	-	-	-	-	-
Educators(total)	18	19	6	9	14	28	18	31	18	30	18	27	10	23
Ex-educators	2	4	-	-	1	2	-	2	-	-	-	-	-	-
Agriculture	12	12	9	13	5	10	5	8	9	15	9	14	1	2
Minor Civil Service	16	17	16	22	7	14	14	24	11	19	8	12	12	28
Higher Civil Service	10	10	5	7	1	2	3	5	2	3	8	12	5	11
Law	2	2	-	-	-	-	-	-	-	-	-	-	-	-
Medicine	6	6	12	17	5	10	1	2	6	10	4	6	7	16
Commerce	3	3	8	11	4	8	6	10	6	10	8	12	1	2
Traditional Sector	10	10	5	7	4	8	1	2	2	3	1	1	3	7
Other	5	5	7	10	-	0	5	8	6	10	3	5	2	5
Not Available	13	14	3	4	10	20	5	8	0	-	1	1	2	5
Total	97	100	71	100	50	100	58	100	60	100	66	100	43	100

Source of Table 7: David B. Abernathy, "Teachers in Politics: The Southern Nigerian Case," in Joseph Fisher (ed.), The Social Sciences and the Comparative Study of Educational Systems, Scranton, Pennsylvania: International Textbook Company, 1970, p. 412.

TABLE 8

COMPOSITION OF FRENCH SPEAKING AFRICAN NATIONAL ASSEMBLIES BY OCCUPATION, 1962

Occupation	Ivory Coast #	%	Mali #	%	Mauretania #	%	Niger #	%	Senegal #	%	Togo #	%	Upper Volta #	%
Education	17	25	22	29	3	8	7	14	22	28	13	25	14	19
Catechiste	-	-	-	-	-	0	-	-	-	-	1	2	-	-
Moniteur	-	-	-	-	-	-	1	2	1	1	1	2	1	1
Instituteur	13	20	18	24	2	5	3	6	4	5	10	19	7	10
Professor	2	3	-	-	1	3	-	-	1	1	1	2	-	0
Directeur c'ecole	1	1	4	5	-	-	3	6	16	21	-	-	6	8
Agent de l'enseignement	1	1	-	-	-	-	-	-	-	-	-	-	-	-
Educators(total)	17	25	22	29	3	8	7	14	22	28	13	25	14	19
Ex-educators	-	-	-	-	-	-	-	-	-	-	-	-	-	-
Agriculture	7	10	-	-	-	-	-	-	1	1	4	8	2	3
Minor Civil Service	11	17	24	32	8	23	9	17	19	24	8	15	18	25
Higher Civil Service	8	12	7	9	11	31	7	13	11	14	6	12	17	24
Law	2	3	-	-	1	3	-	-	10	13	-	-	-	-
Medicine	7	10	12	16	1	3	4	8	6	8	3	5	12	17
Commerce	5	8	5	6	1	3	1	2	3	4	4	8	1	1
Traditional Sector	-	-	4	5	4	11	7	13	1	1	4	8	3	4
Other	4	6	-	-	3	9	-	-	3	4	7	14	2	3
Not Available	6	9	2	3	3	9	17	33	2	3	3	5	3	4
Total	67	100	76	100	35	100	52	100	78	100	51	100	72	100

Source of Table 8: David B. Abernathy, "Teachers in Politics: The Southern Nigerian Case," in Joseph Fisher (ed.), The Social Sciences and the Comparative Study of Educational Systems, Scranton, Pennsylvania: International Textbook Company, 1970, p. 413.

170

The educators-in-politics demonstrated their concern for teacher education by building multiple teacher
training colleges with the exigency to produce teachers
in quantity and quality. Although they failed to attract enough of the more able students, teacher education institutions became important and they multiplied
all through the 1960's. The training colleges were
small and were sometimes located many miles away from
the urban or the densely populated areas. Sifuna
(1974) describes a small teacher training college located in the Kenyan hinterlands that was not easily ac-
cessible by vehicle; he also notes that the teachers
who were being supervised strictly employed the traditional methods of teaching and entertained no
creativity in their teaching patterns. In addition,
there was a need for more teachers, teaching and learning resources. Stein (1976) notes that in Ghana some
teacher training colleges had enrollments of about 200-
300 students. Shrigley (1969) observed in the case of
Nigeria that his student teacher spent "...most of his
time asking questions requiring phenomenal memorization
of facts on the part of the young student."[3] Shrigley
(1970) taught in a Nigerian teachers' training college
where his clients were mere elementary school graduates
who were then trained for five years to be qualified to
teach in elementary schools; in all, they received
twelve years of formal schooling to be elementary
school teachers.[4]

The smallness of the teacher training colleges,
their need for more teaching and learning resources,
buttressed by the increasing demand for more teachers
and especially for more secondary school science
teachers, placed many African countries at a disadvan-
tage in terms of meeting their developmental goals.

171

Thus, Great Britain, the United States of America and
other Western countries provided teachers, teacher
educators, textbooks, and other school paraphernalia.
Anderson (1965) adequately stresses the problem, with
respect to the scarcity of secondary school teachers:

> One of East Africa's most pressing man-
> power needs is for graduate secondary
> school teachers, for without such teachers
> government plans and self-help schemes to
> expand and develop secondary education
> will be hindered...African graduate
> teachers are necessary not only to expand
> secondary education but to take an active
> part in realigning the secondary schools
> to fit them into the philosophy of an in-
> dependent African State and speed up the
> task of nation-building.[5]

Stabler (1969) records that Kagumo Elementary
Training College in Kenya had 163 staff members, 154 of
whom were expatriates; the training colleges could not
keep African graduates who quickly took higher paying
jobs while expatriate teachers departed when their contracts terminated.[6] Cammaerts (1969) shows the number
of non-citizen staff members in Kenyan schools from
1966 to 1968 [see Table 9].

While there was this impending shortage of African
teachers, there was also the concern to improve the
academic standards in the teacher training colleges,
which were barely above academic secondary schools. In
spite of the low academic levels of the students, the
colleges were assigned multiple functions: (1) to
upgrade the academic abilities of the teachers-to-be in
their respective subjects; (2) teach them some instructional methods; (3) teachers were to be able to social-

ize pupils with respect to the new prevailing national
values; and (4) arm them with skills for school management.

TABLE 9

NON-CITIZEN STAFF IN AIDED AND UNAIDED SCHOOLS

IN KENYA - 1966-68

	1966	1967	1968
Schools maintained or assisted	199	206	239
Schools unaided	201	336	362
Staff maintained or assisted schools	2,042	2,320	2,715
Staff in unaided schools	962	1,733	1,929
Non-citizen staff in maintained or assisted schools	1,481	1,632	1,853
Non-citizen staff in unaided schools	485	695	736
Unqualified staff in maintained or assisted schools, citizens.	91	146	183
Non-citizens	290	362	461
In unaided schools, citizens.	246	645	800
Non-citizens	217	430	733

Source of Table 9: F.C.A. Cammaerts, "Priorities for
the Preparation of Secondary Teachers in Kenya," East
Africa Journal, (November, 1969), p. 5.

The newer teacher training colleges were started
in response to the increasing demand for more schools

173

and for mass education. They did not have the liberal
academic tradition as found in the older schools such
as Ibadan, Makerere, Fourah Bay College, Achimota, and
William Ponte, in Nigeria, Uganda, Sierra Leone, Ghana,
and Senegal, respectively. Teachers' colleges were
construed to be 'dignified' secondary schools in the
sense that they trained senior elementary students to
be teachers in elementary schools and most of those who
had not passed well from the high schools to the
university were recruited to be trained for teaching
positions in secondary or middle schools. Fafunwa
(1970) notes this phenomenon succinctly when he explicates the many grades of certificates that teachers
could obtain to qualify them to teach at various levels
in the Nigerian school system depending on their level
of entrance into the teaching profession. Fafunwa
recommends completed secondary school education as
requirement for professional qualification. The pattern of teacher education in Nigeria at this point is
significant as a basis for generalization as this
country 'has' one-fifth of all African teachers and a
fourth of Africa's school-age population.[7] Ogunsola
(1975) describes teacher education programmes in
Nigeria from the 1890's up to the nationalist period;
he, too, notes the variety in teacher education
programmes until the 1960's when the government became
directly involved in the education of teachers in terms
of emphasizing foundation courses, professionalism, and
at the same time focused on the nation's concerns which
were to supply the schools with well-trained teachers
who also must have social and economic development as
priorities. Notwithstanding the desire for qualified
teachers, Lewis (1970) reveals that there were, in the
1960's, many untrained teachers who had to be utilized

174

to barely feed the expanding educational system in Africa. In 1967, for instance, Ghana had as many as 33,000 untrained teachers who also had weak educational backgrounds.[8] Lewis goes on to say that most of the autochthonous teacher educators were recruited on the assumption that since they had teaching experience in elementary and/or secondary schools, this automatically qualified them to be teacher educators; and "one consequence of this...fallacy is that much instruction of teachers-in-training results in the candidates for entry into the profession being taught as small children are taught instead of being treated as adults."[9]

The weak educational background of teachers-to-be, the availability of more higher paying jobs in government or private business, the military and police, which also have likelier promise for promotion in concert with new forms of media and the widespread of general education among the masses, contributed to the loss of status for the African teacher. Omijeh (1976) summarizes the factors contributing to the African teacher's loss of status:[10]

(1) Student-teacher's deprived socio-economic and poor educational background;

(2) the rather limited academic and cultural content of teacher training institutions;

(3) the changing social scene.

African leaders and educators were at this time concerned about the improvement of teacher education, but there was also the fear of "academic empirialism,"[11] since the new countries had to recruit their needed academic staff from the developed countries, usually from the nations of the ex-colonial powers. Nonetheless, Normington (1970) reports that

175

most African countries turned to the United States and other developed countries for aid not only in terms of providing teachers, but also to develop teacher education programmes around subjects perceived to be crucial for social, economic, educational, and technical development. In their belief that qualified teachers would have significant parts to play in national development, the United States government, educational organizations, and some leading American universities in concert with interested funding agencies developed twenty-two projects in fourteen African countries.[12]

Berman (1972, 1977) acknowledges that the United States had contributed to African education in the earlier periods, but that the 1960's presented a vacuum to enhance large scale American involvement especially in the area of teacher education. Livingston (1976) also refers to American influence on African education with specific reference to Liberia and Western Africa in general. With the historic experience of Columbia University in the areas of teacher training and curriculum development, some African graduates were sent to Teachers College and to some other major American universities such as Northwestern University and the University of Chicago. These students returned home as teacher educators or administrators. The project undertaken by the Agency for International Development were, as the concept denotes, developmental in nature in terms of their concern to establish fresh programs aimed to upgrade teachers in such exigent areas as Home Economics, Biological and technical sciences, instructional media and the agricultural sciences.

Evans (1962) states that Africa's educational and technical problems in the 1960's could be solved only with "...provision of massive international assistance from the outside and this, in fact, has recently been supplied by the United States in an exercise commonly known as Teachers for East Africa Program..."[13] West Africa (July, 1961) also documents about American and British educators being sent to Nigeria and Ghana; these teachers were carefully selected and they taught 'key' subjects that were perceived fruitful for African development.[14]

Berman (1979) construes United States' involvement in the development of African teacher education as a neo-colonialist move.[15] Nonetheless, the rising social demands for mass education and subsequently for more qualified teachers presented no likely alternative but to ask for the help of those more experienced in the area of teacher education and who have provided mass education in the type Africa was interested. Britain's teacher education developments had lagged behind that of the United States (Elsbree, 1968; Tomlinson, 1968) for more than fifty years. For instance, while Oxford University officially entertained teacher education in 1832, by 1836 the United States had well established foundations for the systematic training of teachers.[16] British education had been classist oriented where the grammar schools were geared to prepare the children of the gentry for the universities. Beasely (1966) documents that the 11+ examination, which was used to select students for specific secondary schools, was eliminated in the 1960's.[17] African Report (1963) states that with respect to educational problems in Britain,

> there are many possibilities upon which the Americans--indeed many other nations-- are better qualified to advise the British. For, strangely enough, we in

Britain are just beginning to feel acutely
a dilemma in some ways parallel to the
African problem.[18]

A number of studies have been carried out since
the 1960's that have concentrated on African education
and teacher education (Dodd, 1970; Rhors, 1974;
Fafunwa, 1970). Dodd conducted a descriptive survey
study of educational systems in nine African countries
and concluded that irrespective of the peculiar history
of the countries in his study there was, in each nation, urgent concern for quality and quantity of
teachers and that there was a search for a more appropriate curriculum in teacher education institutions.
The type of curriculum sought was one that trained
teachers to be adaptive, imaginative, emphasized subject matter specialization, child studies, and foundation courses that increase the teacher's knowledge
about the socio-cultural environment of African nations. He noted that there was the urgent need for
secondary school teachers, action-oriented research
that tackles immediate classroom problems, and there
was also concern for standards and the status of
African teachers.[19] Fafunwa (1970) also noted that
"...of all the educational problems that beset African
countries today, none is agonizing as the one relating
to the training of teachers...indeed the overall
problem of preparing future citizens of Africa who will
be fully oriented to their environment cannot be effectively accomplished without the aid of competent
teachers."[20] He also noted a significant drop in the
number of untrained teachers among the Nigerian teaching force from 66% in 1966 to less than 50% in 1969,[21]
and this trend will continue until all African teachers

are generally considered adequately qualified. Inser-
vice training programmes will continue to retrain and
upgrade teacher competence as new ideas, technology and
school clientele demand or necessitate.

Hanson (1963) maintains that the African teacher
must be liberally educated and that he should not be
satisfied simply as a task master.[22] Machyo (1969)
states that the role of the African teacher is "...to
produce critical and progressive students...for learning is emulating, and what students subsequently become
will depend above all on the character and intellectual
outlook of their tutors."[23] P'Bitek (1973) asserts:

> Let the people who know our culture teach
> our people. Let us Africanize our cur-
> riculum in a meaningful manner. Let
> African culture form the core of our cur-
> riculum and foreign culture be at the
> periphery....[24]

All these writers are in search of teachers who are
culturally and professionally responsive to Africa's
developmental Zeitgeist.

The coming of the 1970's and the 1980's found many
teacher training colleges as constituent parts of the
newly established national universities as well as the
older ones built during the colonial and missionary
period; the stress is now on the professional educator
and professionalization of the African teacher.

African Teacher Education - 1970's-1980's

While the literature on African teacher education
up to the 1960's emphasize (1) the minimal education of
students enrolled in teacher education programs; (2)

179

inappropriate curriculum; (3) small size of the training colleges; (4) shortage of African graduate teachers
especially for the secondary schools and the subsequent
reliance on expatriate teachers; and (5) the loss of
prestige and social status of the teaching profession,
the literature in the 1970's and 1980's take a more
'encouraging' stance in the anticipation and emphasis
on the professionalization of the African teaching
force.

After delineating the needs for the teacher in
Africa to be a professional, Fafunwa asserts that this
new teacher must also be knowledgeable of the political, sociological, and economic forces besetting
Africa; Obidi (1975) also sees a gradual and the eventual professionalization of the African teacher. In
1970 Professor Espie "...spoke of the four components
of foundation studies namely, philosophy, history,
psychology, and sociology insofar as they are relevant
to the study of education."[25] Wandira (1970) notes
that African teacher education should encompass the
prevalent political and socio-cultural trends. Mazrui
(1971) asserts that national goals and nationalists'
political philosophies be part of teacher education
programs and hence some degree of integration be encouraged among the various groups in African nations.
Mazrui elaborates on his significant points by saying
that the ability to tolerate differences in ethnicity
and race be actively enhanced by teachers.

In 1974, the Association for Teacher Education in
Africa (ATEA) announced itself 'self-reliant' in breaking away from its parent-sponsor (AAA) the Afro-Anglo-
American Programme for Teacher Education in Africa
which had supported ATEA by providing for various
projects, programmes, conferences and the recruitment

of personnel for teacher education institutions in many African countries. African teacher educators and political leaders see the formation of the Association for African Teacher Education as an important step towards making African education suited to African conditions.

The Association had made it possible for African educators to share and view educational problems on continental and regional levels. Between 1972 and 1974, the Association published two books for foundation studies in teacher education institutions in which national unity, identity, and the drive for modernization were emphasized.[26]

Though a few of the writers in the 1970's allude to broader Africa; the majority, however, emphasize their respective countries as their priorities (Fafunwa, 1970; Mwingira, 1970; Mason, 1971; Ogunsola, 1975; Machyo, 1972; Cammaerts, 1969). All of these writers' main concern is with the development of education and teacher education in their respective countries or regions. Regional education for teachers had taken place during colonial times in such universities as Fourah Bay College in Sierra Leone, Makarere College in Uganda, Achimota in Ghana, Fort Hare in Southern Africa, etc., which followed the traditions of the metropoles. With the coming of independence, however, each African country embarked on the establishment of its own national university (Nye, 1963). These national universities are to respond directly to national, regional or Pan-African problems; while some emphasize the national and the regional, others the broader Africa, but all agree and stress the responsibilities of African educational institutions and teachers to African conditions.

Cammaerts (1969) states that

> the important and relevant fact about the
> need for a total change from the British
> model of Education, to a Kenyan, or at any
> rate an East African model, is that this
> cannot be done by expatriate teachers.
> Their judgement of what is needed is
> necessarily impaired by their own ex-
> perience at home in a totally different
> situation.[27]

Although such a writer takes the national and regional approach, various others have taken the Pan-African approach (Nyerere, 1963; Selassie, 1963; Brown, 1963; Wandira, 1970; Lightfoote-Wilson, 1969; Nkrumah, 1961; Brickman, 1963).

In 1963, the Organization of African Unity (OAU) was formed which proposed the political, cultural, and economic unity of Africa (Nkrumah, 1963; Green and Seidman, 1968; Padmore, 1972; Diop, 1978; Nyerere, 1963). In the same year, Selassie advocated the establishment of a Pan-African university in which African students from all African countries would converge and interact.[28] Selassie's premise is that with African unity should come the social integration of African peoples. The 1962 Ghana government also saw that "...African universities should play a role in the achievement of African Unity."[29] Brickman (1963) states that

> African institutions of higher education
> have the duty of acting as instruments for
> the consolidation of national unity. This
> they can do by resolutely opposing the ef-
> fects of tribalism and encouraging ex-
> changes, and by throwing open the univer-

sity to all students who show capacity to
benefit from a university education of in-
ternationally acceptable academic standards, and by resolutely ignoring ethnic or
tribal origins, and political and
religious discrimination.[30]

Nye (1965) sees common schooling as entailing
"...unifying factors..."[31] Since the formation of the
Organization of African Unity African leaders and
educators have advocated the exchange of students and
staff between African educational institutions and
countries (Yoloye, 1970). Nkrumah states that African
students should be allowed the ease of movement from
one African country into another for the purpose of
study and travel.[32]

The 1960's passed with the desire of African
leaders and educators to have African schools
Africanized in terms of staff and curriculum. Although
universal primary education and the complete
Africanization of African educational institutions did
not materialize in the 1980's, the ideology of African
unity persists.

Nyerere (1963) asserts that African nationalism
should be a stepping stone towards African unity and
that African nationalism that is divorced from practical African unity

> ...is meaningless, is anachronistic, and
> is dangerous, if it is not at the same
> time Pan-Africanism. We must use the
> African national states as instruments for
> the reunification of Africa.[33]

Johnson (1965), Lewis (1963), Foy (1979) have all written about attempts made by African governments to integrate Cameroon, Somalia, and Cape Verde and Guinea

Bissau respectively in line with Nyerere's notion of using the African nation states as the basis for larger African unity. Diop (1978) states that

> The days of the nineteenth century dwarf
> states are gone. Our main security and
> development problems can be solved only on
> a continental scale and preferably within
> a federal framework. [34]

A Federal framework for African states would involve the surrendering of their absolute sovereignty and therefore the current political boundaries would have to become merely local administrative demarcations. One of the ramifications of this view means that African teachers from one country could teach in other African countries, and African students would be able to attend schools beyond their autotchonous nations or regions.

Pan-Africanism: Political Arguments

Various writers have raised political arguments about Pan-Africanism (Nkrumah, 1963; Padmore, 1972). Nkrumah, for instance, emphasized the political basis for Pan-Africanism. Although he was cognizant of the economic consideration, in 1963 he was more apparently preoccupied with political unification. Upon closer examination, however, a political kingdom must rest upon an economic infrastructure of which he was aware. The major political argument with respect to Pan-Africanism stems from the subsequent power that would be derived from a large political entity such as the whole of Africa or those that would find consensus to unite. The second political argument relates to the formulation of foreign policy which would be unitary

184

and not fragmentary; it is viewed that a unitary foreign policy from a combined group of African countries would abate balkanization and defend a larger interest. Furthermore, a larger political unit would have a stronger military force to defend its sovereignty in the face of a large arms race. There are other minor arguments such as the respect that a large unitary government would possess in the midst of other large powers; but the political essentials for African unity remain to be the more respectable voice that a United African States would command with the potential to have more say in world events and in the making of policies on the world's political platform. Politically united Africa will also deal with African problems much more effectively.

Pan-Africanism: Economic Arguments

Economists have argued that Pan-Africanism requires an integrated and coordinated economic plan, consideration, and utilization. Writers in this area posit that some African countries are too small to be able to develop industrially. Ola (1979, 1976), Kofi (1976), Seidman and Green (1968), Amin (1977), Diop (1978), and Davidson (1974) have written in support of African economic integration. The central thesis of these writers is that Africa needs to be economically integrated in order to obtain not only economic power and strength, but also to realize social and economic development. Such ideas are founded on the analysis that Africa's relationship with the larger powers has been one of economic dependency and the subsequent political, technical, and cultural dependencies. In their book <u>Unity or Poverty? The Economics of Pan-</u>

Africanism, Seidman and Green realize the economic
potential of continental Africa and assert that small
nation-states are incapable of building and maintaining
large scale industries. Furthermore, the economics of
small African states are outer-directed, mainly towards
the metropoles, and therefore produce more for these
outside markets rather than for their internal consumption. Balkanized African state economies are not only
outer-directed, but also lack an adequate skilled
population required to stimulate economic development
and also because of the absence of diversified wants
and lack in quality manpower to run large industrial
plants. "The optimal size of a modern economic market
is 200 million with at least 25 million dollars G.D.P.
and the whole of Africa is approximately 300 million
strong."[35] Seidman and Green recommend continental
unity on the grounds that this would stimulate economic
development because the diversified natural resources
within the continent can thereby be better organized
and exploited. Furthermore, a continentally planned
economy would reduce duplication of industrial plants
where one plant would be quite adequate; and

> an integrated economy would have a central
> bank and a common currency. Such institu-
> tions would not only facilitate inter-
> state commerce and exchange but also mobi-
> lization and channeling of funds for
> development.[36]

The main arguments of the advocates of Pan-African
economic integration are that: (1) some Balkanized
African states are too small to develop and maintain
large scale industrial plants; (2) the economies of
small states in Africa are outer, rather than inner,
directed; (3) small African states lack the quality

population to give impetus to economic development because of the uniform and non-diversified social and economic wants; (4) Balkanized African states waste efforts in the duplication of industries where one could be sufficient; (5) there is the lack of coordination of resources to handle large scale developmental plans; and (6) most of the forces for African underdevelopment are external with respect to colonialism, neo-colonialism, and the existence of minimal infrastructures that are themselves outerdirected to satisfy the wants of the ex-colonial powers.[37]

Though external factors contribute to African underdevelopment, internal African factors are not immune. Ola (1979) observes that since African countries are at transitional stages, there are instabilities and uncertainties that render African countries susceptible to fluctuations in the world market. Furthermore, the modernizing politicians themselves contribute to instability and economic disorientation.

> All the causes of and origins of decline and underdevelopment cannot be heaped on the shoulders of outsiders. We have to search inside the continent for some explanation and interpretation.[38]

Goody (1971) states that in the development of politics, trade, and art, Africa was not far behind European countries, but that the only scientific productive mechanism by which Europe advanced more than Subsaharan Africa was because Europe invented the plough and that "the so-called feudal systems in Africa lacked a feudal technology, and this absence is of critical importance in the developments of the present day."[39]

Davidson (1974) states that in addition to widespread illiteracy and the absence of technology for large scale industrial development, there are also crises in African social, political, and economic institutions.

> The crisis...is...one of institutions. Those of the past have lost their containing power. Those of the present offer little save confusion. Those of the future have yet to appear.[40]

P'Bitek (1973) blames current African problems on Africa's indigenous ills, the social set-up, and African leadership that is dominated by an educated minority who hold fast onto their unprogressive ideologies. He specifically attacks Nyerere's African socialism as a government where the uneducated Africans have virtually no say or meaningful participation.[41] Babu (1981), an ex-minister in Nyerere's government, has also criticized African socialism and has recommended scientific socialism.[42]

Integration Theories and African Development

Various integration theories were advanced immediately after World War II, and especially after the formation of the European Economic Community; at the time, the United States, Russia and the European Economic Community provided ample basis for the formulation of integration theories. Economic integration or the gradual process of integrating political groupings through economic institutions, form the basis for European integration theorists; United States, Russia and the EEC countries were there to refer to. Using the European Economic Community as a point of reference, European integration theorists deduced that any successful attempt at integration must first utilize the economic approach by using economic institutions. The establishment of a common market, for instance, would culminate into the use of some other social institutions that would affect the lives of the common market members. Laws that govern the economic activities of the common market would affect the populous of the common market members. As the common market infiltrates into the activities of the market members, this would give rise to the establishment of common social institutions which would promote community feeling. Thus "...economic integration would lead to political integration..."[43] Etzioni (1966) states that "Economic integration...affects all societal groups--consumers, producers, management, labour, farmers, small business--and therefore tends to have extensive political repercussions."[44] Etzioni believes that the economic step towards integration should be the first which should then gradually result in the integration of other community institutions.

Etzioni also maintains that for successful unification to occur, the interested parties must have key and similar background factors. A similar stage of economic development, for instance, would be a key background factor. The intellectual elites and interest groups that are in support of integration must have similar ideological stances. These similarities in concert with positive or negative external stimuli would contribute to the integration process. In the case of the European Economic Community, the effects of World war II and Marshall Plan Funds were the negative and positive factors, respectively. The intellectual elites are significant in the integration process, but their success would depend upon whether their aims are too high or too low at the initial stage of the integration. The higher their aims, the lower would be their score.[45] Furthermore, the parties intending to integrate must not allocate resources before integration has been achieved or community-feeling has been realized. If resources are to be allocated before the communities have felt themselves as members of the same large community, the richer regions would tend to withhold their resources for their own local use, because it is the rich which will pay

> ...more taxes and the poor (which will) receive more services. Such reallocation of assets is acceptable to the richer units (e.g., New York State) only after they conceive of the poorer units (e.g., Mississippi) as part of the same community.[46]

Simmel (1902) and Mills (1953) studied the power relationships between three-person groups and assert that two in the group, in such a relationship, are likely to bind themselves together against the third party.

> Systems with three leaders hardly ever survive or maintain stability. Two are likely to form coalition against the other or each goes its different way.[47]

Although these integrationist theories derive their formulations from West European experiences, some of their explanations are applicable to African conditions. The Ghana-Mali-Guinea union did not materialize in part because of the three person relationship which ended in Guinea withdrawing from the union. Furthermore, Ghana came to Guinea's aid with large sums of

money when the latter was in sheer need even though
'community feeling' had not been established between
Ghanians and Guineans. The Ghanaians therefore accused
Nkrumah of being more interested in Africa as a whole
rather than in Ghana per se. A similar case is observed in the attempts to integrate Uganda, Kenya, and
Tanganyika. Uganda, the smallest of the three states,
felt overpowered by Kenya and Tanganyika; Uganda felt
it was richer than the other two states and was therefore wary about sharing its natural resources; it also
felt threatened by the aggressive sizes of the two
other larger states which treated Uganda as less significant because of its size. As one of the Ugandan
representatives remarked, "I am still for federation if
they stop treating us as third place and small."[48] The
validity of the western theory that a grouping of three
aiming for unification would hardly attain its goals is
illustrated in the case of the plans for an East
African Union and also in the attempts to form a Ghana-
Guinea-Mali Union. In the latter case, the absence of
community feeling and the allocation of resources from
Ghana to Guinea and Mali before these three nations
could think of themselves as a community, were more
responsible for the dissolution of the attempts for
achieving unity than their lack of contiguity.

Nye (1965) states that Kenya, Uganda and Tanganyika had already developed a community feeling in
the sense that they had territorial and regional identity.[49] The three territories are contiguous and most
of the modernizing elites had been educated at Makerere
University College in Uganda which was then functioning
as a provincial regional university.[50] Goldthorpe
(1965) provides data to show the representation of

Kenyan, Ugandan, and Tanganyikan students at Makerere College from 1958 to 1960.

TABLE 10

UGANDA, KENYA, AND TANGANYIKA: COLLEGE ATTENDANCE

| | | Number of African Students | | |
		at Makerere College	in U.S.A.	as under-graduates
Uganda	1958-59	259	29	80-90
	1959-60	285		
Kenya	1958-59	285	73	
	1959-60	355	+7 in Canada	40
Tanganyika	1958-59	209	22	
	1959-60	183		26

Source of Table 10:   J.E. Goldthorpe, An African Elite: Makerere College Students 1922-1960, Nairobi: Oxford University Press, 1965, p. 19.

Most of the graduates of Makerere College became teachers, medical doctors, agricultural and veterinary workers in their respective countries.[51] They were the ones who also became the nationalists as well as the ideological leaders within the East African territory. Nye (1965) states that by the early 1960's two-thirds of the Makerere students considered themselves as Pan-Africanists.[52] Thus, the East African territories were not only contiguous, but they also had more common

192

background factors than the Ghana-Guinea-Mali territories which were linguistically, educationally, and
institutionally heterogenous. The common background
factors of the East African territories were many, but
not sufficient to materialize East African Unity. In
addition to their many common background factors, Rotberg (1963) states that the East African countries under colonial rule had been closely interrelated by
colonial administrative strategies based on the desires
of the European settlers and the colonial office in
London to minimize administrative fragmentation. "L.S.
Amery, Viscount Milner's Under Secretary of State for
the Colonies, was anxious that Britain's fragmented
colonial units should, whenever possible, be organized
into larger entities to maximize their economic and
strategic potential."[53] The Europeans viewed that
"...the economic case presented a much more promising
line of approach towards achieving closer union than
any adopted in the past, and that...it appeared
desirable that a statement should be prepared designed
to show that the four territories constituted a single
economic and transport unit."[54]

European theories of integration as deduced from
the European Economic Community experiences and as applied in Africa by the colonials, as in the case of the
East African territories, emphasize the economic approach. The European theory for political and social
integration holds that the economic institutions should
be the first to be integrated which would then have
spill-over effects on the other political and social
institutions. This should eventuate into the establishment and utilization of unitary social and cultural
institutions and eventually lead to a common foreign
policy which should then lead into a common parliament

or other significant political institutions. Since political, cultural and social arguments do not "pay off"[55] on the platform for community integration, they are relegated to the background and do not take precedence in European integration theory. In contrast to this stance, however, African integration theories, as deduced from the integration movements in Africa in the 1960's, emphasize the political and educational institutional approach to African integration. This indeed does not mean that the prime-movers for African integration were incognizant of the significance of economic institutions, but it can be deduced that political and educational institutional integration were foremost. To the Africans, what needed immediate consolidation were their political and ideological institutions before the unification of their economic institutions.

Nye (1965) states that

...paying attention to economic interests when making decisions makes sense only when the ideological and political framework within which interests interact can be taken for granted. When this framework cannot be taken for granted, politics is a necessary first consideration.[56]

For the Europeans, the immediate consideration after World War II was to reconstruct their economic infrastructures which had been destroyed during the war; to the Africans, what they were most apparently deprived of was their political institutions and political leadership. For instance, the Baganda of Uganda opposed federation with Kenya and Tanganyika, in part for reasons of political leadership; "The Baganda are opposed to federation because they feel that it is impossible for the Kabaka to defeat such people like Dr. Nyerere, Mr. Mboya, Mr. B. Kiwanuka, or Mr. Kenyatta, in a presidential election in Eastern Africa."[57] For Uganda,

> A political federation is important to see that economic agreements are respected. We have to feel that we are one big state before funds can be transferred from one country to the other for development.[58]

Uganda was not alone in considering politics as primary for East African unification.

> Ideology is undoubtedly the most important motive in Tanganyika's view of federation. Economics is second in importance and defense is nil...Pan-Africanism is the dominant force behind it (federation). It has little to do with economics. There is absolutely no doubt about this.[59]

Wilde (1971) states that "Ideology plays an extremely important role in the political life of many African countries," and that "...ideology may serve as a guide to action and as a kind of social cement...ideology enables a government to assume the desired image for the benefit of its domestic constituency."[60] It was in part due to the various political ideologies held by African politicians that gave rise to the development of the radical and the moderate groups within the Organization of African Unity.[61]

While Nkrumah and his ideological block wanted an immediate political union, the moderates advocated the gradual, step-by-step approach to African unity. "Nkrumah fears that if newly independent African states do not sacrifice their sovereignty while it is new, they will grow increasingly reluctant to do so."[62]   And

> In direct opposition to the Lagos Charter,
> President Nkrumah advocated immediate
> political union. In his view any delay in
> affecting political integration was dan-
> gerous, since individual African states
> would be vulnerable to the mechanizations
> of neo-colonialist powers.[63]

Nonetheless, "There was practically no support for President Nkrumah's plan."[64]

Welch (1963) states that the difference between the radicals, such as Nkrumah, and the conservatives such as Tubman of Liberia, was one of approach and the timing within which unity was to be achieved.

> Nkrumah and Tubman differed primarily on
> the speed and manner in which unification
> should be achieved. In the opinion of
> Liberian President...Nkrumah's proposals
> and the rapidity with which the Ghanian
> prime minister wished to implement unity
> were unrealistic.[65]

Although there were ideological differences be-tween the African politicians with respect to African unity, there were basic agreements on the necessity for Pan-Africanism. Each ideological camp acknowledged that closer cooperation was necessary to safeguard the newly won independence of each African state; all sup-ported the stance to aid the liberation movements in the African countries that were still under colonialism; each disapproved of South Africa's Apart-heid regime, and all agreed to the formation of OAU. Above all, the formation of the Organization of African Unity prompted the establishment of institutions on na-tional as well as on regional levels, infrastructures to link African countries together and ideas about allowing the ease of movement of people, goods, and services across national boundaries were agreed upon.[66]

The primacy of politics over economics in the case of African integration is perhaps best illustrated in Nkrumah's analysis of the African revolution and political development. He outlined that African political development would go through stages; political unity he put before economic development. "At the All African People's Conference of December 1958, Prime Minister Nkrumah described the African revolution as proceeding in four stages: the achievement of independence, its consolidation, the attainment of political union, the economic and social reconstruction of Africa."[67] Although "'seek ye first the Political Kingdom' may as a slogan have lost some of its popularity...it is well to remember that it is a precept which will continue to guide the actions of the politicians."[68]

Next to the primacy of political institutions as integrative devices, the African nationalists took up education and educational institutions as means to consolidate their newly independent nations and to integrate the various tribes, races, and ethic groups into a cohesive whole. They aimed for a national integration that was not opposed to Pan-Africanism. "National integration...is an expansive concept, implying the creation of durable bonds of unity within a state that are not, however, detrimental to Pan-African or other regional unities..."[69] Educational institutions which had produced the nationalists themselves were found to be inappropriate for the new functions they must perform; furthermore, the power of education was realized by all the nationalists. In the first place

> ...it was education which created the
> small modern elite which gave leadership
> to the independence movements. Educa-
> tion...created many of the aspirations
> which gave popular impetus to the drive
> for independence... It was education
> which played a major role in breaking down
> the isolation and particularism of tribal
> life and thus in helping to create a sense
> of nationalism.[70]

Thus, most of the African leaders put their educational institutions directly under their government peroga- tives where they could be assured to carry out govern- ment concerns. It became fashionable for each African state to have its own university. "To have a national university becomes almost as much a symbol of indepen- dence as having a national airline."[71]

Education and educational institutions became tools for the accomplishment of social, economic, cul- tural, and political plans for the new nations and for the whole of Africa.

> Education must be a tool...of economic and
> social advance. At Alliance High School
> new emphasis is laid on vocational sub-
> jects such as agriculture, business
> management and industrial arts while it
> still maintains a high standard of the
> purely academic subjects.[72]

Educational development became closely correlated with economic and social development; it was believed that

education made persons more productive and since technology was what Africa lacked, technical schools and
manpower studies proliferated.[73]

The universities are to produce African graduates
who are not photocopies of their metropolitan counterparts. "The hope is that the universities would assist
in the development of the new nations of Africa not
only by providing them with well-educated men and women
who are urgently needed...but also that these educated
men and women should be truly African and not pale
carbon copies of their former imperial masters and
mistresses."[74] The universities are not only to include studies of African history, Arts, Literature, and
other cultural subjects, but they are also to deal with
the "...problems of emergent nations and of African
unity."[75] West Africa (1961) states "...that universities should play a role in the achievement of African
unity."[76] Brickman (1963) makes a similar statement
with regards to African universities contributing to
national integration:

> African institutions of higher education
> have the duty of acting as instruments for
> the consolidation of national unity. This
> they can do by resolutely opposing the ef-
> fects of tribalism and encouraging ex-
> changes, and by throwing open the univer-
> sity to all students who show capacity to
> benefit from a university education of in-
> ternationally acceptable academic stand-
> ards, and by resolutely ignoring ethnic or
> tribal origins, and political and
> religious discrimination.[77]

The recognition of educational institutions as instruments for social integration was illustrated in

May, 1961, during the meeting of more than thirty
African states in Addis Ababa to discuss plans for the
development of education in Africa; this was followed
in 1962 by another conference of African states on
educational plans for Africa.[78] These conferences
revealed the low level of education in Africa and the
necessity to accelerate educational diffusion; educational expansion became a priority for the new African
states. Although many African states were receiving
teachers from Western countries, "eventually it will be
necessary for the new African nations to depend more
and more upon their own teachers and administrators."[79]
Cammaerts (1969) claims that

> There are many excellent young men and
> women from overseas countries who are
> fully aware of the need for change, but
> both by judgement and by length of service
> their contribution can be of only limited
> significance. Their judgement of what is
> needed is necessarily impaired by their
> own experience at home in a totally dif-
> ferent situation. They can say 'this is
> all wrong,' but they cannot stay long
> enough to be able to say 'this is what is
> right'[80]

There was thus concern for the Africanization of the
teaching staff and the school curriculum; the African
teacher was charged with the responsibility to
safeguard viable African traditions and at the same
time orient his students to the contemporary social
Zeitgiest.[81]

The African teacher was seen as an agent for the
transmission of traditional as well as the contemporary
social values. Castle (1965) states that

more and more children from different
tribes and races will be educated in the
same class, and more teachers from different tribes will teach in the same
school. In these circumstances it will
not be wise or even possible to use the
school to emphasize tribal or racial
differences: The aim of the African
teacher should be to help Africans and
other races to work and play together and
to understand each other.[82]

Schools are institutions where social integration
should occur since this is one of the major places
where tribal, social, racial, and cultural diversities
converge and teachers are to be agents of political
socialization. Nye (1965) asserts that "...shared
educational experience was a source of unity among the
East African elite."[83] Selassie (1963) recommends a
Pan-African university so that African students could
come to interact with each other for the purpose of the
impending possibilities of a United Africa.[84] Nyerere
(1963) states that each African nation should aim for
the ultimate unity of African states.[85] Wandira (1970)
states that teachers and teacher education institutions
have crucial parts to play for the achievement of
African unity "...which looms so large on the minds of
African leaders."[86] Brown (1966) asserts that African
education should reflect the moves for African unity
and that teachers should be instruments for the
realization of the ideology of Pan-Africanism.[87]

The predominant concern for the use of African
educational institutions and teachers for the integration of Africa has had a long history; furthermore,
Pan-Africanism as a concept was started by a teacher by

201

the name of Sylvester Williams.[88]   It was taken over by African nationalists, the most significant of whom had been teachers.[89]

This prevailing concern over teachers and educational institutions as instruments for the integration of Africa can be contrasted with the integration movements in Europe where economic institutions take precedence. Arnold (1979) states that cultural considerations are not at the top of the list of European politicians with respect to the integration of European communities because cultural policies do not 'pay off'; any cultural policy must, therefore, be subsumed under economic considerations.[90]

Mujuju (1972) asserts that European politicians emphasize the utilitarian aspects of education because they govern societies that have already had long histories of establishment and relatively have stable values, cultural, and political systems.

> The old and industrialized countries are probably right to emphasize the utilitarian aspects of education, especially as they concern industry. Their political systems are relatively more stable and, although crises still occur, they have survived some major ones. Their values and procedures are a lot more identifiable. They have in addition, acquired a sophistication in technology unequaled in history, which is indeed part and parcel of their culture. When they stress the relevance of their education to the needs of industry they are only responding to an impelling presence.[91]

In contrast to African countries, Mazrui (1972) and Davidson (1974) emphasize the fluidity in African cultural values[92] and instability of cultural and political institutions in Africa.[93] It seems therefore that until African cultural values and political institutions are entrenched and identifiable, educational institutions and teachers would continue to be salient instruments for the transmission of cultural, social, and political values.

Educational Institutions and Teachers as Agents of Political Socialization for the Integration of Africa

Several attempts have been made to integrate African peoples; such efforts have originated within and without Africa (Phelps-Stokes Commission on Education in Africa, 1923, 1925; Kilson, 1961; Conference of African States on the Development of Higher Education in Africa, 1962, Malinowski, 1943; Washington, 1913; Bascom, 1962, Brown, 1964, African Ministers of Education Conference, 1962; Smith, 1973; Cameron, 1970; Berman, 1971, 1979; King, 1971; Lindsay and Harris, 1976; Nkrumah, 1963, Azikiwe, 1968, Selassie, 1963).

A landmark attempt to integrate African peoples by means of education is revealed in Kings's Pan-Africanism and Education: A Study of Race Philanthropy and Education in the Southern States of America and East Africa. The attempts accounted for in this book utilized curriculum content, teaching methods and procedures, philosophy of education, teachers and teacher education institutions so as to ensure not only the implantation of the philosophy of educational adaptation in Africa, but also that "Racial unity and compromise...would be enhanced through such means."[94] Schools were established in the early 1920's to ensure that the education received by black Americans in the southern states of North America, primarily in Tuskegee and Hampton Institutes, is also received by Africans on the African continent. The Jeanes Industrial teacher in Kenya, for an instance, was taught using the philosophy of educational adaptation. The Jeanes teacher taught recreational skills, health, industrial, agricultural, and his wife was trained in child care and household management skills. The emphasis was not to change but to adapt to the environment. Thus the Jeanes teacher was not expected to be a political activist but would teach his clients skills to make them economically self-sufficient. Mumford (1930) describes Malangali School in Tanzania which attempted to use African traditional ways of teaching, recreational practices, etc. and the student wore African attire.[95] Cameron (1939) had maintained that educational adaptation was to make the African a good African and it was meant to protect his environment and culture which were not to be radically changed or destroyed.[96]

Berman (1972) points out that a model of Tuskegee Institute was established in Liberia and that this was done to apply the system of education of the blacks in the American south to those in Liberia. "...the people of Africa are dependent and black, like those in the Southern United States; ergo, the same policy that works so well there should work in Africa."[97] Washington (1913) had earlier likened the social, economic and political conditions of American blacks to African blacks in Africa,[98] and "the Phelps-Stokes fund had...pan-African education at the heart of its work from the very beginning," and that is to say "the education of Negroes, both in Africa and the United States."[99]

By the 1930's, however, educational adaptation was being criticized, by some Africans as well as some

Westerners, as an inferior sort of education designed to keep African peoples collectively subservient.[100] In the late 1940's and 1950's the colonial governments took an active interest in providing regional educational institutions for Africans.[101] Cameron (1970) states that Makerere in East Africa had its own institute of education in 1949, five years after the McNair Report.[102] Students from the three East African countries of Kenya, Uganda and the then Tanganyika were to attend the same school of education, and the institute was to actively participate in the education of teachers from each of the three territories. Lewis (1965) states that a similar institute had been recommended for the West African British territories.[103] All through the colonial period, Makerere University College, Fourah Bay College, The University College of Rhodesia, Fort Hare, William Ponty, and Achimota each graduated African students from various African territories. Although these institutions graduated teachers to teach in secondary schools and teacher training colleges, prepared minor bureaucrats and clerks, surveyors and foresters, the number of graduates were minimal enough for African countries in the 1960's and 1970's to importunately request aid from Canada, the United States, New Zealand and other developed nations in the form of secondary school teachers, teacher educators, manpower planners and other professionals African development desperately lacked.

Simultaneously, questions of academic imperialism and the Africanization of Africa's school systems surfaced. As Ashby (1964) noted, the university colleges that had been recommended by the Asquirth Commission prior to African independence were vivid expressions of

British parochialism; the Commission's basic assumption had been that "a university system appropriate for Europeans brought up in London and Manchester and Hull was also appropriate for Africans brought up in Lagos and Kumasi and Kampala."[104] These universities were in Africa, but they were European universities and showed no "sign of adaptation to the African environment."[105]

The question of the Africanization of African schools was also debated for it was viewed that African teachers, who were in high demand, would be in better cultural and political frames to transmit the appropriate cultural, political, and social values being espoused by the new African nationalists. While the Africanization of the African teaching force was being debated, questions of academic standards were also exigent issues.[106]

Carr-Saunders (1963) studied the staffing patterns in African universities to determine sources of staff members with respect to their nationalities [Tables 11, 12, 13, 14].

TABLE 11
STAFF MEMBERS IN AFRICAN UNIVERSITIES:
EXPATRIATES AND AFRICANS

Year	Total # of University Staff	Locally Born	Expatriates	% Expatriates	% Expa-African
1961-1962	2,166	594	1,572	73%	27%

TABLE 12

STAFF MEMBERS IN AFRICAN UNIVERSITIES:
COUNTRIES REPRESENTED

Countries Represented	No. of Staff From Each Country
Britain	702
France	257
Belgium	135
U.S.A.	107
India	50
South Africa	48
Canada	29
Australia and New Zealand	26
Netherlands	22
19 Other Countries	771

TABLE 13

PREDICTION OF EXPATRIATE TEACHERS NEEDED FOR
ENGLISH SPEAKING AFRICAN UNIVERSITIES

Year	No. of Expatriates Needed
1961-1962; 1965-1966	2,200
1966-1967; 1970-1971	2,000
1971-1972; 1975-1976	900
1976-1977; 1979-1980	300

TABLE 14

PREDICTION OF EXPATRIATE TEACHERS NEEDED FOR

FRENCH SPEAKING AFRICAN UNIVERSITIES

Year	No. of Expatriates Needed
1961-1962; 1965-1966	800
1966-1967; 1970-1971	600
1971-1972; 1975-1976	200
1976-1977; 1979-1980	less than 100

Source of Tables 11, 12, 13, 14: A.M. Carr-Saunders, "Staffing African Universities," Minerva, 1, 3 (Spring, 1963), p. 304.

Carr-Saunders predicted that "the proportion of African staff members will rise steadily and will be nearly one hundred percent by 1980-81."[107]

Adams (1972) found increments in the representation of African faculty members at Makerere University College between 1963 and 1972 [Table 15]; the increment in African staff members was a result of the desire to Africanize the educational institutions. However, in contrast to Carr-Saunders' prediction, Adams points out that "at the current rate it would be 1986-1987 before half of Makerere's faculty would be African...and of course, not all these would be East Africans or Ugandans."[108] Nonetheless, Adams went on to assert that members of the East African Association mean Uganization when they speak of Africanizing the staff and that the practice has been"...the elimination of expatriates and non-citizens...."[109] Although the desire to Africanize, or in Adams' terms to indigenize, is there, Adams notes that very few African graduates aspire for university teaching. Furthermore, certain African governments and school authorities still prefer the services of expatriates in their universities.[110] To this latter reason preventing the total Africanization of African schools, a good number of educated and qualified Africans "feel as Americans would feel in Cambridge, Massachusetts, if sixty percent of their faculty were British; or (the British) would feel in Cambridge, England, if sixty percent of (their) dons were American."[111]

TABLE 15

PROPORTION OF AFRICAN TEACHERS AT MAKERERE 1963-1972

Year	No. of Faculty	No. of African Faculty	Proportion of African Faculty
1963-1964	101	10	10%
1965-1966	123	13	11%
1967-1968	139	25	18%
1969-1970	147	30	20%
1970-1971	181	44	24%
1971-1972	156	41	26%

Source of Table 15: Bert N. Adams, "Africanization and Academic Empirialism: A Case Study in Planned Change and Inertia," East African Journal, (May, 1972), p. 28.

Kilson (1961) also illustrated this low representation of African staff members [Table 16] for five
African universities.

TABLE 16

AFRICAN UNIVERSITIES TEACHERS: EXPATRIATE AND AFRICAN

African Universities	Expa- triate	African
1. University College of Rhodesia and Nyasaland	62	1
2. University College of East Africa	150	8
3. University College of Ghana	132	13
4. Ibadan University College	253	15
5. University College of Sierra Leone	58	19

Source of Table 16:   Martin Kilson in African and the
United States, Images and Realities, U.S. National Commission for UNESCO, 1961, p. 67.

Biobaku (1963) studied the nationality representation of the staff members at the Institute of
African Studies at Ibadan, Nigeria.   His findings are
arranged in Table 17.   According to Biobaku, this representation is a "...practical demonstration of the
belief that in selecting staff the only relevant
qualification must be interest in Africa and ability to
contribute in a special way to the study of Africa,
without undue preoccupation with nationality."[112]

210

TABLE 17

STAFF MEMBERS IN AFRICAN UNIVERSITY 1963

Total # of Staff	Nations	Number of Staff	Percentage	Percentage: African
10	Nigeria	2	20%	30%
	Sudan	1	10%	
	Great Britain	2	20%	
	West Indies	1	10%	
	America	2	20%	
	New Zealand	1	10%	
	Brazil	1	10%	

Source of Table 17: Sabari Biobaku, "African Studies in an African University," Minerva, 1, 3 (Spring, 1963), pp. 285-302.

Eyoloye (1970) looked into three Nigerian universities to determine the representation in the student body for Africans other than Nigerians and the course of studies the non-Nigerian students pursued. He further considered (1) the extent of student exchange, (2) staff exchange, (3) examiners, and (4) teachers of modern languages. Although his study examined mostly the exchange within the four categories in the three Nigerian universities, his findings in Tables 18 and 19 reveal that there is 'low' representation of students from other West African countries in the three universities. Furthermore, only one of the 'foreign' students in the Nigerian schools was listed as attending the Department of Education. Eyoloye cites Professor Week's comments that there is very little exchange of students between African countries because of (1) language barriers, (2) lack of understanding and knowledge about other African countries, (3) institutional differences, (4) unguided nationalism and (5) inertia.[113] Thus, the Africanization meaning indigenization, of Africa's teaching staff is up-to-date incomplete, not to mention their Pan-Africanization, which is as farther away as practical Pan-Africanism.

Southall (1972) and Kofele-Kale (1978) have both viewed the feeling of strong nationalism in the current balkanized African countries as a hindrance to African unity and therefore larger African integration; Nye (1965), however, asserts that common schooling gave 1963 East African leaders a similar political outlook during their moves for East African integration.[114] Furthermore, that education, educational institutions including teachers can contribute to mitigate the strong feeling of nationalism has been postulated by several writers and substantiated by knowledge derived from socialization research.

TABLE 18

WEST AFRICAN STUDENTS IN THREE NIGERIAN UNIVERSITIES
BY COUNTRY

Country	Ibadan	Lagos	Ife	Total	Percent
Cameroon	22	1	8	31	49.3
Dahomey	--	-	1	8	1.6
Gambia	7	-	-	7	11.1
Ghana	3	1	-	4	6.3
Guinea	--	13	-	13	20.6
Senegal	--	1	-	6	1.6
Sierra Leone	5	1	-	6	9.5
Total	37	17	9	63	100.0

TABLE 19

SUMMARY OF FOREIGN STUDENTS IN THREE
NIGERIAN UNIVERSITIES

	University			
	Ibadan	Lagos	Ife	Total
West Africans	37 (1.4%)	17 (1.3%)	9 (0.7%)	63 (1.2%)
Total Foreign	74 (2.8%)	45 (3.5%)	11 (0.9%)	130 (2.6%)
Total	2,559	1,227	1,252	5,088

Note: The percentages are of the total enrollments in
each of the Universities studied.

Sources of Tables 18 & 19: E.A. Eyoloye, "Educational
Exchange Between West African Countries," West African
Journal of Education, October 1970, pp. 172-174.

Political Socialization

Political socialization research in the United
States as well as in Africa has shown that educational
institutions and teachers, and undoubtedly, in addition
to the home, church, peer, and civic groups, are significant agents of political socialization. Although
the strength of the contribution that schools and
teachers make is not easily and has not been precisely
identified, the literature suggests that schools and
teachers are significant elements in the transmission
of political, cultural, and social values.

213

Hyman (1959) first made into popular use the term 'political socialization' to mean the learning about the political systems in which one lives and as a process during which an individual is inducted into a particular political system.[115] This is also done through the media, in the home, church, as well as in formal educational institutions where children meet other children, teachers, and administrators. Jones (1971) refers directly to teachers 'as agents of political socialization,' and defines the concept "...as the process that both fosters the acceptance of traditional political norms and values and encourages the development of skills and abilities that will enable one to adapt to his rapidly changing society.[116] Although the traditional norms and values, in the context of Africa, are themselves undergoing rapid changes, Jones' idea of including in the socialization process 'self-development by acquiring skills and abilities to successfully adapt to his changing society,' is in order, especially in the case of Black Africa where formal schooling is relatively new.

Political socialization research has traditionally concentrated on the examination of textbooks, school curriculum, attitudes and perceptions of students, but the examination of the teacher has increasingly become a preoccupation. "The teacher is the medium through which topics of controversy are given meaning, substance, and relevance."[117]

In the older nations, such as Great Britain, Germany, and France, where political institutions have been entrenched, there is hardly any need for active political socialization in the schools; there are, in these nations, active socialization agents outside of the school systems that are capable of compensating the schools' inadequacies. "It is important to remember that the more advanced civilizations have institutions as the home, the church, the press to supplement the omissions and correct the errors of the schools."[118] African countries, on the contrary, are emerging nations and the schools are basically and intricately political institutions. Similarly, unlike British,

> American schools are highly political institutions. One of their primary tasks is to train young people to be 'good citizens,' that is to be 'good Americans'; only about three percent of England's secondary school children attend public schools, and almost all these children come from middle and upper-middle class families.[119]

Corresponding to American development, American schools are too becoming well defined with respect to the sort of socialization they must perform while the informal socialization agents correct and recompense the omissions of the schools. The radical Farber (1969) states that

> By and large our schools are in the hands of the most entrenched and rigidly conservative elements in society. In the secondary and elementary schools, students, of course, have no power and teachers have little power.[120]

This is because there are in American society other developed and entrenched means of socializing the youth other than the schools. Teachers who indeed fail to change with the prevailing winds of change, such as the movements of the 1960's, the dynamic development of new technologies and economies, etc. will undoubtedly be, and readily viewed as, conservatives.

The fanatical use of schools and educators as agents of political socialization, however, could lead to catastrophe, as in the case of Hitler's regime in which

> ...no one could teach who had not first served...in Labor Service. Candidates for instructorships in the universities had to attend six weeks in an observation camp where their views and character were studied by Nazi experts and reported to the Ministry of Education which issued licenses to teach based on the candidate's political reliability.[121]

The African leaders of the 1960's, nonetheless, expected their schools and teachers to be active participants in transmitting their political views and ideologies which they saw were appropriate for the developmental Zeitgeist. Some African countries implemented National Service requirements before students could proceed to the university or field of employment.[122]

Political socialization researchers in Africa have consistently shown teachers and schools to be significant agents for the transmission of political, social, and cultural values (Koff and Von Der Muhll, 1967; Dunajaiye, 1970; Weeks, 1963, Dawson, Prewitt, and Dawson, 1969, King, 1976; Nye, 1963, Mwingira, 1969, Smith, 1973) and authoritative opinions on socialization concur with these research findings (Selassie, 1963; Wandira, 1970; Allport, 1954).

In their comparative study of political socialization of high school students in Kenya and Tanzania,

Koff and Von Der Muhll found teachers and schools to be effective instruments for instilling norms of good citizenship in the students; the pupils saw schools as a means to success and teachers, among others, as agents from whom knowledge about the country can be learned. According to the data for both countries, more secondary school students have trust in teachers than they do in government leaders. (See Tables 20, 21, 22, 23). Religious leaders and fathers are also ranked higher than government leaders by most of the secondary school students in the two countries.

TABLE 20

PERCENTAGE OF STUDENTS WHO SAY THAT MEMBERS
OF DIFFERENT GROUPS CAN BE TRUSTED "ALWAYS"
OR "USUALLY"

Agents	Kenya Schools		Tanzania Schools	
	Primary	Secondary	Primary	Secondary
Fathers	78	92	85	87
Teachers	80	79	86	77
Religious Leaders	74	82	90	84
Government Leaders	72	57	89	63

TABLE 21

PERCENTAGE OF STUDENTS MENTIONING DIFFERENT
AGENTS AS THE BEST WAY TO LEARN ABOUT WHAT
IS HAPPENING IN THE COUNTRY

Agents	Kenya Schools		Tanzania Schools	
	Primary	Secondary	Primary	Secondary
Radios and Newspapers	85	96	60	96
Teachers	9	54	33	48
Parents and Relatives	2	3	5	3
Older People in the Home Area	4	3	2	6
Classmates (secondary only)		9		12

TABLE 22

STUDENTS' RANK ORDER OF PURPOSES OF

SCHOOLS BY WEIGHTED INDICES

Purposes:	Schools	
	Kenya	Tanzania
Teach students to be good citizens	869	867
Teach students skills necessary to get jobs	622	630
Teach students the important things to know for the examinations	579	585
Teach students to be religious (good Christians, etc.)	547	428
Teach students about the important African traditions and customs	353	400

TABLE 23

STUDENTS' PERCEPTIONS OF WAYS TO SUCCESS

Ways to Success:	Secondary Schools	
	Kenya	Tanzania
Be well educated	87	82
Work hard	79	75
Have friends in government	13	15
Belong to a certain tribe	6	2
Come from a rich family	4	4
Be willing to break laws	3	3
Other	3	3

Sources of Tables 21, 22, & 23: David Koff and George Von Der Muhll, "Political Socialization in Kenya and Tanzania: A Comparative Analysis," The Journal of Modern African Studies, 5, 1 (1967), pp. 13-51.

Weeks (1963) studied friendship patterns among the students at Lubiri Secondary School in Mengo-Kampala, Uganda. The school was started as a private institution of the Kabaka, supported by the Buganda government, and was initially mostly attended by members of the Baganda tribe; it later accepted students from Kenya, Tanganyika, and Northern Rhodesia. Although it remained predominantly Baganda, the minority tribes, due to the emphasis on academic performance rather than on tribe per se, were able to become friends with members of the dominant tribe. Weeks observed that language differences were a barrier, but academic tutoring, communication of secrets, discussion of personal problems, revelation of relationships with girls, sharing of cigarettes, drinking, and going to the movies together, etc. were shared experiences that promoted the development of cross-tribal friendships[123] "...it might be concluded that Baganda students becoming friends with non-Baganda students in the school helps to alter their attitudes towards minority students;"[124] the Baganda students who had friendship relations with non-Baganda students would like to see more non-Bagandas admitted into the school.[125]

Nye (1963) randomly selected 180 African male college students for an interview to determine their attitudes towards plans for an East African federation. His sample consisted of 50 Kenyans, 50 Tanganyikans, and 80 Ugandans, 30 of whom were from the Baganda tribe; of the 180 students selected, he interviewed 126. Thirty Kenyans, of whom fourteen were Kikuyu, were interviewed and all were for East African unity; 70% of the sample was for federation, 16% were opposed, and 14% undecided. Even though "...it is debatable whether their view twenty years" since 1963 "...will be the same as the one they held in College,"[126] Nye remarks elsewhere that common schooling was in part responsible for the unity of outlook among the East African leaders in Kenya, Tanganyika, and Uganda.[127]

Smith (1973) writes that the principal of Alliance High School in Kenya deliberately made a plan to integrate the school which was attended by students from various tribes and regions of the country; the students, because of tribalism, were "hereditary enemies."[128] This plan to integrate the students

> ...was a tricky experiment as there were
> no teachers-in-training from whom he
> usually obtained his older and more reli-
> able prefects...Yet mixing worked well to
> begin with although there were sporadic
> outbursts before it was finally accepted
> as normal.[129]

Sass (1950-1960) states that integrated schooling, especially at the elementary school level, could subsequent in 'mixed bloods' particularly if the integration is supported by teachers and administrators.[130] Allport (1954) supports the stance that schools and teachers have influence in the process of integration of racial or ethnic groups. He states that

> ...emotional valuations are learned from
> teachers and parents and are ready-made.
> The mode of teaching ordinarily stops the
> process of an enlargement...Beyond the na-
> tive land there is only the domain of
> 'foreigners'--not fellow men. Most
> children never enlarge their sense of
> belonging beyond the ties of the family,
> city, or nation. The reason seems to be
> that those with whose judgement he mirrors

221

do not do so...While the national orbit is
the largest circle of loyalty that most
children learn, there is no necessity for
the process to stop there.[131]

Allport goes on to elaborate that

prejudice...may be reduced by equal status
contact between majority and minority
groups in the pursuit of common goals.
The effect is greatly enhanced if this
contact is sanctioned by institutional
support (i.e., by law, custom, or local
atmosphere), and provided it is of a sort
that leads to the perception of common interests and common humanity between members of the two groups.[132]

Smith and others (1969) and Bowker (1968) have all been
concerned about the integration in the schools of
America and England respectively and stress that
teachers can enhance the process of social integration.[133]

A.C. Mwingina, Tanzania Minister of Education, asserts that "The teacher, we recognize, is the key factor in educational reform, whether it be short-term
changes in school administration, or long-term reorien-
tation of the school curriculum."[134]

Other African statesmen, writers, and researchers
have emphasized educational institutions and teachers
as significant for the realization of African integration and larger African unity. Durajaiye (1970) inves-
tigated the occupational and social psychological perceptions of 196 secondary school pupils in Nigeria.
Due to the students' high class background in concert
with the international climate of their school, which
was staffed and attended by school boys from various

222

tribes, ethnic groups, races, and nationalities, the students

...admirably demonstrated an international outlook towards place of occupation. They said they would like to work anywhere.[135]

Mazrui (1971) asserts that some degree of integration among African peoples be encouraged in the schools and by teachers. Selassie (1963) advocates the physical integration of African students in a Pan-African University specifically for the purpose of materializing African unity and development. Brown (1966) asserts that the ideology of African unity be implemented in African schools by teachers. In his frame of perceptions, as Africans look "...forward to a free and united Africa..." so also must they stop "...giving...children an essentially European-type education which has contributed to the national divisions of Europe and has cut the continent of Africa up as though it were a cake."[136] Wandira (1970) states that Pan-African ideology "...which looms so large in the minds of African leaders must find its place in the scheme of African teacher education."[137] In Ghana, "undergraduates" were "to follow in their first year a course in African courses" 'stressing the unity of the African continent in all its aspects.'"[138]

Wandira (1970), Brown (1966), Selassie (1963), and Mazrui (1971) all denote that African teachers should be agents of the 'prevailing' African ideology. National integration and larger Pan-Africanism have been the desired goals of African political leaders since the 1960's[139] and must therefore be part of African education.[140] Apple (1978) establishes that schools are microcosms of the larger society.[141]

This chapter has shown abundantly that educational institutions and teachers are highly considered with respect to their capacities to enhance political, cultural, and social integration. Teachers, as agents of political socialization and as part of the macro-Africa culturally, politically, and ideologically are not oblivious to the African social Zeitgeist.

Africa, in contrast to the already developed western world, is in a transitional stage and it seems would continue to be so for a good number of years. The developed western world has had a longer history of entrenched institutions which have successfully defined the western personality. For Africa to have a defined Pan-African personality, it must establish Pan-African educational institutions to enhance the feat. Even though the African nationalists of the 1960's and 1970's established numerous schools, colleges and universities, the majority of Africa still remains illiterate and balkanized. Literacy has been modestly achieved in some African countries, but the African continent as a whole remains the most backward educationally.[142]

Chapter eight presents some criticisms of African education under African leadership; Chapter Nine describes Pan-African education as the last stage of educational developments in Africa.

Notes

CHAPTER SEVEN

[1]J. Stephen Smith, The History of Alliance High School (Nairobi, Kenya: Heinemann Educational Books, 1973), p. 9.

[2]William Conton, The African (Heinemann Educational Books Ltd., 1969), p. 21.

[3]Robert L. Shrigley, "Student Teaching in Nigeria," Peabody Journal of Education, 46 (January 1969), p. 204.

[4]_____, "Teacher Education in Africa," Peabody Journal of Education, 47, 4 (January 1970), pp. 221-223.

[5]John Anderson, "Training Teachers for East Africa," East Africa Journal (June 1966), p. 21.

[6]Ernest Stabler, Education Since Uhuru: The Schools of Kenya (Middletown, Connecticut: Wesleyan University Press, 1969), pp. 58-76.

[7]A. Babs Fafunwa, "Teacher Education in Nigeria," West African Journal of Education, XIV, 1 (February 1970), pp. 20-26.

[8]L.J. Lewis, "Getting Good Teachers for Developing Countries," International Review of Education, XVI (1970/74), p. 394.

[9]Ibid., p. 398.

[10]Matthew Omijeh, "Training Primary School Teachers in Nigera: Problems and Prospects," Education in Eastern Africa, 6, 1 (1976), p. 14.

[11]Bert N. Adams, "Africanization and Academic Emperialism: A Case Study in Planned Change and Inertia," East African Journal, 9, 5 (May 1972), p. 23.

[12]Louis W. Normington, Teacher Education and the Agency for International Develonment, [AACTE, 1970], p. 19.

[13]P.C.C. Evans, "American Teachers for East Africa," Comparative Education Review, Vol. 6, No. 1 (June 1962), p. 69.

[14]"Peace Corps for Ghana" and "British Teachers for Nigeria," West Africa (July 1, 1961), p. 730.

[15]Edward H. Berman, "Foundations, United States Foreign Policy and African Education, 1945-1975," Harvard Educational Review, 49, 2 (May 1979), pp. 146-179.

[16]Willard S. Elsbree, "History of Teacher Education in the United States," in Kalil I. Gezi, Teaching in American Culture (Holt, Rinehart and Winston, 1968), pp. 35-49.

[17]L. Beasley, "London Eliminates the 11+: The Transfer Document Becomes the Basis for Secondary Selection," Comparative Education Review, Vol. 10, No. 1 (February 1966), pp. 80-81.

[18]"African Universties at the Crossroads," Africa Report (November 1963), p. 4.

[19]W.A. Dodd, Recent Trends in Teacher Education in Developing Countries of the Commonwealth (London: Commonwealth Secretariat, 1970).

[20]A. Babs Fafunwa, "Teacher Education in Nigeria," West Africa Journal of Education, XIV, 1 (February 1970), p. 20.

[21]Ibid.

[22]J.W. Hanson, "On General Education for the African Teacher," Teacher Education, 3, 3 (February 1963), pp. 181-188.

[23]Chango Machyo, "The University, Its Role in Africa," East Africa Journal (February 1969), p. 21.

[24]Okot P'Bitek, Africa's Cultural Revolution (Nairobi, Kenya: MacMillan Books for Africa, 1973), p. 102.

[25]Quoted by Asavia Wandira, "Foundation Studies in Teacher Education in Africa," Education in Eastern Africa, 1, 2 (January 1970), p. 15.

[26]The Editors, "Whither ATEA," West African Journal of Education, XVII, 2 (June 1974), p. 94.

[27]F.C.A. Cammaerts, "Priorities for Preparation of Secondary Teachers in Kenya," East Africa Journal (November 1969), p. 9.

[28]Haile Selassie, "Towards African Unity," The Journal of Modern African Studies, 11, 3 (1963), pp. 281-291.

[29]West Africa (July 22, 1961), p. 791.

[30]William W. Brickman, "Tendencies in African Education," The Educational Forum, Vol. XXVII, No. 4 (May 1963), p. 408.

[31]Joseph S. Nye, "Unity and Diversity in East Africa: A Bibliographical Essay," The South Atlantic Journal, Vol. LXV, No. 1 (Winter 1966), p. 113.

[32]Colin Legum, Pan-Africanism: A Short Political Guide (London: Pall Mall Press, 1962), p. 249.

[33]Julius K. Nyerere, "A United States of Africa," The Journal of Modern African Studies, 1, 1 (1963), p. 6.

[34]Cheikh Anta Diop, Black Africa: The Economic and Cultural Basis for a Federated State (Connecticut: Lawrence-Hill and Company, 1978), p. 11.

[35]Reginald H. Green and Ann Seidman, Unity or Poverty? The Economics of Pan-Africanism (Penguin Books, 1968), p. 79.

[36]Opeyemi Ola, "Pan-Africanism: An Ideology for Development," Presence Africaine, No. 112 (4th Quarterly, 1979), p. 82.

[37]Walter Rodney, How Europe Underdeveloped Africa (Washington, D.C.: Howard University Press, 1974).

[38]Opeymei Ola, "Pan-Africanism: An Ideology for Development," Presence Africaine (4th Quarterly, 1979), p. 92.

[39]Jack Ran Kine Boody, Technology, Tradition, and the State of Africa (London: Oxford University Press, 1971), p. 76.

[40]Basil Davidson, Can African Survive? (Boston-Toronto: Little Brown and Company, 1974), p. 6.

[41]p'Bitek, Op. Cit., p. 7.

[42]Abdul Rahman Mohamed Babu, African Socialism or Socialist Africa (Dar es Salaam, Tanzania Publish House, 1981).

[43]Leon N. Lindberg, "Interest Group Activities in the E.E.C.," in Paul A. Tharp (ed.), Regional Internal Organizations/Structures and Functions (New York: St. Martin's Press, 1971), p. 11.

[44]Amitai Etzioni, "The Dialects of Supranational Unification," in Anchor Books Edition, International Political Communities (New York: Anchor Books, 1966), p. 141.

[45]Ibid., p. 179.

[46]Ibid., p. 189.

[47]Theodore M. Mills, "Power Relations in Three Person Groups," American Sociological Review, Vol. 18, No. 4 (August 1953), p. 335.

[48]Quoted in Joseph S. Nye, Pan-Africanism and East African Federation (Cambridge, Massachusetts: Harvard University Press, 1965), p. 192.

[49]Nye, Op. Cit., p. 11.

[50]J.E. Goldthorpe, An African Elite: Makerere College Students, 1922-1969 (Nairobi, Kenya: Oxford University Press, 1965).

[51]Ibid., p. 63.

[52]Nye, Op. Cit., p. 32.

[53]Robert I. Rotberg, "An Account of the Attempt to Achieve Closer Union in British East Africa," Makerere Institute of Social Research, Conference Papers (January 1963), p. 2.

[54]Ibid., p. 7.

[55]Hans Arnold, "Cultural Exchange and European Polity," Universitas, Vol. 21, No. 3 (1979), p. 170.

[56]Nye, Op. Cit., p. 25.

[57]"Attitudes of Makerere Students Towards the East African Federation," Proceedings of the East African Institute of Social Research (January 1963, p. 3.

[58]Ibid., p. 5.

[59]Ibid., p. 207.

[60]Patricia Berko Wild, "Radicals and Moderates in the OAU: Origins of Conflict and Basis for Co-existence," in Paul A. Tharp (ed.), Regional International Organizations/Structures and Functions (New York: St. Martin's Press, 1971), p. 37.

[61]Ibid., pp. 36-50.

[62]Joseph S. Nye, Pan-Africanism and East African Integration (Cambridge, Massachusetts: Harvard University Press, 1965), p. 14.

[63]Wilde, Op. Cit., p. 40.

[64]Ibid.

[65]Claude E. Welch, Dream of Unity: Pan-Africanism and Political Unification in West Africa (Ithaca: Cornell University Press, 1966), p. 306.

[66]Christopher T. Baunn "Highways and African Unity," West Africa (December 30, 1961), p. 1439; see also West Africa (November 4, 1961), p. 1233; "What ECOWAS Says" (May 19, 1975), p. 558, and Simon Anekwe, "Hundreds Rejoice as OAU Acquires Office Building," New York Amsterdam News, Vol. 72, No. 45 (Sat. No. 7), 1981, p. 33.

[67]Welch, Op. Cit., p. 336.

[68]Arthur Hazlewood, "Problems of Integration Among African States," in his edition of African Integration and Disintegration (Oxford University Press, 1967), p. 25.

[69]Richard L. Sklar, "Political Science and National Integration," The Journal of Modern African Studies, 5, 1 (1967), p. 3.

[70]E.A. Ayandele, A.E. Figbo, et al., The Growth of African Civilization: The Making of Modern Africa, Vol. 11, 1971, p. 28.

[71]Laing Gray Cowan, Black Africa: The Growing Pains of Independence (New York: Foreign Policy Association, Inc., 1971), p. 41.

72Smith, Op. Cit., p. XIV.

73William L. Gaines, "Some Thoughts about African Man-power and U.S. Educational Assistance to Africa," in R. Pierce Beaver (ed.), Christianity and African Education (Grand Rapids, Michigan: William B. Eerdmans Pub-lishing Company, 1965), p. 97.

74Saburi Biobaku, "African Studies in African Univer-sities," Minerva, Vol. 1, No. 3 (Spring 1963), p. 301.

75Ibid., p. 291.

76West Africa, "Reorganizing Ghana's Colleges" (July 1961), p. 791.

77William W. Brickman, "Tendencies in African Educa-tion," The Educational Forum, Vol. XXVII, No. 4 (May 1963), p. 408.

78Ibid., p. 399.

79Ibid., p. 402.

80F.C.A. Cammaerts, "Priorities for the Preparation of Secondary Teachers in Kenya," East Africa Journal (November 1969), p. 9.

81George C. Urch, "Africanization of Schools in Kenya," Educational Forum, 34 (March 1970), p. 376, see also Jane and Idrian Resnick, "Tanzania Educates for a New Society," Africa Report, Vol. 16, No. 1 (January 1971), pp. 26-29.

82Edgar Bradshaw Castle, Principles of Education for Teachers in Africa (Nairobi, Kenya: Oxford University Press, 1965), p. 18.

83Nye, Op. Cit., p. 80.

84Haile Selassie, "Towards African Unity," The Journal of Modern African Studies, Vol. 11, No. 3 (1963), pp. 281-291.

85Julius K. Nyerere, "A United States of Africa," The Journal of Modern African Studies, Vol. 1, No. 1 (1953), p. 6.

86Asavia Wandira, "Foundation Studies in Teacher Education in Africa," Education of Eastern Africa, 1, 2 (1979), p. 14.

[87]G.N. Brown, "Education for Responsibility--The Teacher's Role," West African Journal of Education, X, 2 (June 1966), p. 66.

[88]Owen Charles Mathurin, Henry Sylvester Williams and the Origins of the Pan-African Movement, 1869-1911 (Westport, Connecticut, 1976).

[89]Rupert Emerson and Martin Kilson (eds.), The Political Awakening in Africa (Englewood Cliffs, New Jersey: Prentice-Hall, Inc., 1965), pp. 169-174.

[90]Hans Arnold, "Cultural Exchange and European Policy," Universitas, Vol. 21, No. 3 (1979), p. 170.

[91]Akiiki B. Mujuju, "A Critique of Education for Development," East Africa Journal (June 1972), p. 5.

[92]Ali A. Mazrui, "The Educational Implicatiors of National Goals and Political Values in Africa," Education in Eastern Africa, Vol. 2, No. 1 (1971), pp. 38-55.

[93]Basil Davidson, Can Africa Survive? (Boston-Toronto: Little Brown and Company, 1974), p. 6.

[94]Beverly Lindsay and J. John Harris, "A Review of Pan-Africanism and Education," The African Review, Vol. 6, No. 2 (1976), p. 266, see also Kenneth King, Pan-Africanism and Education, p. 3.

[95]Bryant W. Mumford, "Malangali School," Africa, 3 (July 1930), pp. 265-290.

[96]Donald Cameron, My Tanganyika Service and Some Nigeria (London: George Allen and Unwin, Ltd., 1939, pp. 92-93; see also Anton Bertram, The Colonial Service (Cambridge University Press, 1930), p. 82; W.B. Mumford, "Native Schools in Central Africa," Journal of the African Society, Vol. XXVI, No. CI (October 1926), pp. 237-244, O.W. Furley and T. Watson, "Education in Tanganyika Between the Wars: Attempts to Blend Two Cultures," The South Atlantic Quarterly, Vol. LXV, No. 4 (Autumn 1966), pp. 471-490, and Fielding A. Clarke, "An Experimental School in Nigeria," Journal of the Royal African Society, 39 (January 1940), pp. 36-50.

[97]Edward H. Berman, "American Philanthropy and African Education: Toward an Analysis," African Studies Review, Vol. XX, No. 1 (April 1977), p. 75; see also

E.H. Berman, "Tuskegee-In-Africa," The Journal of Negro Education, XLI (1972), pp. 99-112.

[98]Booker T. Washington, "David Livingstone and the Negro," International Review of Missions, Vol. 2 (1913), p. 233.

[99]King, Op. Cit., p. 3.

[100]Nnamdi Azikiwe, "How Shall We Educate the African?" Journal of the African Society, Vol. 33 (April 1934), pp. 143-151.

[101]L.J. Lewis, "Education in Africa," The Yearbook of Education (London: Evans Brothers, 1949), pp. 312-337.

[102]John Cameron, The Development of Education in East Africa (New York: Teachers College Press, 1970), Chapter IX.

[103]L.J. Lewis, Society, Schools and Progress in Nigeria (Institute of Education, University of London: Pergamon Press, 1965), pp. 105-117.

[104]Eric Ashby, African Universities and Western Tradition (Cambridge, Massachusetts: Harvard University Press, 1964), p. 19.

[105]Ibid., p. 30.

[106]Ibid., pp. 44-49.

[107]A.M. Carr-Saunders, "Staffing African Universities," Minerva, 1, 3 (Spring 1963), p. 304; for a further discussion on the Staffing of African Universities, see Eric Ashby, African Universities and Western Traditions (Cambridge, Massachusetts: Harvard University Press, 1964), pp. 49-53.

[108]Bent N. Adams, "Africanization and Academic Empirialism: A Case Study in Planned Change and Inertia," East African Journal (May 1972), p. 28.

[109]Ibid., p. 23.

[110]Eric Ashby, Op. Cit., p. 52.

[111]Ibid., p. 51.

[112]Sabari Biobaku, "African Studies in African University," Minverva, 1, 3 (Spring 1963), p. 295.

[113]Cited by E.A. Eyoloye, "Educational Change Between West African Countries," West African Journal of Education, XIV, 3 (October 1970), p. 175; see also Rocheforte L. Weeks, "Inter-African Cooperation," in The Development of Higher Education in Africa (UNESCO: Report of the Conference on the Development of Higher Education in Africa Tananarive, 1962), pp. 214-216.

[114]Joseph S. Nye, Pan-Africanism and East African Integration (Cambridge, Massachusetts: Harvard University Press, 1965), p. 83.

[115]H.H. Hyman, Political Socialization (Glencoe, Illinois: The Free Press, 1959).

[116]Ruth S. Jones, "Teachers as Agents of Political Socialization," Education and Urban Society, Vol. IV, No. 1 (November 1971), p. 99.

[117]Ibid., p. 100.

[118]Ibid.

[119]Paul R. Abramson, "Political Socialization in English and American Schools," The High School Journal, Vol. LIV, No. 1 (October 1970), p. 70.

[120]Jerry Farber, The Student as a Nigger (California: Contact Books, 1969), p. 16.

[121]William L. Shirer, The Rise and Fall of the Third Reich (New York: Simon and Schuster, 1960), p. 249.

[122]N.J. Small, "Getting Ideas Across: Limitations to Social Engineering in a New State," African Affairs, Vol. 77, No. 309 (October 1978), pp. 531-553 and Jane and Idrian Resnick, "Tanzania Educates for a New Society," Africa Report, Vol. 16, No. 1 (January 1971), pp. 26-29.

[123]S.G. Weeks, "A Preliminary Examination of the Role of Minority Students at a Day Secondary School in Kampala, Uganda," East African Institute of Social Research (January 1963), p. 4.

[124]Ibid., p. 7.

[125]Ibid., p. 8.

[126]Joseph S. Nye. "Attitudes of Makerere Students Towards the East African Federation," East African Institute of Social Research (January 1963), p. 1.

[127]_____, Pan-Africanism and East African Integration (Cambridge, Massachusetts: Harvard University Press, 1965), p. 80.

[128]Smith, Op. Cit., p. 84.

[129]Ibid., pp. 84-85.

[130]Ravenel Sass, "Mixed Schools Mixed Bloods," The Annals of America (Encyclopedia Britannica), Vol. 17 (1950-1960), pp. 373-378.

[131]Gordon Allport, The Nature of Prejudice (Cambridge, Massachusetts: Addison-Wesley, 1954), pp. 45-46.

[132]Ibid., p. 281.

[133]Gordon Bowker, The Education of Colored Immigrants (Longmans, Green and Co., Ltd., 1968); Othanel O. Smith, Teachers for the Real World, The American Association of Colleges for Teacher Education (AACTE), 1969.

[134]Quoted in Richard Jolly (ed.), Education in Africa: Research and Action (Nairobi, Kenya: East African Publishing House, 1969), p. 68.

[135]M.O.A. Durajaiye, "School Education and Occupational Choice: Social Psychological Research in a Nigerian International Secondary School," West African Journal of Education, XIV, 1 (February 1970), p. 63.

[136]G.N. Brown, "Education for Responsibility--The Teacher's Role," West African Journal of Education (June 1966), pp. 65-66.

[137]Asavia Wandira, "Foundation Studies in Teacher Education in Africa," Education in Eastern Africa, 1, 2 (January 1970), p. 15.

[138]Ashby, Op. Cit., p. 63.

[139]Julius K. Nyerere, "A United States of Africa," The Journal of Modern African Studies, 1, 1 (1963), p. 6.

[140]Asavia Wandira, "Foundation Studies in Teacher Education in Africa," Education in Eastern Africa, 1, 2 (January 1970), p. 15.

[141]Michael W. Apple, "The New Sociology of Education," Harvard Educational Review, Vol. 48, No. 4 (1978), p. 496.

[142]Emmanuel A. Ayandele, "Africa: The Challenge of Higher Education," Daedaeus, Vol. III, No. 2 (Spring 1982), p. 168.

CHAPTER EIGHT
SOME CRITICISMS OF AFRICAN EDUCATION UNDER NATIONALIST
AFRICAN LEADERSHIP: 1960's - 1980's

(1) Irrespective of the multiplicities of universities, colleges, secondary and elementary schools on
the African continent in the 1960's and 70's under
African leadership, African education remained closely
aligned with Western academic paradigms.   The universities that were established were European universities
built simply on African soil "...to enable a generation
of Africans to accept the superiority of the Western-
oriented, democratic capitalist development model over
its socialist counterpart."[1]   In these nationalist
universities, questions about the establishment of
African studies programs were debated[2] as if these were
inferior fields of study.   The lead universities established in Ethiopia, Nigeria and Zaire were

> to play important roles in the creation of
> a leadership, which...would help sustain
> 'the orderliness of economic growth.   The
> objective is one that engages directly the
> self-interest of the economically more ad-

vanced peoples and calls for their understanding and assistance'[3]
Thus, most of the 1960's 'nationalist' universities
were deliberate results of western governments and
their interested multinational co-operations to keep
African nationals in check in terms of their aspirations for other types of regimes such as socialism or
communism.

> Ford and fund officials thought they could
> nurture, through training offered in elite
> United States Universities, potential
> leaders whose outlook and values would en-
> sure their support of the dominant United
> States social, economic, and political in-
> stitutions. These ford-nurtured leaders
> would then assume their places as execu-
> tives of major African institutions, where
> they would continue to uphold the inter-
> ests of society's dominant classes.[4]

(2) The school culture in the new African universities did not reflect the dominant aspirations of the
African masses; they in fact encourage elitism, ar-
rogance on the part of the small educated elite who,
upon their graduation, find themselves heading departments of government, business or schools. Often, at
the university, their clothes had been laundered, bed
spread[5], and given regular government allowance at the
expense of the masses of Africans whom they will continue to exploit as government officials by lavishly
spending government funds on themselves.[6]

(3) Most African countries at the time of independence were already infested with African bourgeoisie
bureaucrats, military and police personnel, and other
professionals who had been mostly responsible to their

colonial masters culturally, intellectually, linguistically, etc., but few African leaders instituted schools
to counteract their concomitant colonial mentalities.
When in 1961 Nkrumah established an ideological institute at Winneba to counteract the pervasive colonial
mentality in Ghana, the school was one of the first institutions to be attacked by the police and military
men who engineered the 1966 coup that removed Kwame
Nkrumah and his CPP from the political scene to retard
his socialist revolution.[7] Thus, all efforts were made
to deter any progressive movement to get Africans
thinking in a radical way so as to achieve African
unity under socialism. The colonial mentality was so
ingrained that even when...

> hundreds of students (were sent) to places
> like Russia, it was plain that they
> despised the Russians. They attempted to
> desecrate Lenin's tomb, and they looked
> down on the people.
> It was the result of wanting to change
> colonial institutions overnight, but not
> having the qualified staff to do it. This
> was the anatomy of our misery, that we had
> nobody trained to implement our aims.[8]

(4) In the 1960's as soon as individual African
countries attained political independence, a national
university shortly followed; this retarded the integration of African students from various African countries
in terms of African students attending a centrally located university such as Fourah Bay College for English
speaking West Africa, the university at Senegal for
French speaking West Africa, Makerere for English
speaking East Africa as these centers had functioned

during Colonial times; thus pre-independence Pan-Africanism died with the achievement of independence. After independence was achieved Africans developed an intense feeling of national pride and belonging. The Africans were deeply proud to be Kenyans, Malawians, Ghanaians, Zimbabweans, Nigerians, etc.[9]

(5) The new national universities recruited most of their staff and academic paradigms from their ex-colonizers or from the United States of America, and there was therefore present in African Schools of higher learning the most diversified body of staff members than any school systems in the world. It was then predicted that African schools would be Africanized in terms of staff, but this has not up to date been accomplished. And in fact, when these African schools spoke of Africanization, they meant indeginization,[10] not Pan-Africanization, and that de facto stance is still functional today. In essence, African Universities implicitly, by such means, balkanized Africa academically, psychologically and intellectually.

(6) In the 1960's and the 1970's teacher training colleges mushroomed all over the African Continent, but most of these colleges were so ill-equipped that they could hardly thoroughly prepare the academically ill-equipped teacher trainees. The lack of school supplies such as books and other educative materials continue to plague these teacher training colleges.

(7) African teachers continue to be poorly paid in African countries and thus, the teaching profession has not been attractive to the more ambitious element of the educated Africans. Those who graduate from African national Universities are more attracted to 'lucrative' employment sectors such as banking, business, government bureaucracy; or they go for higher studies in

Western countries, or migrate to other African countries perceived to be politically and economically more conducive for their material aspirations. African University professors are not immune to the low salaries paid the African teaching profession; those professors who do not agree with government policies often migrate to developed countries or are co-opted into the political machinery of their respective nations.

(8) It is a well known fact in African countries that those university students who opt to protest against government mismanagement of funds, bad food on campuses and living conditions, have been summarily expelled and in certain cases several African governments have closed their national universities to show their displeasure over student displeasures and their subsequent protests. These closing of schools have often retarded students' progress in their studies.

(9) Some African universities still require too high and strict entrance requirements before students can be admitted to their 'limited' programs and 'limited' places, so that those students who have not performed exceptionally well, (even though these students often have the ability to do college work) are left without opportunities to advance their studies in their countries; some of these students often obtain placements in Western universities where they successfully go on to advanced degrees after which they decide to remain abroad. Though brain drain is as yet not a problem as is in Asian and Latin American countries, Africa cannot afford to lose any of its skilled manpower such as college graduates in technology, teaching, management, agriculture, health and nutrition, etc. In essence, African colleges and universities

have not been flexible enough to recruit even those students who have the desire and often the ability to improve themselves within their own countries, and there are virtually no other opportunities to attend other African universities. Those students who can afford to go to America and other Western countries are often those from the middle class; those college graduates from lower classes are relegated to remain at home and often take jobs in which they are frustrated and thus negatively affecting their performance at a job that seems to be a dead end. In most African countries, if one does not go through the university levels, there are very few other opportunities left for self-advancement (except, maybe in the smuggling of goods across national boundaries).

(10) The universal primary education that was projected to be achieved by the 1980's at the 1961 UNESCO Ministers of Education Conference has not been obviously met. Even though the number of elementary schools and elementary school children almost doubled between 1961 and 1968, the 1970's experienced large number of drop-outs and no corresponding development in industry was affected to absorb the large drop-outs. Certainly, the failure in African education is dependent on other factors such as economics, political ideology of African leaders, international financial aid, etc. which in turn affect the type of education Africa has been providing.

(11) Generally, contemporary African education has been affected by educational paradigms such as community development, assimilation, adaptation, independent African schools and schools for national integration;[11] the latter aim, national integration,

241

has not been completely achieved, not to mention community development or educational adaptation. The national integration of each independent African nation has only been superficially attained for tribalism and regionalism still remain dormant especially in areas of employment and in certain cases access to higher education; most African universities are still predominantly male dominated in terms of student body and staff membership.

(12) Even though the process of education and educational institutions have been known to be able to abate the feeling of tribalism, a good percentage of African students continue to think in tribal and nationalistic terms;[12] furthermore, no attempt has been made to establish and institutionalize Pan-African educational institutions as suggested by Haile Selassie in 1963.[13] As early as 1961, almost two years before the formation of the Organization of African Unity (OAU), there were talks about the exchange of students and staff between African Universities, the intensive study of French in English-speaking Africa, and English in French-speaking Africa, starting at the secondary level, the establishment of common academic standards[14] and to form an all "West African Institute of Cultural Research which would be international in its administration and personnel;"[15] but these suggestions emphasize the regional aspects of Pan-African education with little or no attention paid to other African regions.

(13)

> The open-door policy of Dakar University beckoned citizens of neighboring Francophone countries in West Africa, but

national pride, defined by colonial boundaries, led them to choose national universities. And despite the high promise that
the University of East Africa would become
a mega-multiversity for the whole region,
after six years of experiment, Kenya ap-
propriated the campus in Nairobi, Uganda
that in Kampala, and Tanzania that in Dar
es Salaam. And in the name of evenly
sharing the 'national cake,' the Federal
Republic of Nigeria has decided to
punctuate each of its nineteen states with
a federal university, in total disregard
of cost and integrated national planning.[16]

The call for Africans to cooperate in educational matters has been numerous, but there has been far less
talk about the total integration of all African
schools, and much less emphasis on functional cooperation and integration.   There are still divisions between the British, French, Portuguese and American
spheres of influence and lack of Pan-African education
to mitigate these well established spheres of influences.   "...the pre-existing colonial forms of
African unity, such as those for scientific research
and pestology amongst the French and British West
African Countries,"[17] have all been nationalized in the
name of national sovereignty and to abate fear of sub-
version from non-nationals.

(14) African education is up to date not adequately
diffused within African nations; the urban areas, the
first sites for western educational institutions,
remain the best places, to receive better education.
In Kenya for instance, "most of the top ten schools are

243

located in Central province"[18] which supply the most students to Kenyan universities because of their superior educative resources; other areas undoubtedly have had secondary schools, but these are qualitatively nowhere near the older schools established by missionaries and the various colonial governments. Thus, while the Europeans were asked to leave or were expelled from some African countries, their well established school systems were left practically unaltered. In fact, most of the newer schools that were established after independence were nowhere good enough for the sons of ministers and other top level civil servants; most of these schools were for the sons and daughters of the illiterate peasants whose children saw school walls for the first time; these were children most of whom would soon join the growing number of drop-outs and the unemployed youth.

(15) Even though technical schools were widely established in Africa in the 1960's and 70's, these schools remain less popular for the technically or mathematically bright student. These technical schools continue to recruit those students who have not passed very well to be admitted in the national universities. In Africa, technical education still seem to be less prestigious than the study of law and medicine, a residue of colonial tradition, especially in British Africa.

> ...the unavailability of places at the University of Nairobi whose facilities are so limited that the majority of those who attain university entrance requirements do not get admittance and the result has been that many of those who can afford it go to overseas for further studies. Until the

244

late seventies, the majority of students
used to go to the United States and
Britain, where costs are high, but, some-
what suddenly, India was discovered as a
cheaper alternative and today, up to 40
percent of all Kenyan students going
abroad for studies go to India.[19]

Thus, generally, African students can be found all over
the world, bringing back into Africa various shades of
ideologies, expectations, life-styles, languages, etc.
but not cohesiveness in thought in terms of the solving
of African problems. Thus, there are in Africa, Mar-
xists, scientific Socialists, Leninists, Maoists, Ghan-
dists, Capitalists, and others not so easily
categorized and the effect has been suspicions between
African leaders and intellectuals and the subsequent
inertia. It is not a wild hunch that Africa has become
the tower of Babel of the modern world in terms of the
presence of all sorts of alien ideologies other than
those that should accelerate African development.

(16) African universities continue to concentrate
on the study of other peoples other than African
peoples within Africa and those in the diaspora;

...their curricula in the arts and social
sciences focus on peoples in the Wider
World, giving students a more informed and
healthier understanding of man in Europe
and North America than one finds in
universities in these developed regions.
...the global nature of the content of
study in African universities is one leaf
their counterparts in the developed
societies could borrow with profit.[20]

It is not that African universities should not study other societies in depth, but this should not be at the expense of African conditions that need urgent attention at all fronts.

(17)

> In the academic area of curriculum-design, in which they should excel, African universities have been rather a disappointment, for they have not operated within the parameters of the desire and struggle of contemporary Africa for self-realization and self-creation. They simply are not in the vanguard of the cultural renaissance that should pervade....[21]

Furthermore,

> ...many African academics lack an adequate emotional attachment to the African past, and therefore not committed to a detailed and comprehensive survey of the cultural heritage of African society. True, the curriculum in the arts and social sciences is impressively Africa-oriented, but it is yet to be African-oriented. It is not an accident that most of the materials in which the academic merits of the curriculum rest have been authored by non-Africans. Indeed, Africa is par excellence a region where most of the textbooks in the secondary schools and tertiary institutions are the work of non-Africans - that is, Europeans and American.[22]

And because most African academics still must be 'approved' by western scholars and institutions, their writings are mainly in the western paradigm, and the junior African scholars continue to imbibe the inherited paradigm.

> ...in comparative terms, only a few publications by African scholars can be celebrated as tours de force. Hence, the economist or sociologist has yet to discover theories or models and produce vocabularies evolving out of the peculiar situation, to be learned by American or French scholars.[23]

(18) Irrespective of the seemingly massive efforts of African leaders of the 'sixties' and the 'seventies' to mass-educate Africa,

> ...in education, generally, Africa is the most backward region of the world. Its universities, unit by unit, are the smallest in number of any other major world region, and continues to have the lowest ratio of students enrolled as a percentage of the twenty-to-twenty-four-year age group, Asia having four times the number of university students per capita, and Latin America five.[24]

If one were to compare Africa to America in terms of the number of students and educational institutions, Africa would be seen to have accomplished little.

(19) Perhaps Africa's backwardness in education can best be illustrated by the level of illiteracy in African countries (Table 25).

TABLE 24

AFRICAN LITERARY RATES, 1985

COUNTRY	% OF MALES	% OF FEMALES	OFFICIAL LANGUAGE
Angola	36	19	Portuguese
Benin	43	17	French
Botswana	37	44	Setswana/English
Burundi	39	16	Kiscroli/French
Cameroon	55	25	French
Cape Verde	54	34	Portuguese
Central African Republic	48	20	French
Chad	12	1	French
Comoros	66	52	Shoari
Congo	30	3	French
Djibouti	5		French
Ethiopia	35-40		Amharic
Equatorial Guinea	38		Spanish
Gabon	22	5	French
The Gambia	29	12	English
Ghana	43	18	English
Guinea	14	4	French
Guinea Bissau	25	13	Portuguese
Ivory Coast	45	24	French
Kenya	60	35	English
Lesotho	58	82	English
Liberia	30	12	English
Madagascar	41	27	Malagassy
Malawi	48	25	English
Mali	13	1	French
Mauritania	17	-	French
Mauritius	86	72	English

AFRICAN LITERARY RATES, 1985 (continued)

COUNTRY	% OF MALES	% OF FEMALES	OFFICIAL LANGUAGE
Mazambique	44	23	Portuguese
Namibia	45	31	English/Afrikaans
Niger	14	8	French
Nigeria	46	23	English
Rwanda	62	37	French
Sao Tome Principe	5-10		Portuguese
Senegal	31	14	French
Sierra Leone	10	4	English
Seychelles	56	60	English/French
Somolia	60 (1978)		Somali
S. Africa	99 (whites)		Afrikaan/English
	50 (Africans)		
Sudan	38	14	Arabic
Swaziland	57	53	English
Tanzania	78	70	English
Togo	27	7	French
Uganda	65	40	English
Upper Volta	18	5	French
Western Sahara	20		Arabic
Zambia	79	58	English
Zaire	77	39	French
Zimbabwe	78	64	English

Source of Table 25: Compiled from Jane Martin (ed.), Global Studies: Africa (Guilford, Conn.: Dushkin Publishing Group, Inc. 1985).

Even though some African countries, such as Tanzania, Botswana, Lesotho, etc. have attempted to increase the literacy level of both males and females, most African countries can be seen to have largely illiterate societies, especially the female population. Until illiteracy is eliminated in Africa, African peoples will continue to be politically, technically, and economically backward. The majority of Africans will continue to be peripheral to the political process, the choosing of political leadership, and thus the existence of corrupt and individualistic leaders such as Mobutu of Zaire[25] and even the continued existence of Apartheid South Africa and a discriminated Black America. The following quotation concerning illiteracy could illuminate the predicament of the mass of African peoples.

> Illiteracy...is not only a disqualification from better-paid employment in offices or factories. It is not only a cultural deprivation, an exclusive from national life, and in some countries even from voting. ...To be illiterate is to be helpless in a modern state run by a way of complex laws and regulations. The man who cannot read or write is at the mercy of those who can. He is totally dependent on the sometimes questionable honesty and competence of lawyers and officials. ...He is a sitting duck for exploitation and fraud.
> Illiteracy, like other forms of educational disadvantage, weighs heaviest on the groups who are already disadvantaged

in other ways.   ...Illiteracy is concentrated among lower-income groups, the
marginal masses and women.[26]

The masses of people starving in Africa are the illiterates, the half-educated are those who have prema-
turely dropped out of school and remain perpetually
unemployed and frustrated. The African illiterates and
half-educated are the ones who continue to suffer from
malnutrition, bad housing and other 'primitive' standards of living. Until African leaders implement massive programs to eradicate illiteracy, their peoples
will continue to be the least developed in the world
and whose natural resources will continue to develop
other areas of the globe other than Africa itself.[27]

(20) African education in the 1960's and 1970's did
not integrate continental Africa, nor did it eliminate
tribalism and colonial mentality within individual
African countries. African schools have not been used
to attack the most salient and massive problems of
starvation, malnutrition, underdeveloped agriculture
and political primitiveness of the masses of African
peoples. The 'mis-educated' minority continue to exploit, misdirect and mis-manage Africa's natural
resources.

> The problems that African (schools) face
> are bigger than can be solved on in-
> dividual basis or on national platform
> alone. International cooperation, both on
> regional and continental levels is not
> only long overdue, but imperative. The
> necessity for a united effort was per-
> ceived as long ago as the early days of
> independence when it was hoped that higher
> education would 'ensure the unification of

Africa' and that expensive facilities like medicine and veterinary science would be joint enterprises across national boundaries. But the prospect of concerted effort in... education remains today as remote as it did in 1961 when this wish was so ardently and hopefully expressed.[28]

Chapter 9 suggests pan-African education which is not posited as a wish, a hope, or a desire for cooperation between African nations, but a necessary constituent for pan-African integration and continental African development. Until African countries establish pan-African educational institutions expressly for the achievement of African unity, suspicions between African peoples and their leaders, multiple external interference in continental African affairs, and the large scale exploitation of Africa's natural resources for the benefit of non-Africans and a few African bourgeoisies, Africa as a continent would remain poor and powerless, and African peoples will remain the most ignorant ideologically and politically.

Notes

CHAPTER EIGHT

[1]Edward H. Berman, "Foundations, United States Foreign Policy and African Education, 1945-1975," Harvard Educational Review, Vol. 49, No. 2 (May 1979), p. 154.

[2]Ibid.

[3]Ibid.

[4]Ibid.

[5]Lyson P. Tembo, "The African University and Social Reform," African Social Research, No. 25 (June 1978), pp. 379-397.

[6]David Lamb, The Africans (New York: Vantage Books, 1987), pp. 43-54.

[7]Kwame Nkrumah, Revolutionary Path (Thomas Nelson and Sons Ltd., 1957), pp. 161-162.

[8]Ras Makonnen, Pan-Africanism from Within (Oxford University Press, 1973), p. 248.

[9]Godfrey N. Brown and Mercyn Hiskett, Conflict and Harmony in Education in Tropical Africa (London: George Allen and Unwin Ltd., 1975), p. 417.

[10]Bert N. Adams, "Africanization and Academic Imperialism: A Case Study in Planned Change and Inertia," East Africa Journal, Vol. 9, No. 5 (May 1972), pp. 23-28.

[11]Brown and Hiskett, Op. Cit., p. 417.

[12]Otto Klineberg and Marisa Zavallons, Nationalism and Tribalism Among African Students: A Study of Social Identity (Mouton, Paris: The Hague, 1969), pp. 27-30.

[13]Haile Selassie, "Towards African Unity," The Journal of Modern African Studies, 1, 3 (1963), pp. 281-291.

[14]International Seminar on Inter-University Cooperation in West Africa held in Freetown, Sierra Leone, The West African Intellectual Community (New York: Africana Publishing Corporation, 1961), p. 101.

[15]Ibid., p. 102.

[16]Brown and Hiskett, Op. Cit., p. 422.

[17]The West African Intellectual Community, Op. Cit., p. 101.

[18]The Weekly News Kenyan (July 20, 1984), p. 11.

[19]Ibid.

[20]Emanuel A. Ayandele, "Africa: The Challenge of Higher Education," Daedalus: Journal of the American Academy of Arts and Sciences, Vol. 111, No. 2 (Spring 1982), p. 169.

[21]Ibid., pp. 170-171.

[22]Ibid., p. 171.

[23]Ibid., p. 172.

[24]Ibid., p. 168.

[25]David Lamb, The Africans (New York: Vantage Books, 1987), pp. 44-47.

[26]Paul Harrison, Inside the Third World: The Anatomy of Poverty (Penguin Books, 1982), pp. 304-305.

[27]Sophie Bessis, "The Fruits of Independence," in Global Studies: Africa (ed.), Jane Martin, (Guilford, Connecticut: Dushkin Publishing Group, 1985), pp. 16-17.

[28]Ayandele, Op. Cit., p. 176.

CHAPTER NINE

PAN-AFRICAN EDUCATION:

THE LAST STAGE OF EDUCATIONAL DEVELOPMENTS IN AFRICA

Pan-African education is the education of Africans for larger, continental African citizenship; this education goes beyond 'education for nation-building' that was so adamantly espoused in the 1960's and has led to the intellectual, geographical and psychological balkanization of the African continent. Pan-African education mitigates racial, tribal, ethnic, religious and geographical boundaries currently entrenching themselves between the peoples of Africa. Pan-African education goes beyond the mere exchange of 'privileged' students between two or more African countries or universities; it calls for the integration of African schools, colleges and universities without regards to race, color, religion or nation in which one happened to be born; it would give the African people "...new objects or models with which to identify."[1] This involves the instilling in African peoples new Pan-African consciousness other than solely nationalism,

tribalism, regionalism, and other forms of
Parochialisms. As Kenneth Kaunda of Zambia has stated:

> At all costs, our young men must be edu-
> cated to see Africa whole...no greater
> disservice could be done to the African
> cause than the implanting in young minds
> of seeds of suspicion of other states
> based upon matters of historical rivalry
> which must be buried forever.[2]

He goes on to specify that what must be emphasized to
the African youth "...is the people's Africanness...a
sense of solidarity which transcends national boundaries, drawing substance from the struggles and vic-
tories of African leaders and their people all over the
continent."[3] Gabral Abdel Nasser, speaking on behalf
of Egypt states:

> We cannot look stupidly at a map of the
> world not realizing our place therein and
> the role determined to us by that place.
> Neither can we ignore that there is an
> Arab circle surrounding us and that this
> circle is as much a part of us as we are a
> part of it, that our history has been
> mixed with it and that its interests are
> linked with ours. These are actual facts
> not mere words.
>
> Can we ignore that there is a continent of
> Africa in which fate has placed us and
> which is destined today to witness a ter-
> rible struggle on its future? This
> struggle will affect us whether we want or
> not.[4]

Ahmed Sekou Toure of Guinea, the first African leader to provide in his constitution a plan to surrender Guinea's sovereignty to a larger African unity, states: "...in the fields of history, geography, political economy, in a word everything that is not purely scientific and universal, the educational raw materials can only be drawn from Africa."[5] President Toure sought "...a bilingual state as a means of adding substance to... and furthering... larger Pan-African unity..."[6]

Other African leaders and educators have expressed their commitments to African unity and have recommended the establishment of Pan-African educational institutions. The cases of Haile Selassie, Kwame Nkrumah, Julius Nyerere, Nnamdi Azikiwe are fairly well-known and have been dealt with in chapter six. This chapter recommends institutionalized Pan-African education in extending Haile Selassie's advocation of a Pan-African university.[7]

As "...the purpose of European education is to Europeanize...,"[8] so also will Pan-African education Pan-Africanize. The process in the Pan-Africanization of African peoples must involve the establishment of specific, Pan-African educational institutions to accomplish the feat. It would involve changes in curriculum, curriculum content, staffing patterns, student body, publications, school personnel, administration of schools, examination systems, and the establishment of integrative mechanisms, strategies and procedures that are conducive to school and larger social integration.

African universities, colleges and other schools will be integrated in terms of their student body, faculty members, administrative personnel and others employed by Africa's educational institutions. These workers will be recruited irrespective of their national origin, tribal affiliations, regional or religious background. Even though elementary schools need not be so integrated with respect to student body, teachers and the administrative personnel, they should employ other African nationals. An African youth socialized in a Pan-African environment would be a more 'renascent'[9] African than one exclusively educated by autochthonous teachers and administrators. When the African child is introduced to Africans from various African countries and finds, through the secondary grades and higher education that Pan-African integration is the norm, he would be most unlikely to be anti-other-Africans; and when the integration process is institutionally and professionally supported by the administrators and teachers, the student becomes even more confident concerning his pro-integration attitudes.

This is not the case in most African schools at the present; all African schools, colleges, and universities are at present predominantly nationalized institutions, overwhelming attended and taught by the autochthonous or the native born and their European counterparts. It could even be asserted that some African universities and colleges would often rather recruit Americans, French, English and other Westerners than African nationals from other African countries even though as qualified as the Western nationals, and perhaps more culturally compatible to the African environment, not to mention dedication! If African societies are to be integrated, the intellectual institutions must demonstrate practical integration by practicing the ideology of practical Pan-Africanism; "The masses are Pan-Africanist all the way!"[10]

Some African leaders, such as Nyerere and Kaunda, have spoken about the exchange of students between African universities and other institutions of higher learning; however, the level of integration being advocated here goes beyond the mere exchange of students between two neighboring African countries to advocate: (1) the establishment of a Pan-African university as suggested by Haile Selassie in 1963; (2) that the Pan-African university be established at Bangui in the Central African Republic; (3) French and English be the language of instruction in the Pan-African university; (4) that the Pan-African University be a model for other African national universities in terms of the recruitment of staff, student body and other school personnel; (5) that African educational institutions build intensive language institutes where French speakers can learn English within a short period of time and English speakers French; (6) that Africans be trained and educated to be citizens of Africa; (7) that Africans be trained and educated to the economic, social, political, cultural and international realities of Africans and the African continent; (8) that African schools, especially at the levels of higher learning, establish departments of Black American Studies, Caribbean Studies, Latin American Studies, West European Studies, North American Studies, Asian Studies, East European Studies, and (9) that these various departments be conducted with a Pan-African perspective.[11] The curriculum in Pan-African education will be Pan-African centered, not European or narrowly nationalistic-centered.

The predominant presence of western teachers in African schools, sometimes comprising "up to fifty-percent of the teaching staff..."[12] is an academic as

well as a cultural problem; and Africa seems to be the
only continent, (or <u>nation</u> in the views of a true Pan-
Africanist), whose schools are so overwhelmingly
staffed by their ex-colonizers. Pan-African education
will recruit staff members not only from various
African countries, but also from the diaspora in the
United States of America, the Caribbean and Latin
America; Westerners, or Europeans will not be excluded,
but their ratio will greatly be reduced and will be
employed to teach mostly in non-cultural subject areas.

Pan-African education is closely associated with
Nkrumah's brand of Pan-Africanism in which he submitted
that the African continent be united under socialism
and to have "...a common African citizenship."[13]
Nkrumah believed that in the long run no African, irrespective of his nation or region of birth, should be
considered an alien in another African country or
region. Unlike the other Pan-Africanists who believed
in the regional and gradual approach to African integration, Nkrumah asserted that any delay in African
unity will make it extremely difficult in the future to
affect unity, as it has become painfully clear since
1963 when the current OAU was founded; that 1963 OAU
charter "...was a Charter of <u>intent</u>, rather than a
Charter of <u>positive action</u>."[14] It must now evolve to
positive action.

In a sense, Nkrumah wanted a Union of African
States similar to that of the United States of America,
USSR, but not (OAS) Organization of American States, as
the 1963 OAU turned out to be; for Nkrumah, "...Pan-
Africanism and socialism are organically complementary;
one cannot be achieved without the other."[15] He advocated that French and English be taught in African
schools so that the integration process is accelerated,

and completely rejected the domination of African school systems by Western countries.[16] In Pan-African education, science, tropical medicine, nutritional sciences, agricultural education and research into the various African social, linguistics, political, and economic conditions will be emphasized and stress will "...be laid on the cultural and social features common to African countries, thus strengthening African unity and helping the countries of the continent to get to know each other better."[17]

In actuality, the forces that unite Africa are much more than those that divide the continent.[18] For instance,

> The practices of child rearing and the educational attitudes appear most homogeneous across the African con-tinent... Black African religion and thought have shown that the way the... African perceives the world and reacts to it is different from that of other cul-tures, and it displays quite a remarkable degree of homogeneity.[19]

One only needs to read John S. Mbiti's <u>African Religious and Philosophy</u>, Jomo Kenyatta's <u>Facing Mount Kenya</u>, Achebe's <u>Things Fall Apart</u>, Kaunda's <u>Zambia Shall Be Free</u>, Camara Laye's <u>The Dark Child</u>, P'Bitek's <u>Song of Lawino</u>, just to mention a few, to concur with the above observations.[20] Although there are, un-doubtedly, particular local idiosyncrasies, as these must be so, the overwhelming similarities must be in-stitutionalized in the Pan-African education cur-riculum, as, say, American Studies is institutionalized in American schools.

In addition to the fundamental similarities among Africans on the continent, the West - its institutions, ideology, belief systems and attitudes towards Africans have been overwhelming singular; this singular treatment of African peoples by west Europeans has contributed to Africans looking at themselves as more alike than different and has enlarged the Africans' loyalty. Ashby (1964) recognized that

> At the core of an African's loyalty lie his extended family and his tribe. Outside this core his loyalty extends far beyond the frontiers of his nation; it covers the Black African people, their oral traditions and religions, their dance and music, their liberation from foreign control and their ultimate political unity.[21]

Pan-African education will fundamentalize Pan-African loyalty. Some might argue that Pan-African loyalty will isolate Africa; on the contrary, Africa has never been isolated, nor will it be isolated from the rest of the world, for the rest of the world is now vibrant in Africa; there are Europeans, Asians, Muslims and Christians in Africa, Capitalism and Socialism are in Africa aside traditional African religions and the extended family. Pan-African education will be cognizant of Africa's unique, transitional predicament and synthesize the various elements within the continent to produce the renascent African. "...the social purpose of a university in Africa differs from its traditional social purpose in Europe."[22] While "In Europe universities have stood for continuity and conservation; in Africa universities are powerful instruments for change."[23] Pan-African education will be one of the most powerful instrument of change and will continue to be of change until African unity is entrenched in the social, political, economic, and psychological lives of Africans.

Sociologists, Anthropologists, educators and other related professionals agree that any given community or political entity has its own particularly congruent educational systems that enhance and perpetuate the life of the society of which they are a part, and the better educated in the society control those educational institutions which are carriers of the political, social, economic, and cultural values of the educated leadership and the macro-society. It is mundane to even allude that educational systems that perpetuate anachronistic and inapropos social values such as tribalism, racism, and balkanization in Africa are destined to create anome.[24] One only needs to observe the current balkanized Africa, racism in South Africa, extreme nationalism that manifests itself in the expulsion of Africans from one African country into another, tribalism and regionalism in education and in the employment sector, etc. to concur that anachronistic values are rampant on the continent, and to a large measure deter development.

Colonial educational systems in Africa worked, and continue to do so in the hands of Africans subjected to colonial education, to negate the educated African from his culture, his 'illiterate' brethren, and to a certain extent render him impotent in his ability and strength to develop Africa.

Regardless of which meaning one embarks upon, the ultimate aim of Pan-African education is for the cultural, social, economic, and of no less importance, the psychological integration of Africa and African peoples. These levels of integration require deeper levels of commitment and interaction than the mere technical, cultural, and economic cooperations advocated in the 1963 charter of the Organization of African Unity (OAU).

Economic, political, social and cultural integration being the ultimate aim of Pan-Africanism and Pan-African education, mere rhetoric about African unity or the actual visitations of particular African countries by particular African leaders and business men, and the 'full' attendance of OAU summit conferences are not in themselves enough to ensure an integrated Africa. These conferences and visitations must be substantiated with established educational institutions that will work educatively for the achievement of an integrated Africa. These institutions must be planned and established in the country of each African leader and aided committedly by other socializing mediums and personalities. It must be noted that cultural and technical cooperations and exchanges can take place even between countries that ascribe to contrasting political ideologies and cultural values. The exchanges and cooperations in this latter conception do not ensure the integration of the masses; here one can mainly speak of the integration of the political and business elites who already directly benefit from such contacts at the expense of the populous who remain alienated from even their next door neighbors.

In contrast to that form of integration, that is the integration of the political and business elites, Pan-African education aims at the integration of the masses of Africans including those in the diaspora. Those in the diaspora need not necessarily be physically integrated, but they must be mentally integrated.

The mental integration of African descents in other
parts of the world must not be construed only as the
mere recognition of their existence in outlandish lands
and cultures where their citizenship is dubious at
best.   To mentally integrate something, a concept, is
to internalize that thing or concept.   This internalization culminates into empathy.   The Puerto Ricans
in New York City need not go back to Puerto Rico, but
they are actively alert to the political Zeitgeist of
the island and they pursue specific actions in accordance with their frames of references.   Equally so, all
Jews need not go back to Israel, but their academic,
religious, cultural interests in Israel cannot be questioned.   The Israeli government has in turn been alert
to the conditions of Jews everywhere, and some Black
Jews in Ethiopia have been moved to Israel for settlement, because in part, Jews in Ethiopia were perceived
to have been living under horrible conditions.
Africans on the continent must likewise be concerned
with those in the diaspora, and vice versa.

Two important things must be realized by African
leaders and educators: firstly that those African
peoples in the diaspora are oppressed, humiliated and
discriminated against because they are African descendents.   Morally, Africa and all Africans must shoulder
this humiliation and be propelled to iron out such
blatant incongruencies; secondly, African leaders and
educators have relentlessly and blindly pursued educational arrangements that have explicitly balkanized
Africa socially, economically and psychologically, for
the comfort of those who benefit from African disunity.

Any major movement on the lines of Pan-African
education would give rise to radical changes and improvements in the conditions of those in the diaspora

and in Africa itself. The image the world has about
Africa and Africans, the image that Africans have about
themselves because of the world's image of Africa and
Africans, would all be transformed. Pan-African education then is not only for those on the continent, but
also for those in the diaspora and the non-African
peoples within Africa.

From observations, however, Pan-Africanism, while
an ideology on the minds of most African leaders,
educators and some academicians, it does not seem at
the moment an overriding and exigent concern as pre-
occupations with individual national problems. Each
African leader has been intimately more preoccupied
with the economic, social, cultural and educational
developments of his own country with only slight
references here and there to larger Africa and with
that much collaboration or parity with neighboring
countries. If this trend persists and entrenches itself, some African countries will develop much faster
than others which could further deter unity on the
premise that the more developed neighbors would tend to
keep their own resources to themselves. McWilliams and
Polier (1964) have observed that between African
countries,

> The temptation to engage in competition to
> obtain economic advantages over other
> states is a marked one. This, of course,
> does not include the very obvious fact of
> differential wealth and revenue between
> African states, and the temptation of the
> relatively wealthy and prosperous states
> to retain their wealth for domestic pur-
> poses.[25]

266

The reservation of wealth and educational facilities for domestic consumption in individual African countries has become a marked one with their concomitant "micro-nationalism;"[26] paradoxically, the colonialists had explicitly recommended and affected integration of African countries under their jurisdictions; in the case of Eastern Africa, Makerere University was to enroll 26 percent of its students from each of the East African countries,[27] and it must be recalled that a call for a West African University was sounded earlier so that some form of integration would be affected among the West African countries. All these developments came to a halt in the 1960's and 70's when individual countries began to build their own national colleges and universities. By the late 1970's "The ideologies and personalities of Nyerere, Kenyatta, and Amin differed so much that there was little to encourage the three leaders to solve the problems..."[28] of the East African community that had once been integrated to the extent that

> Peoples moved freely across the borders of the three states in the community. The links between the three countries were so important in the early 1960's that President Nyerere of Tanzania proposed that Tanzania wait to become independent until Kenya was given freedom, in hopes that the two countries would then join together.[29]

Although there are talks that people in East Africa should "Think East Africa,"[30] the different political ideologies that have begun to entrench themselves in individual African countries could further deter collaboration and unity between African countries if they continue to follow the path of balkanization by pursuing different political ideologies, educational systems, and economic development strategies other than Pan-Africanism.

In East Africa, the Kenyan approach to development embarks on the development of an indigenous entrepreneurial class based on private enterprise and capitalism while Tanzania is institutionalizing African socialism based on the doctrine of firstly improving the community by which means the individual will be improved. The two value systems are similar only in that they both might eventuate in general development, but they differ to such an extent that one might not abandon its approach for the other; one is capitalistic and individualistic, the other is socialistic and communalistic. When the two value systems eventually entrench themselves, the peoples from the two different regimes might speak the same languages - English and Swahili - but would speak from two different vantage points of interests.

The colonial educational residues that continue to function in most African countries would continue to produce classes based on who are educated at the universities and those who are not. Colonial educational systems have not only created classes in Africa in areas where classes did not exist before, but they also directed students from specific African countries to specific metropolitan countries in accordance with the colonization patterns.

> The lines of the partition of Africa naturally affected the education of the colonized Africans. Students from English-speaking territories went to Britain as a matter of course, just as those from French-speaking territories

268

went to France as a matter of course. In
this way, the yearning for formal education, which African students could only
satisfy at great cost of effort, will, and
sacrifice was hemmed in within the confines of the colonial system.[31]
This pattern was slightly altered in the late 1960's
and throughout the 1970's when America, India, USSR and
other nations began to attract African students thus
making the African continent the recipient of diversified body of academicians and trained personnel
tainted with diverse experiences they had undergone in
socialist as well as in capitalist countries. The
norms of academic excellence no longer belonged in the
ex-colonial metropoles and in universities such as
Makerere and FBC, but in various other places such as
in the United States of America, India, Canada, the
USSR, etc. Pan-African education dictates the mitiga-
tion of this trend of making Africa the Tower of Babel
of educational experiences. Pan-African education will
produce Pan-Africanists, not 'intelligent' sociologists
such as Kofi Busia who claims: "I am a Westerner...I
was educated in the West."[32]

The aim of a Pan-African educational system is to
produce Pan-Africanists; this is in agreement with the
aims of other political, ideological, cultural, and
educational systems in other countries. The Russian
and American educational systems produce citizens who
are loyal to these political systems and individuals
and groups that assert negative pressures are quickly
liquidated in many ways than one.

The nature of African tribal and colonial legacies
dictate that the Pan-Africanist be a polyglot and
therefore a mobile person mentally and physically.

This inevitably requires the ability to tolerate idiosyncrasies other than one's own group or groups. Regardless of the region in which the Pan-Africanist decides to reside in Africa, it is dictated that he speaks more than one language.[33] Language differences, ipso facto, have been used by westerners and even by some 'enlightened' Africans as the major stumbling block obfuscating African unity. Some Africans have internalized the idea that if only Africa could, out of some mysterious force, speak one language, the road to unity would have been paved. These individuals underestimate other binding forces such as the methods of exploitation of nature, the references to God, the universal denouncements of Africans, African culture and artifacts, the common desire among Africans for economic and social development and the effects of institutionalized multi-lingual institutions.

The common place fact is that Africa's composition and history are unlike West and East European countries and these facts must be dealt with, with Africa's history and composition in mind. The Pan-Africanist must be able to deal with many more diversities than the Westerner. The 'mental construction' of the Pan-Africanist should consist of many more 'compartments' to accommodate not only the various idiosyncrasies within Africa itself, but also the western and the eastern. Some of the accommodation of African idiosyncrasies by African peoples within Africa is already taking place chiefly through schooling and this needs to be institutionalized at the continental level. Speaking in a similar vein, Mazrui explicates:

> ...there is the diversity of cultural
> backgrounds confronting anyone who studies
> African countries and the composition of

their societies. These different traditional cultures need never fully merge to
form one national heritage, but some
degree of integration needs to be encouraged so that the groups can evolve
gradually a shared universe of ideas and
values.[34]

Shared ideas and values are in part obtained in
schools and in the case of Africa, schools become of
utmost importance in the face and desires for political
and social developments and the projection for universal primary and secondary education. In the 1960's,
schools became so exigently important that Africa was
offered aid and advice from American philanthropic and
multinational corporations in concert with professional
educational organizations with the sublime intents to
affect Africa's academic orientations.[35] These efforts, however, have not educationally integrated
Africa on a Pan-African level.

Perhaps it has been more in the west where various
Africans from diverse African countries have met
chiefly in schools and on university campuses. African
students in western schools come in contact with students from both French and English-speaking Africa including West Indians and Black Americans. It was in
France that Senghor and Cesaire discovered a bond they
termed Negritude. After similar encounters with
various African students, Nkrumah remarked:

In meeting fellow Africans from all parts
of the continent, I am constantly
impressed by how much we have in common.
It is not just our colonial past, or the
fact that we have aims in common, it is
something which goes far deeper. I can

271

best describe it as a sense of oneness in
that we are all Africans.[36]
Though one is equally capable of observing differences
between Africans, as one can between Europeans, it is
important to note that it is the dissimilarities that
have been over-emphasized by the enemies of African
unity.

One variable that has been over-emphasized by
enemies of African unity is the language differences
between Africans.   The multiplicity of languages in
Africa is primordial and must be dealt with not as a
liability, but as an asset. The Pan-Africanist will be
a polyglot and will be educated to be tolerant of the
peculiarities of the African continent, thus making him
one of the most mobile in the world today.   In some
African countries such as Cameroon, students are able
to speak French and English in addition to their tribal
languages and a lingua-franca.   Through intensive language study, African students from French-speaking
African countries are able to attend U.S. universities
and take higher degrees in research and the sciences.
This can be institutionalized under Pan-African educational system.

Mobility and tolerance for diversity must be institutionalized in Pan-African education; this becomes
significant in light of the eventual fall of apartheid
South Africa that will make the African continent truly
multi-racial.   The existence of Animism, Christianity,
Islam and other Asian religions in Africa compel the
Pan-Africanist to be tolerant and to guard against
tribalism, regionalism and other forms of
Parochialisms. Indeed, the Pan-Africanist must be com-
mitted to diversity, and this does not mean apathy.
Toil and teamwork are imperative values that must be

fostered in the school socialization process under Pan-African education.

There is an additional sense which requires the Pan-African person to be mobile mentally and physically namely that he does not only have to deal with Westerners, Chinese, Indians, and the Lebanese in their respective cultures, at the international, political and economic spheres, but also in Africa's cultural and political contexts. For instance, he must be able to deal with Indian festivities in Eastern Africa which seemingly are celebrated at the wrong times of the year according to the native East African cultural calendar,[37] but which should become an integral part in a truly multi-cultural society. The Pan-Africanist should be socialized (educated, in other words) acquainted with the various groups in Africa not in any way superficially, but intimately in order to master the interrelationships.

One of the greatest challenges to African leaders, educators and other cultural agents is to practicalize Pan-Africanism as suggested by Nkrumah. As it has been stated elsewhere, the Charter of the OAU signed in 1963 fell far too short from Nkrumah's position; it was a compromise on the part of the radical group. It is "...an ambivalent charter," and "a case" can be made "for charter revision,"[38] if continental unity is to be achieved. And to make Pan-Africanism perpetuate itself, appropriate educational institutions are necessary to prepare Pan-Africanists.

The Pan-Africanist will be mobile and will be socialized to tolerate diversity of cultures in Africa which is appropriate for the future world's political and cultural Zeitgeists. In the cultural and academic spheres, the Pan-Africanist cannot negate himself from

the rest of the world; he will be acquainted with the
music, literature, politics, economics and the social
conditions of African descendents in the diaspora. In
Nkrumah's scheme of Pan-Africanism, the African
diaspora belongs to the African nation! Furthermore,
all those cultural aspects of Eastern, Western, and
Asian countries that contribute to the re-affirmation
of the African will be selected and Africanized. The
Pan-Africanist will selectively reject any attempts at
his mental and cultural re-enslavement and will not be
inundated by Europeanism.

There is broad agreement amongst concerned African
educators, students, academics and leaders that tribal,
Islamic, colonial and neo-colonial educational institutions in Africa are incapable of integrating continental Africa as they have shown themselves to be.
Tribalistic education is discriminatory as well as Islamic education. Even though

> The African and the Muslim forms of educa-
> tion had certain similarities; e.g. both
> believed strongly in training children in
> good manners towards elders and visitors,
> owing to the importance of personal rela-
> tions, major difference lay in the Islamic
> literary emphasis upon the Holy Koran as
> the core of Islamic teaching.[39]

Pan-African education will be secular, and therefore
Islamic education cannot be imposed in Pan-African
educational institutions. Colonial educational systems
in Africa de-nationalized the African and attempts were
made to Europeanize the educated. For instance, the
African educated under colonialism was indoctrinated to
hate his own culture and to embrace the European culture that enslaved him. He was led to believe that his

274

dress and dance, just to mention two, were primitive. Thus,

> The educated moved away from traditional
> dancing and were converted more and more
> into ballroom dancing. Traditional danc-
> ing - regarded by most Europeans as primi-
> tive - lost the respect of the new west-
> ernized Africans.[40]

National educational systems that sprouted up in Africa in the 1960's have emphasized micro-nationalism and have entrenched balkanization. Pan-African educa-tion is the last stage of educational developments in Africa that offers a curriculum that is continentally focused.

> The Chinese are Chinese, the East Indians
> are East Indians, the English are English.
> And this in spite of other cultural in-
> fluence.[41]

Africans likewise need to selectively select from other cultures responsibly. For instance, the Normans once defeated the English and imposed the French language on them. "Norman French was made the status language and was substituted for English wherever the vernacular had been used in the school."[42] The English became uneasy under this French domination and freed themselves to later subdue the Africans, a condition they had once rebelled against. To take another example, the French Revolutionary government of 1792-1795 created educa-tional institutions in accordance with their views of New France emphasizing "...that French as a whole...learn to think like (a) republic..."[43] The Americans could not tolerate any form of British domination and they therefore developed and substan-tiated their own form of school systems in accordance with the type of society they wanted to create. Africa has the obligation to free herself mentally through Pan-African education and all peoples associated with her culturally, racially and historically. African politicians, educators and other socialization or cultural agents are charged with the responsibility to develop and integrate Africa.

Obstacles to Pan-Africanism and Pan-African Education:

One of the greatest stumbling blocks preventing the achievement of Pan-Africanism, one that Europeans refer to, one that friends and enemies of African unity refer to concern the polyglot nature of African societies. Sometimes they spend so much time expounding on differences that they lose sight of the fact that this skepticism about language differences is a manifestation of colonial mentality which construes polyglotness as liabilities. European history and cultures do not tolerate language differences. The French hold on to their language as though it were the most supreme; the English and some mis-educated Africans refer to English as the 'queen's' language! In both English and French cultures language is used to determine class, one's station in life, and even who can marry whom. The point here is that since these metropoles do not tolerate polyglotness, they have controlled the African mind to be skeptic about language differences while the fact of the matter is that Africans have to be polyglots! A common sense hunch is that men are more likely to go to wars over ideological differences than over language differences per se. Another assertion is that even if Africa were to, through the power of some mysterious force, speak one

276

language today, this in itself would not ensure African unity with the presence of ideological, educational, and class differences and their subsequent ramifications.

As alluded to earlier, one of the basic requirements for Pan-Africanism is the ability to speak more than one widely spoken and written language in Africa. The ability to speak two or three written languages in Africa will not only open the doors to other countries of the world, but also to neighboring African countries as well. The educated African under Pan-African education will be able to speak any combination of the widely spoken and written languages in Africa depending on the region in which he is inclined to reside. To educate a Pan-African person, and therefore a mobile person, clearly demands integrated efforts by the educational institutions, the media, politicians, teacher education, the family, and other infrastructures that have heavy inputs in the socialization process; to neglect any of the such socializing agents would create anomie for the Africa youth.

There are more obfuscating factors preventing African unity. These factors include (A) Tribalism; (B) Nationalism; (C) Regionalism; (D) African-metropolitan relationship pattern; (E) Afrikaaner Nationalism or Apartheid; (F) Different Ideological approaches regarding Pan-Africanism; and (G) the absence of institutionalized Pan-African educational system and other salient unifying infrastructures such as roads. To take the example of regionalism,

> The African countries north of the Sahara are destined to have an ambivalent attitude regarding Pan-Africanism and Pan-Arabism. Most of them are members of the

Organization of African Unity and the Arab
League. Their real dilemma will occur if
at any time in future both hopes materialize and each country has to decide which
side to take.[44]

As it could be seen, various levels of commitments
and loyalties would have to be transcended partially or
wholly before Pan-Africanism can be realized. However,
the building of Trans-African highways and the establishment of Pan-African educational institutions are
undoubtedly moves in the direction for Pan-African integration.

The Pan-African University:

Much education reformation and development in
Africa take place at the elementary and secondary
school levels. Individual African countries boast of
the number of elementary and secondary school boys and
girls in attendance, but the type of education given is
never thoroughly scrutinized. These schools are in
Africa, but they are not African schools (Tembo, 1978)
as one could speak of the American schools in Sierra
Leone, Guam, or Egypt. It is important to note that
schools being in Africa ipso facto does not make them
African; it is the culture of the schools that makes
them African or European.

The establishment of a Pan-African university in
Africa or a branch of it elsewhere does not make it
African if, for instance, it were to be staffed with
unsympathetic expatriates or Europeanized Africans.
Nonetheless, a Pan-African university would be a
centralizing force both physically and mentally; it
would mitigate the influx of African students into

European schools simply because they are European or Western.

It is not uncommon to find African students in the west working at odd jobs they will never dream of doing in Africa. They do these jobs in order to obtain a western diploma which carries more mystic than the African certificate. Part of the reason stems from the colonial mentality that whatever the West has to offer has to be the best. This myth is ingrained not only into the students' psychics, but also their parents' who celebrate their children's return from abroad as if they were returning from another planet. Psychologically, there is mystic around being schooled abroad, but that mystic illustrates colonial mentality in both the educated African and the illiterate.

Generally, most African students find it difficult to go through school, especially through the stages that pay back in money and prestige. In Africa, some students have to walk many miles to and from school to return home at night and attempt to study in unacademic climates. Having struggled thus hard, whether abroad or at home, graduated Africans come to see themselves as a special group of talents who should deserve this and that for their studies much of which they can never use. Mazrui understands this phenomenon very well: "What should be remembered is that the harder it is to acquire an education, the more it will be regarded as a passport to a future life of leisure."[45] That graduated Africans construe their credentials as heading them for the good life cannot, however, be explained by the lone truth that it is because they had worked hard at their studies. Whatever is considered good, if not inherited, is not attained at ease. Another partial explanation is that the attainment of

279

educational credentials has and is constantly being portrayed to the African youth as the only thing needed for the good life. The teacher who exhorts his students to go back to the village to help their parents will hardly be heeded if he, the teacher, himself scorns village life and in all his behaviors demonstrate Europeanism.

It seems then that any educative attempt at educational improvements in Africa should start at the right place - the higher levels of education; to start at the lower levels would hardly accomplish anything, if for instance, teachers continue to teach in ways they always have. Since the African youth is economically and socially reinforced to emulate the educated classes, not any other social sector, to change the direction of emulation one must first change the emulated.

The Pan-African university is a partial attempt to alter the influx of Africans into Western or Eastern universities and for the training of African personnel for African schools, administrations, the media and other educational institutions. The university will contribute not only at the lower levels of African education, but also at the college and university levels in the education of African teachers, lawyers, doctors, architects, preachers, professors, musicians, television personalities, journalists, and all those that have inputs in the socialization process. The university will not only be an ideological institution in the broader sense of culture, but it will also be the highest African academic institution, such as Peking University in China, that would set up standards for African educational processes. It will conduct scientific, psychological, and sociological research germane to the African stage of development and contribute recommendations for educational and cultural affairs. The Pan-African university will be the largest university in Africa and serve as the repository for all literature that has been written by, for, and against Africa and Africans; in essence, the university library will hold most of the knowledge and thereby must abate the impetus for study outside of Africa. In science and technology, the university will collaborate with the more technologically advanced nations that are in ideological positions to do so. The Pan-African university will be staffed with the best African academicians, supported by all African countries, and seen as a point of reference for academic and cultural epitome.

The Pan-African university does not mean that individual African countries would not develop their own universities with high academic and cultural standards, but as the largest and station for excellence, the All African University will function as a point of reference and exemplum and therefore a centripetal force. At least Africa will be intellectually better off in terms of minimizing the presence in African schools of varied, ideologically opposing nationalities.

The Pan-African University will be integrated in terms of drawing its students, staff, and other school personnel from all African countries. The universities, colleges, and other types of schools in individual African countries will likewise draw their students, staff members, and other school personnel from various African countries. The location of the Pan-African University would be a university city, preferably in Bangui in Central Africa, vibrating with diversity, tolerance, and vivacity. Each university would emulate the Pan-African life. Until such integrationistic measures are made concrete, OAU conferences will remain political and academic picnics while each African country develops according to its own image. The choice is not between pan-Africanism or no pan-Africanism, the choice for Africa is to unite on its own plans, or on pre-fabricated plans from outlandish lands, especially from those that benefit and rejoice over Africa's underdevelopment, ignorance and stagnation.

Social and Cultural Integration Begins at Home

Perhaps the most embarrassing and apparent contradiction that exists in the countries of most pan-Africanist politicians is that, even though they make convincing speeches during OAU conferences in support of programs for African integration, they neglect the fact that their home people are rigidly disintegrated into classes based not only on naked physical wealth, but also on the lines of those who are educated and those who are not, between those who first came in contact with formalized European educational systems and the late arrivals to the schooling scene. In this system, it is easier for the sons of the educated and well-to-do to do well in school on the premise that they have inherited the academic culture and can afford to provide prerequisite skills that are conducive to European school learning. Explicitly, those children whose parents can read and write English, French, or what have you, are steps ahead in terms of their home background being congruent with the school culture; and this perpetuates itself. The earlier arrivals into the

school culture have already adapted themselves to the
expectations of the Europeanized school's social milieu
and reading and writing are already primordial. This
does not mean that the latest arrivals in the school do
not do well; what it means is that the newer students
have to spend much more energy and end up construing
school learning, by emulating their pioneers, as a
passport to leisure life. It also means that those
among the late arrivals who do not have the stamina or
financial resources to persist drop out in limbo between education and no-education. Furthermore, since
the type of schooling system is one that does not internalize social facts, the dropouts refuse to go back
to the bush preferring to experience anomie in jobless
African cities.[46]

Another aspect of this phenomenon is that some
Africans construe western education, especially the
British and the French types, as better and depreciate
the American and Russian systems despite the fact that
these systems have implemented mass education and de-
emphasize classicism in principle. Thus, those educated in the former metropoles, regardless of the
metropole's philosophy and practice of the philosophy,
have no equals at home.

> This link dates back to colonial
> times....All over London there are
> numerous colleges whose unhealthy lecture
> rooms are packed with black faces willing
> to pay incredible sums in order to obtain
> one certificate or the other. There are
> lots of people who live off the African's
> quest for knowledge.[47]

While he is being educated thus, he imitates "...the
non-vital externals of that culture - the readily

visible stylized forms, not the substance that these forms both conceal(ed) and express(ed)."[48]

The Americo-Liberian ruling class that claimed to be closely linked to the Carolinas in North America was rudely awakened by a group of the newly arrivals to the school scene. The crime of the Americo-Liberian ruling class was that it drew its examples of excellence from without Africa and the rest of the society was lured to imitate the alien life. In this century, it is pretty much Africans who have to look outside of themselves for leadership type, examples of standards of living, academic and social standards. For this deep seated psychological inclination, radical education is exigent.

With respect to the rigid class formation that is confirming itself in Africa's social milieu, which is often based on who speaks the metropolitan language better and exhibits western patterns of behavior more effectively and which are subsequently rewarded economically, J.M. Kariuki in Kenya exhorted:

> In years to come we are in danger of
> having a class of the very rich and a
> class of the very poor. If this situation
> continues there is going to be an upris-
> ing.[49]

But as experience has shown such farsighted Africans are easily obliterated. Mazrui again understands this phenomenon quite well:

> It is not simply a question of how long a
> government stays in power. Some African
> governments have been known to stay in
> power longer than they would have done in
> some of the more developed societies of
> the world. A few governments have been

284

known to stay in power too long. Political stability, however, is not to be
measured purely in terms of duration of
office; it has to be measured by the
yardstick of predictable duration of office.[50]

With this as baseline, one can almost accurately pre-
dict those governments that are next in line for the
falling; and the falling will come about because of the
governments' tolerance of rigid class structure and
their satisfaction with the provision of minimal educational opportunities to the populace. The occasional
giving away of money to the peasants at election times
is not the solution and disguises the dynamics of the
fate of the masses; the building of elementary and/or
secondary schools in one's constituency serves no
perennial purpose if the builder sends his children
abroad for what is perceived as better education.

Mass Education

The very idea of pan-African education denotes
mass education. When pan-African education is viewed
not only as an end in itself, but also as means for the
cultural, political, and social integration of African
peoples, then mass education, as defined by Figuera
(1963) becomes ineluctable. Figuera does not only include popular education in his definition of mass
education, but also that such education must concern
itself with political, cultural, and psychological
education.[51] These aspects of education increase the
individual' awareness of not only himself but also of
his social, cultural, political, physical, economic and
psychological environments.

285

The educational systems African countries have inherited, traditional and colonial systems alike, are wholly anachronistic compared to pan-African education. Tribalism can no longer be tolerated, nor should regionalism be. European educational systems are based on class and tends to perpetuate classicism. Education based on class and class origin perpetuates inflexible differentiation and restricts, creates barriers, and is intolerant of newcomers into the scene. However,

> one cannot speak of human learning today in solely an elitist context, that a minority of fortunate citizens of a few fortunate countries blessed with the resources to develop formal education. There are below this level men in all stages of moral and mental development who are striving to survive in conditions of life becoming steadily more complex.[52]

African countries should not tolerate educational systems that perpetuate tribalism, racism, classicism and intolerable diversity; rather, they must evolve to pan-African education that integrates. Africa's contemporary desires to improve human life, establish communication infrastructures, and concern for others must be reflected in the types of education provided the youth.

Mass education is not limited to the youth; it extends to the adult and female population. It is dubious whether Africa would rapidly develop without the collaboration of the female whom tradition has asked to play subservient roles. Pan-African education demands popular input and participation from both sexes.

286

The starting point for mass education is not the youth, but the already educated classes; it is the educated classes the youth emulate, sometimes only to find out that other things are involved, other than being schooled. The African university student who sees himself as privileged and as specially talented must be made accountable to the public at whose expense he is being educated. Tembo (1978) alludes that African college students in Zambia sometimes live at higher living standards than a large sector of the public (and this is often true for most African universities) and have their rooms cleaned by government employees.[53] All along the way they are made and encouraged to see themselves as a special group of people, and thus their subsequent alienation from the masses, who, not having gone through the institutionalized privileges, are considered rustic. Angered over this matter, P'Bitek states:

> I have seen apes on bicycles and have laughed. The thought that educational institutions in the country continue to produce cultural apes at the taxpayer's expense is painful beyond bearing.[54]

The whole blame must not be thrown on to the shoulders of the African university students. Those academic professors who show all signs of Europeanism, for they too take part in perpetuating the classicist spirit and mentality, must be re-educated. Nicol (1963) for instance, asserts that since he was not accorded the privilege of dining with his academic professors while he attended Cambridge, so also will he refuse to dine with African students in an African university.[55] The 'crime' is not mostly that he refuses to dine with his students, but mostly the illfortune of transplanting this anarchronistic mentality from institutions, cultures, and traditions behind time even in America. There are a lot of academic professors in America who (go out of their way to) have social interactions with their students. The academician is first of all a human being and to elevate him a step above that is hero worship, a superstitious behavior, and manifests master-servant relationship.

The sad case about Nicol and his tribe of scholars is that they get emulated by their students more so than not, for they are construed as the epitome. When members of this tribe entrench themselves, moves for African integration become ineluctably difficult. The place then to start pan-African education is at the upper levels, that is, those stratum that influence the mentality of the masses. Some African politicians (notably Nkrumah and Nyerere) seem to be further ahead of African educators with respect to their articulation of the appropriate routes African education must take. For instance, Nkrumah established an ideological institute in Ghana and replaced West European lecturers with East Europeans even though there were excruciating frictions between the students at the institute and those at the old University of Ghana for the two groups began to speak two different, unrelated, languages; the graduates of the institute were falsely construed as spies. The new institute was not only an alternative, but was also a threat to standards and philosophy of the inherited colonial educational systems. The institute at Winneba was a challenge to a university whose aim had been to accentuate the class system. As pointed out earlier, Makerere, a colonialist institution, was timid over academic standards during the move

288

for the establishment of an East African university. Similar schools had been suggested for West African countries, but skepticisms, distrusts, inertia, (which are usually blamed on the lack of money), and concerns for academic standards have provided opportunities for neo-colonialism and delayed action from Africans themselves. The inertia is largely the result of having to look outside of Africa for standards of excellence; pan-African education does not have to look outside to borrow standards. Through research on continental basis, pan-African education will focus and attack areas that need exigent attention. Furthermore, it will set its own academic standards, standards based on Africa's political and cultural Zeitgeists. At least in this way, African schools would terminate producing cultural apes!

The Education of Teachers for Pan-Africanism

Social, cultural, and economic developments in Africa are, for obvious reasons, closely linked with the improvement of African teachers. Africa's ineluctable desire to improve her people has made her to place emphasis on the education of not only competent teachers, but also teachers who are to be responsive to the emergent needs of Africa and to be conscious of the contributions they can make towards African development. Correctly then, African teacher educators have emphasized the education of more qualified persons to be professional teachers. Indeed, the idea that the academician ipso facto can teach effectively and fruitfully is no longer tenable.[56] The least African teacher educators can require is to demand African teachers to be professional graduates. Elementary

289

schools, which have been taught largely by non-graduates, should be staffed by graduates and the 'better' teachers. The type of education the child receives in the early, maleable years could largely impede or make easy for further education. The unsound education elementary school children receive could in part explain the large dropout rate in most African countries especially at the higher elementary and secondary levels.[57]

The education of teachers for pan-Africanism recognizes the exigency of professional graduates to man African schools. One added dimension here is to expand the cultural base of African teachers so that they are qualified to teach in any African country and feel at ease doing so, and not to feel as native foreigners. To accomplish this feat, they must first be liberally educated in African cultures with specific reference to pan-Africanism. Secondly, they must be educated in integrated schools of education. An integrated school of education in this respect refers to the educational institution that is composed of administrators, teachers, and students from various African countries. Such a setting will bring face-to-face similarities and dissimilarities between African peoples and with institutional support, in both curriculum and administrative planning, problems and desires facing Africans become manifest. In an integrated setting, the ability to tolerate other people unlike oneself becomes a fact if for nothing else but for survival. More importantly, however, Africans would discover that their differences are not as great as they have been magnified. If Europeans and other third world people can live together, irrespective of some abrasive frictions and occasional upheavals, that

Africans can live in integrated settings must be put to a test!

In an integrated setting the common fate of humanity is made explicit. When this is made explicit to the African teacher and he's made conscious of the part he can play to achieve pan-Africanism, then, he would have had an added reason for professional education. The African teacher's contribution to Africa's economic, social, and for the attainment of pan-Africanism in particular, is unquestionable; he is the one who is in daily contact with the African youth not only for academic, but also for socio-cultural reasons.[58] He will not have realized half of his duties if he continued to construe his profession strictly in academic and economic terms.

The consciousness of the impact of one's actions comes about succinctly during varied social interactions and the ability to see the interrelations between oneself and the others, between the micro and the macro, and between African countries in concert with the rest of the world is a fruitful state for the African teacher. Hanson (1963) recommends that the African teacher should be liberally educated and not simply as a task master.[59] If he is trained wholly as a task master he'll be parochially minded, not responsible for the consequences of what he does and how this would affect his clients. In essence, he would be like the irresponsible factory worker who, not made conscious of the impact of his tardiness, would continue oversleeping and taking too many breaks. Nkrumah's foresight that Ghana's independence was meaningless while other African countries remained colonies is derived from a mentality that sees the intricate interrelationships between socio-cultural events and social entities. One would have to be myopic and selfish to continue consuming conspicuously in the midst of poverty, oblivious to the fact that his leisure is obtained at the expense of some nearby malnourished child.

There is a great difference between construing education solely for one's improvement and that which is solely for community improvement. In the case of Africa, the former would be an irresponsibility. And,

> Prevailing irresponsibility has certain characteristics. First it takes little thought for the future. Secondly, it is little concerned with significant social issues. Thirdly, it is individualistic and selfish. Does education contribute to the mess or seek to remedy it?[60]

Consciousness of the needs of the community forms the basis for pan-African education - Africa needs 'selfless' teachers whose mental constructs include the predominant desire for Africa's improvement as opposed to the inclination for individual improvement at the expense of the community. Some would argue that self-improvement is community improvement, but surely the slave does not seize to be one as a result of his master's economic improvement which in fact could lead to more intricate forms of domination. There is an ingrained likelihood of exploitation in the ideology of individual improvement as a priority. Furthermore, there is also the likelihood that one whose priority is solely for self-improvement would justify his accumulations and status in the name of his special abilities and build all sorts of defense mechanisms about him. It should also be noted that self-improvement need not take place in one's community of birth, or origin; it can be accomplished in an alien community to which one is not morally, intellectually, or emotionally attached. The last point should be clear to Africans with the cases of the Lebanese in West Africa, the Asians in East Africa, the Europeans in South Africa, and Africa's general experience with the colonialists; it is evident in individual cases of educated Africans who remain in the West after their schooling, which in their view offers them more money, psychological, and intellectual satisfaction for their work. This tribe of African intellectuals has been educated for the West and not for Africa and even when they return to their native countries are unable to decline Western patterns of conspicuous consumption and recreational patterns.

One pertinent question that emerges in relation to this is the how to impart the feeling of social responsibility to the African teacher, this feeling of concern for the whole of Africa as opposed to the predominant concern for the self, tribe, village, the immediate community, country, or region of the continent. There are five viable ways in which to accomplish the feat: (1) by integration; (2) direct teaching; (3) exemplification; (4) elucidation; and (5) planning. If African politicians are genuinely devoted to achieve pan-Africanism, this should be exemplified in planned, integrated educational institutions. In the case of teacher education, the schools of education should be integrated in terms of staff, students, and other school personnel. Teacher candidates would see that pan-Africanism is practically expressed in the school's faculty and student body. Some faculty members will directly teach pan-Africanism as Democracy and Communism are taught in their appropriate social

entities in so many ways, although not necessarily under the explicit topics of democracy or communism. The
faculty members will impart the ideology of community
development as the priority by exemplifying it. There
is a great difference in credibility between the following three professors, or lecturers: (1) Professor X
who teaches in the mornings and conducts adult education classes in the evenings; (2) Professor Y who is
negated from community affairs and retires strictly
with members of his tribe in terms of educational
level, and (3) Professor Z who lectures enthusiasti-
cally against Europeanism but in class and at home
demonstrates all forms of Europeanism. Indeed, con-
tradictions are readily apparent, and thus attract more
attention regardless of the skillfullness of the actor
or actress to remain incognito. Audiences are usually
enlightened enough to empathize with the actor or allow
him to build cases against himself. With respect to
elucidation, the teacher can explicitly organize his
classes in such a way that the students become coopera-
tive or competitive. The skillful teacher thinks of
himself as a politician with the power to respectively
reward and punish those behaviors that are to be maintained and those that are to be terminated. The
teacher can give group assignment or individual assignments, demand reports on individual or group projects.
Either strategy is based on the ideology of the teacher
and the school and they give different results. At the
macro level, planning is in the hands of African
politicians to build schools specifically geared to enhance pan-Africanism. At the micro level, however,
teachers and administrators are the ones who have to
carry out practices that enhance integration or
tribalism.

Other Educational Mediums to Enhance Pan-Africanism

Journalists, dramatists, playwrights, novelists, broadcasters on radio and television, all have crucial parts to play in enhancing African integration. Journalists, for instance, should, as they are now doing in African Concord: The Premier Pan-African Weekly, cover more stories from other African countries. The items should cover the stories in depth and must not be stuck in some corner of the newspaper, or magazine, where no one will have the opportunity to read them. To bring African countries closer to each other such items should be treated as though the native foreign country were not alien as it should be. It is not inconceivable, for another example, to integrate radio, television, and newspaper staff. Playwrights and novelists should make their protagonists pan-Africanists as opposed to local boys and girls. "It is important to remember that the more advanced civilizations have institutions as the home, the church, the press to supplement the omissions and correct the errors of the schools."[61] All of these are done to transmit appropriate cultural values and political ideologies. Lenin never saw television but he honored the power of any form of media that reached the masses. Television can be used effectively in the classroom or in the boarding homes to get the students in touch with other lives within Africa dissimilar or similar to their own.

Conclusions

Rather than getting entangled here and there concerning the most appropriate definition of pan-African education we called a spade a spade by stating that the ultimate aim of Pan-African education is to educate for the cultural, social, political, and psychological integration of African peoples including those in diaspora and especially at the psychological level at that. We noted the many divisive factors that obfuscate the achievement of pan-Africanism but that these should not present unsurmountable problems. Educational institutions, including the pan-African university, and teacher training colleges should be integrated and designed to promote African integration. The transmission of cultural values and the pan-African ideology should not only be taught in the schools, but should also be reflected in African novels, plays, newspapers, radio, and television. The establishment of pan-African infrastructures would counteract the entrenchment of micro-nationalism that is destined to postpone African unity. Pan-African education will graduate African students for the broadest African citizenship. The African student educated under pan-African education would be more mobile than Africans are now and would attain a universalistic outlook with a vivacious concern for the whole of Africa as opposed to one focusing on the self and the immediate community. It is at this point appropriate to again quote at length Selassie's views on African education at the formation of the Organization of African Unity:

> Education abroad is at best an unsatisfactory substitute for education at home. A massive effort must be launched in the educational and cultural field which will not only raise the level of literacy and provide a cadres of skilled and trained technicians requisite to our growth and development, but, as well, acquaint us one

with another.... Serious consideration
should be given to the establishment of an
African university, sponsored by all
African states, where future leaders of
Africa will be trained in an atmosphere of
continental brotherhood. In this African
institution...African life would be emphasized and study would be directed
toward the ultimate goal of complete
African unity.[62]

Pan-African education is the ultimate stage for
the educational developments in Africa. It is more advanced than traditional forms of education that emphasized tribalism, regionalism, and also parochialism
which are inappropriate for contemporary African
political and cultural Zeitgeists. It is superior to
colonial systems of education that educate the African
out of his environment and culture and has mentally,
psychologically and culturally balkanized Africa.

Notes

CHAPTER NINE

[1]Kenneth Kaunda, A Humanist in Africa (London: Longmans, Green and Co. Ltd., 1966), p. 131.

[2]Ibid., p. 98.

[3]Ibid.

[4]Gabral Abdel Nasser, The Philosophy of the Revolution (Buffalo, New York: Economica Books, Smith, Kaynes, and Marshall Publishers, 1959), pp. 59-60.

[5]Cited in Victor D. DuBois, "Guinea Educates a New Generation," Africa Report (1968), p. 3.

[6]Ibid., p. 4.

[7]Haile Selassie, "Towards African Unity," The Journal of Modern African Studies, Vol. 1, No. 3 (1963), pp. 281-291.

[8]Watson, T. and O.W. Furley, "Education in Tanganyika Between the Wars: Attempts to Blend Two Cultures," The South Atlantic Journal, Vol. LXV, No. 4 (Autumn 1966), p. 471.

[9]Nnamdi Azikiwe, Renascent Africa (London: Frank Cass and Co. Ltd., 1968).

[10]Shibobaw Yimenu, "Pan-Africanism and African Economic Development," The Black Scholar (May 1975), p. 39.

[11]See George O. Cox, Education for the Black Race (New York: African Heritage Studies Publishers, 1974), pp. 160-170.

[12]Ali A. Mazrui, Political Values and the Educated Class in Africa (Los Angeles: University of California Press, 1978), p. 203.

[13]Kwame Nkrumah, Revolutionary Path (New York: International Publishers, 1973), p. 247.

[14]Ibid., p. 249.

[15]Ibid., p. 127.

[16]Nkrumah, Africa Must Unite (New York: International Publishers, 1970), p. 49.

[17]Richard Greenough, Africa Calls (Paris-Place de Fontenory, UNESCO, 1961), p. 35.

[18]Nkrumah, Revolutionary Path, Op. Cit., p. 227.

[19]Pierre Erny, The Child and His Environment in Black Africa (Nairobi, Kenya: Oxford University Press, 1981), pp. 27-28.

[20]These and other literature from across the African continent demonstrate the similarities between Africans on the continent, educated or illiterate. See J.D. Ojo, "Supernatural Powers and Criminal Law: A Study with Particular Reference to Nigeria," Journal of Black Studies, Vol. 11, No. 3 (March 1981), pp. 327-348.

[21]Eric Ashby, African Universities and Western Tradition (Cambridge, Mass.: Harvard University Press, 1964), p. 3.

[22]Ibid., p. 98.

[23]Ibid.

[24]Musa T. Mushanga, "Education and Frustration," East African Journal (February 1970), pp. 39-46.

[25]Wilson C. McWilliams and Jonathan Wise Polier, "Pan-Africanism and the Dilemmas of National Development," Phylon, Vol. XXV, No. 1 (Spring 1964), p. 53.

[26]West Africa (February 7, 1983), pp. 305-309.

[27]Roger J. Southall, "The Federal University and the Politics of Federation in East Africa," East African Journal (November 1972), pp. 38-43. See also John Cameron, The Development of Education in East Africa (New York: Teachers College Press, 1970), Chapter IX. For the case of West Africa, see P.T.O. Arie J. VanderPloeg, "Africanus Horton and the Idea of a University for West Africa," Journal of African Studies, Vol. 5, No. 2 (Summer, 1978), pp. 185-204.

[28]Jane Martin (ed.), Global Studies: Africa (Guilford, Conn.: The Dushkin Publishing Group, Inc. 1985), p. 128.

[29]Ibid.

[30]Ibid., p. 129.

[31]Kwame Nkrumah, Consciencism: Philosophy and Ideology for De-Colonization (New York: Monthly Review Press 1964), pp. 1-2.

[32]Cited in Bob Fitch and Mary Oppenheimer, Ghana: End of an Illusion (New York: Monthly Review Press, 1964), p. 64.

[33]J.O.O. Abiri, "Preparation of the Secondary School Mother Tongue Teacher," West African Journal of Education, Vol. XX, No. 1 (February 1976), p. 10.

[34]Ali A. Mazrui, "The Educational Implications of National Goals and Political Values in Africa," Education in Eastern Africa, Vol. 2, No. 1 (1971), p. 38.

[35]Edward H. Berman, "Foundations, United States Foreign Policy, and African Education, 1945-1975," Harvard Educational Review, Vol. 49, No. 2 (May 1979), pp. 146-179.

[36]Nkrumah, Cited in James Jennings, "Pan-Africanism: Reconsidered," Pan-African Journal, Vol. VI, No. 3 (Autumn, 1973), p. 134.

[37]A case in point is the celebration of Diwali festivals in Kenya in which the Hindu constituent uses fireworks that keep some of the native Africans awake all night. For a detailed discussion of this and other cultural differences, see Mougo Nyaggah, "Asians in East Africa: The Case of Kenya," Journal of African Studies, Vol. 1, No. 2 (Summer 1974), pp. 205-233.

[38]West Africa (May 23, 1983), p. 1219.

[39]O.W. Furley and T. Watson, A History of Education in East Africa (New York: NDK Publishers, 1978), p. 29.

[40]Ali A. Mazrui, Political Values and the Educated Class in Africa (The University of California Press 1978), p. 301.

[41]F.G. Joseph, "Mental Therapy: A Consideration of the African Cultural Background," Pan-African Journal, Vol. VII, No. 1 (Spring 1974), p. 51.

[42]I.N. Thut and Don Adams, Educational Patterns in Contemporary Societies (New York: McGraw-Hill Book Company, 1964), p. 141.

[43]Robert J. Smith, L'Ecole Normale Superieure and the Third Republic (Albany, New York: State University of New York Press, 1982), p. 5.

[44]Mohamed E. Abdel-Rahman, "Interactions Between Africans North and South of the Sahara," Journal of Black Studies, Vol. 3, No. 2, (December 1972), pp. 143-144.

[45]Ali A. Mazrui, "The Educational implications of National Goals and Political Values in Africa," Education in Eastern Africa, Vol. 2, No. 1 (1971), p. 45.

[46]Mushanga, Op. Cit., pp. 39-46.

[47]Mazrui, "Education as Commodity," West Africa (October 1979), p. 1886.

[48]Chinweizu, "Towards a Liberated African Culture," East African Journal (September 1972), p. 20.

[49]Quoted in M. Tamarkin, "The Roots of Political Stability in Kenya," African Affairs, Vol. 77, No. 308 (July 1978), p. 315.

[50]Mazrui, Op. Cit., p. 38.

[51]John J. Figuera, "Teacher Training for Mass Education in Africa," The Yearbook of Education (1963), p. 558.

[52]Charles R. Reid, Environment and Learning: The Prior Issues (Granbury, New Jersey: Associated University Presses, Inc., 1977), p. 26.

[53]Lyson P. Tembo, "The African University and Social Reform," African Social Research, 25, (June 1978), pp. 379-397.

[54]Quoted in Tembo, Ibid., p. 397.

[55]Davidson Nicol, "Politics, Nationalism and Universities in Africa," African Affairs, Vol. 62, No. 246 (January 1963), p. 27.

[56]John E. Horrocks, "The Relationship Between Knowledge of Human Development and the Ability to Use Such Knowledge," Journal of Applied Psychology, 30 (1946), pp. 501-507.

[57]Archibald Callaway, "Unemployment Among African School Leavers," The Journal of Modern African Studies, 1, 3 (1963), pp. 351-371.

[58]Thomasyne Lightfoote-Wilson, "Teaching for National Development," West African Journal of Education (October 1969), pp. 145-147.

[59]John W. Hanson, "On General Education for the African Teacher," Teacher Education, 3, 3 (February 1963), pp. 181-188.

[60]G.N. Brown, "Education for Responsibility - The Teacher's Role," West African Journal of Education (June 1966), p. 65.

[61]Phelps-Stokes Report on Education in Africa (London and Southampton: The Camelot Press Ltd., 1962), pp. 46-47.

[62]Haile Selassie, "Towards African Unity," The Journal of Modern African Studies, 1, 3 (1963), pp. 287-288.

SELECTED BIBLIOGRAPHY

Abdel-Rahman, Mohamed E. "Interactions Between Africans North and South of the Sahara," Journal of Black Studies, Vol. 3, No. 2 (December 1972), pp. 131-147.

Abernathy, David B. "Teachers in Politics: The Southern Nigerian Case," in The Social Sciences and the Comparative Study of Educational Systems, Joseph Fisher (ed.), Scranton, Pennsylvania: International Textbook Company, 1970, Chapter 10.

_____. The Political Dilemma of Popular Education: An African Case. Stanford, California: Stanford University Press, 1969.

Abramson, Paul R. "Political Socialization in English and American Schools," The High School Journal, Vol. LIV, No. 2 (November 1970), pp. 63-67.

ACCRA Correspondent. "School for African TV Producers," West Africa (January 29, 1979), pp. 159-160.

Adams, Bert N. "Africanization and Academic Imperialism: A Case Study in Planned Change and Inertia," East Africa Journal, Vol. 9, No. 5 (May 1972), pp. 23-28.

Adams, Don and Thut, I.N. Educational Patterns in Contemporary Societies. New York: McGraw-Hill Book Company, 1964.

"Africa's Common Market," West Africa (June 16, 1975), p. 678.

"African Development Bank," Africa (1969/1970), pp. 127-129.

"African Universities at the Crossroads," Africa Report (November 1963), p. 4.

Alldridge, T.J. Sierra Leone: A Transformed Colony. Westport, Connecticut: Negro Universities Press, 1970.

Allport, Gordon. The Nature of Prejudice. Boston, Massachusetts: Addison-Wiley Publishing Co., Inc., 1954.

Amin, Samir. Imperialism and Unequal Development. New
York: Monthly Review Press, 1977.

_____. Neo-Colonialism in West Africa. New York:
Monthly Review Press, 1973.

Anderson, C. Arnold. "Dilemmas Arising from the Link-
ing of Education to Economic Planning," in Christianity and African Education, R. Pierce Beaues
(ed.). Grand Rapids, Michigan: William B.
Eerdmans Publishing Company, 1965.

Anderson, John. "Training Teachers for East Africa,"
East Africa Journal (June 1966), pp. 21-27.

Anise, Emmanuel Oladunjoye. "A Broad Examination of
Pan-Africanism as an Ideology of African Unity."
Master's Thesis, Syracuse University, Maxwell
Graduate School, 1969.

Apple, W. Michael. "The New Sociology of Education:
Analyzing Cultural and Economic Reproduction,"
Harvard Education Review, Vol. 48, No. 4 (November
1978), pp. 495-503.

Arensberg, M. Conrad. "The Community-Study Method,"
The American Journal of Sociology, Vol. IX, No. 2
(September 1954), pp. 108-124.

Armstrong, Earl. "Teacher Education," in Higher Education in the United States, Allan M. Carter (ed.).
Washington, D.C.: American Council on Education,
1965.

Arnold, Hans. "Cultural Exchange and European Policy,"
Universitas, Vol. 21, No. 3 (1979), pp. 169-180.

Asante, S.K.B. "Trade Problems and Prospects," West
Africa (May 1982), p. 1369.

Ashby, Eric. African Universities and Western Tradition (Cambridge, Massachusetts: Harvard University Press, 1964).

Ayandele, E.A., A.E. Afigbo, R.J. Garin and J.D. Omer
Cooper. The Growth of African Civilization: The
Making of Modern Africa. New York: Humanities
Press, 1971.

Azikiwe, Nnamdi. Renaiscent Africa. London: Frank
Cass and Company, Ltd., 1968.

_____. "How Shall We Educate The African?" Journal of the African Society, Vol. 33 (April 1934), pp. 143-151.

Babu, Abdul Rahman Mohamed. African Socialism or Socialist Africa (Dar es Salaam: Tanzanian Publishing House, 1981).

Balassa, Bela. The Theory of Economic Integration. Homewood, Illinois: Richard D. Irvin, Inc., 1961.

_____. European Economic Integration. Amsterdam: North-Holland Publishing Co., 1975.

Balogh, T. "Catastrophe in Africa: UNESCO's Colonial Style Plan," The Times Educational Supplement (January 5, 1962), p. 8.

Barber, Xenophon Theodore. Pitfalls in Human Research: Ten Pivotal Points. New York: Pergamon Press, Inc., 1976.

Battle, M. and Charles H. Lyons (eds.). Essays in the History of African Education (New York: Columbia University Press, 1970).

Beasley, L.K. "London Eliminates the 11+: The Transfer Document Becomes the Basis for Secondary Education," Comparative Education Review, Vol. 10, No. 1 (February 1966), pp. 80-86.

Beaver, Pierce (ed.). Christianity and African Education. Grand Rapids, Michigan: William B. Eerdman's Publishing Company, 1965.

Berdie, Douglas R. and John F. Anderson. Questionnaires: Design and Use. Metuchen, New Jersey: The Scarerow Press, Inc., 1974.

Berman, Edward H. "Tuskegee-In-Africa," The Journal of Negro Education, Vol. XLI, No. 2 (Spring 1972), pp. 99-112.

_____. "American Philanthropy and African Education: Toward an Analysis," African Studies Review, Vol. XX, No. 1 (April 1977), pp. 71-85.

_____. "Foundations, United States Foreign Policy, and African Education, 1945-1975," Harvard Educational Review, Vol. 49, No. 2 (May 1979), pp. 146-179.

_____ (ed.). African Reactions to Missionary Education (New York: Teachers College Press, 1975).

Bertrom, Anton. The Colonial Service. London: Cambridge University Press, 1930.

Biesheuvel, S. "Methodology in the Study of Attitudes of Africans," The Journal of Social Psychology, Vol. 47 (May 1958), pp. 169-184.

Billingsley, Andrew. Black Families in White America (Prentice-Hall, Inc. 1968).

Biobaku, Saburi. "African Studies in an African University," Minerva, Vol. 1, No. 3 (Spring 1963), pp. 285-301.

Block, James H. "Teaching, Teachers, and Mastery Learning," Today's Education (November-December 1973), p. 35.

Boas, Franz. The Mind of Primitive Man. New York: The Free Press, 1938.

Boateng, Felix. "African Traditional Education: A Method of Disseminating Cultural Values," Journal of Black Studies, 3 (1983), pp. 321-336.

Bond, Horace Mann. "Forming African Youth: A Philosophy of Education," in Presence Africaine, Africa as Seen by American Negro Scholars. New York: The American Society of American Culture, 1963.

Bowker, Gorden. The Education of Colored Immigrants. London: Longmans, 1968.

Boyd, Julian P. (ed.). The Papers of Thomas Jefferson, Vol. 8. New Jersey: Princeton University Press, 1953.

Brickman, William W. "Tendencies in African Education," The Educational Forum, Vol. XXVIII, No. 4 (May 1963), pp. 399-416.

"British Teachers for Nigeria," West Africa (July 1961), p. 730.

Brown, G.N. "Education for Responsibility - the Teacher's Role," West African Journal of Education, Vol. 2 (June 1966), pp. 65-67.

_____. "The Development of Universities in Anglophone Africa," West African Journal of Education, Vol. XV, No. 1 (February 1971), pp. 41-49.

Brunner, Christopher T. "Highways and African Unity," West Africa (December 30, 1961), p. 1439.

Caldwell, John Charles. African Rural-Urban Migration: The Movement to Ghana's Towns. Canbera: Australian National Universty Press, 1969.

Callaway, Archibald. "Unemployment Among African School Leavers," The Journal of Modern African Studies, Vol. 1, No. 3 (1963), pp. 351-371.

Cameron, Donald. My Tanganyika Services and Some Nigeria. London: George Allen and Unwin, Ltd., 1939.

Cameron, John. The Development of Education in East Africa. New York: Teachers College Press, 1970, Chapter IX.

Carr-Saunders, A.M. "Staffing African Universities," Minerva, Vol. 1, No. 3 (Spring 1963), pp. 302-318.

Carter, G.M. Politics in Africa: Seven Cases. New York: Harcourt, Brace and World, 1966.

Castle, Edgar Bradshaw. Principles of Education for Teachers in Africa. Nairobi, Kenya: Oxford University Press, 1965.

Charton, A. "French Tropical and Equatorial Africa," The Year Book of Education. London: Evans Brothers, 1949.

Chinweizu. "Towards a Liberated African Culture," East Africa Journal, Vol. IX, No. 9 (September 1972), pp. 20-26.

Clarke, A. Fielding. "An Experimental School in Nigeria," Journal of the Royal African Society, Vol. 39 (January 1940), pp. 36-40.

Clifford, Mary Louise. The Land and People of Sierra Leone. New York: J.P. Lippincott Co., 1974.

Clignet, Remi. "Inadequacies of the Notion of Assimilation in African Education," The Journal of African Studies, Vol. 8, No. 3 (1979), pp. 425-444.

Clignet, Remi and Philip Foster. "Potential Elites in Ghana and the Ivory Coast, a Preliminary Comparison," The American Journal of Sociology, Vol. LXX, No. 3 (November 1964), pp. 349-362.

Coltart, James M. "The Influence of Newspaper and Television in Africa," Journal of the Royal African Society, Vol. 62, No. 248 (July 1963), pp. 202-210.

Conference Reports. "Goals of Educational Development in Africa," School and Society (October 20, 1962), pp. 379-381.

Conton, William. The African. London: Heinemann Educational Books, Ltd., 1960.

_____. "The Educational System of Sierra Leone," Journal of Education (Ministry of Education, Government of Sierra Leone) Vol. 1, No. 1 (April 1966), pp. 3-7.

Counts, George S. "What is a School of Education?" Teachers College Record, Vol. 30 (October 1928-May 1929), pp. 647-655.

Cowan, Laing Gray. Black Africa: The Growing Pains of Independence. New York: Foreign Policy Association, Inc., 1972.

Cox, George O. Education for the Black Race (New York: African Heritage Publishers, 1974).

Cox, Richard. Pan-Africanism in Practice, An East African Study: Pafmecsa, 1958-1964. London, New York: Oxford University Press, 1964.

Crowder, Michael. West Africa Under Colonial Rule. Evanston, Illinois: North Western University Press, 1968.

Cudjoe, Selwyn R. Resistance and Caribbean Literature (Athens, Ohio: Ohio University Press, 1980).

Davidson, Basil. Can Africa Survive? Boston, Massachusetts: Little, Brown, 1974.

_____. The African Genius: An Introduction to African Social and Cultural History (The Atlantic Monthly Press, 1969).

Dawson, Richard E. and Kenneth Prewitt. Political Socialization. Boston, Massachusetts: Little, Brown, 1969.

Deutsch, Karl W. Nationalism and Social Communication: An Inquiry Into the Foundations of Nationality. Cambridge, Massachusetts: M.I.T. Press, 1962.

Dillon, Wilton S. "Universties and Nation-building in Africa," The Journal of Modern African Studies, Vol. 1, No. 1 (March 1963), pp. 75-89.

Diop, Anta Cheikh. The Cultural Unity of Black Africa. New York: Third World Press, 1978.

_____. The African Origin of Civilization: Myth or Reality. New York: Lawrence Hill and Co., 1974.

Dodd, W.A. Recent Trends in Teacher Education in Developing Countries of the Commonwealth. London: Commonwealth Secretariat, 1970.

Doob, Leonard W. Patriotism and Nationalism: Their Psychological Foundations. New Haven and London: Yale University Press, 1964.

DuBois, Victor D. "The Death of Kwame Nkrumah," West African Series (Ghana), Vol. XIV, No. 4 (June 1972), pp. 1-11.

Duroyaiye, M.O.A. "School Education and Occupational Choice: Social Psychological Research in a Nigerian International Secondary School," West African Journal of Education, Vol. XIV, No. 1 (February 1970), pp. 60-64.

_____. "The Need for Research in Child Rearing Practices in East Africa," East Africa Journal, Vol. 7, No. 10 (October 1970), pp. 17-22.

"Ecowas Milestone," West Africa (May 22, 1982), p. 1359.

"What Ecowas Says," West Africa (June 16, 1975), p. 679.

The Editors. "Whither ATEA," West African Journal of Education, Vol. XVII, No. 2 (June 1974), p. 94.

Education and Development in Sierra Leone (The Government of Sierra Leone). Paris: UNESCO, 1980.

Ehman, Lee H. "The American School in the Political Socialization Process," Review of Educational Research, Vol. 50, No. 1 (Spring 1980), pp. 99-119.

Elsbree, Willard S. "History of Teacher Education in the United States," in Teaching in American Culture, Kabil I. Gezi (ed.). New York: Rinehart and Winston, 1968.

Emerson, Rupert and Martin Kilson. The Political Awakening of Africa. Englewood Cliffs, New Jersey: Prentice-Hall, Inc., 1965.

Emory and Ross Myrta. Africa Disturbed. New York: Friendship Press, 1959.

Erney, Pierre. The Child and His Environment in Black Africa: An Essay in Traditional Education (Nairobi, Kenya: Oxford University Press, 1981).

Etzioni, Amitai. "The Dialects of Supranational Unification," in International Political Communities. New York: Anchor Books, 1966.

_____. "European Unification: Strategy for Change," in International Political Communities. New York: Anchor Books, 1966.

Evans, Maurice S. Black and White in South East Africa, A Study in Sociology. New York: Longmans, Green and Co., 1911.

Evans, P.C.C. "American Teachers for East Africa," Comparative Education Review, Vol. 6, No. 1 (June 1962), pp. 69-77.

Eyoloye, E.A. "Educational Exchange Between West African Countries," West African Journal of Education, Vol. XIV, No. 3 (October 1970), pp. 172-176.

Fafunwa, Babs A. "Teacher Education in Nigeria," West African Journal of Education, Vol. XIV, No. 1 (February 1970), pp. 20-26.

_____. "The Preparation of Teachers for African Universities," West African Journal of Education (February 1975), pp. 159-168.

Farber, Jerry. Student as a Nigger. California: Contact Books, 1969.

Fedler, Frederick. Main Currents of West African History - 1940-1978. London: The MacMillan Press, Ltd., 1979.

Feld, Werner J. The European Community in World Affairs. New York: Alfred Publishing Co., 1976.

Ferron, O.M. "Curricular and Extra Curricular Interests of Secondary School Children in Freetown," West African Journal of Education, Vol. XVII, No. 2 (June 1973), pp. 229-240.

_____. "Education for Responsibility: The Teacher's Role," West African Journal of Education (June 1966), pp. 65-66.

Fisher, John H. "Our Changing Conception of Education," Phi Delta Kappan (October 1969), pp. 16-19.

Fisher, Joseph (ed.). The Social Sciences and the Comparative Study of Educational Systems. Scranton, Pennsylvania: International Textbook Co., 1979, Chapter 10.

Foray, Cyril P. Historical Dictionary of Sierra Leone. London and New Jersey: The Scarecrow Press, 1977.

Foster, Phillip. Education and Social Change in Ghana. Chicago: University of Chicago Press, 1965.

Fougeyrollas, Pierre. "Acculturation Phenomena Among the Students of the University of Dakar," in Readings in African Psychology from French Language Sources, R. Frederic (ed.). East Lansing, Michigan: African Studies Center, Michigan State University, 1967.

Fox, Frederic. 14 Africans vs. One American. New York: The MacMillan Co., 1961.

Foy, Colm. "'Unity' Between Bissau and Cape Verde," West Africa (February 1979), pp. 326-327.

Fyfe, Christopher. A Short History of Sierra Leone. Hong Kong: Commonwealth Printing Press Co., Ltd., 1979.

_____. A History of Sierra Leone, London: Oxford University Press, 1962.

Fyle, Clifford. "A National Languages Policy and Teacher of English in Sierra Leone," Journal of Education (Ministry of Education, Government of Sierra Leone), Vol. 1, No. 2 (October 1975), pp. 1-8.

Gaines, William L. "Some Thoughts about African Man- power and United States Educational Assistance to Africa," in Christianity and African Education, R. Pierce Beaver (ed.). Grand Rapids, Michigan: William B. Eerdman's Publishing Co., 1965.

Geroge, Betty Stein. Education in Ghana. Washington, D.C.: United States Printing Office, 1976.

Glaser, William A. The Brain Drain: Emigration and Return. New York: Pergamon Press, 1978.

Goddard, Thomas Nelson. The Handbook of Sierra Leone. New York: Negro Universities Press, 1969.

Golthorpe, J.E. "An African Elite: A Sample Survey of Fifty-Two Former Students of Makerere College in East Africa," The British Journal of Sociology, Vol. VI, No. 1 (March 1955), pp. 31-47.

_____. An African Elite: Makarere College Stu- dents 1922-1960. Nairobi, Kenya: Oxford Univer- sity Press, 1965.

Gordon, H.L. "The Mental Capacity of the African," Journal of the African Society, Vol. XXXIII, No. LXXXII (July 1934), pp. 226-242.

Gould, W.T.S. Africa and International Migration. Liverpool: The University of Liverpool, Depart- ment of Geography, 1974.

Government of Sierra Leone. Education and Development in Sierra Leone. Paris: UNESCO, 1980.

Green, Reginald H. and Ann Seidman. Unity or Poverty: The Economics of Pan-Africanism. Baltimore, Maryland: Penguin Books, 1968.

Hanson, J.W. "On General Education for the African Teacher," Teacher Education, Vol. 3, No. 3 (February 1963), pp. 181-188.

_____. Is the School the Enemy of the Farm: The African Experience. East Lansing, Michigan: Michigan State University, 1980.

_____. "The Spirit of the Teacher," in Education in Nigeria, Okechukwu Ikejiani (ed.). New York: Frederick A. Praeger, 1965.

Harrell-Bond, Barbara. "Local Languages and Literacy in West Africa," West Africa Series, Vol. XVIII, No. 2 (November 1977), pp. 1-8.

Harris, Sheldon H. "An American's Impressions of Sierra Leone in 1811," Journal of Negro History, Vol. XLVII, No. (January 1962), pp. 35-41.

Hass, Ernst B. "International Integration: The European and the Universal Process," in International Political Communities: An Anthology. New York: Doublday and Co., Inc., 1966.

_____. The Uniting of Europe. Stanford, 1958.

Hayford, J.E. Casely. Ethiopia Unbound: Studies in Race Emancipation. London: Frank Cass and Co., Ltd., 1969.

Hayward, Fred M. "Correlates of National Political Integration: The Case of Ghana," Comparative Political Studies, Vol. 7, No. 2 (1974), pp. 165-192.

Hazlewood, Arthur. African Integration and Disintegration. London: Oxford University Press, 1967.

Heintz, Peter. "Education as an Instrument of Social Integration in Underdeveloped Societies," International Social Science Journal, Vol. 19, No. 3 (1967), pp. 378-386.

Hooker, J.R. Henry Sylvester Williams - Imperial Pan-Africanist (London: Rex Collins, 1975).

Horton, James Africanus. West African Countries and People (London: Edinburgh Unversity Press, 1969).

313

Hoskyns, Catherine. "Pan-Africanism and Integration," in African Integration and Disintegration, Case Studies in Economic and Political Integration, Arthur Hazlewood (ed.). London: Oxford University Press, 1967.

Hughes, A.J. East Africa: The Search for Unity Kenya, Tanganyika, Uganda, and Zanzibar (Baltimore, Maryland: Penguin Books, Ltd., 1963).

Hunter, John M. "Teaching to Eliminate Black-White Racism: An Educational Systems Approach," Journal of Geography, Vol. LXXI (February 1972), pp. 87-95.

Huxley, Elspeth. White Man's Country. London: Chatto and Windus, 1953.

Hyman, Herbert Hiram. Political Socialization: A Study in the Psychology of Political Behavior. Glencoe, Illinois: The Free Press, 1959.

Hyman, Herbert Hiram and Paul B. Sheatsley. "Attitudes Toward Desegregation," Scientific American, Vol. 211, No. 1 (July 1964), pp. 16-23.

Jahoda, Gustav. "Nationality Preferences of National Stereotype in Ghana Before Independence," The Journal of Social Psychology, Vol. 50 (November 1959), pp. 165-174.

_____. "The Social Background of a West African Student Population: Part One," The British Journal of Sociology, Vol. V, No. 4 (1954), pp. 355-365.

_____. "The Social Background of a West African Student Population: Part Two," The British Journal of Sociology, Vol. 6, No. 1 (1955), pp. 71-79.

Jaros, Dean. Socialization to Politics. New York: Praeger Publishers, 1973.

Johnson, Willard R. "African-Speaking African? Lessons from the Cameroon," African Forum, Vol. 6, No. 2 (Fall 1965), pp. 65-77.

Jolly, Richard. Planning Education for African Development: Economic and Manpower Perspectives. Nairobi, Kenya: East African Publishing House, 1969.

314

_____. Education in Africa: Action and Research. Nairobi, Kenya: East African Publishing House, 1969.

Jones, Eldridge. "Choices in Africa Education," Journal of Education (Ministry of Education, Government of Sierra Leone) Vol. 2, No. 2 (October 1963), pp. 1-6.

Jones, Ruth S. "Teachers as Agents of Political Socialization," Education and Urban Society, Vol. IV, No. 1 (November 1971), pp. 99-114.

Jones, Thomas Jesse. Education in East Africa: A Study of East, Central and South Africa. New York: Negro Universties Press, 1925.

_____. The Phelps-Stokes Report on Education in Africa. Southampton and London: The Camelot Press, 1962.

Joseph, F.G. "Mental Therapy: A Consideration of the African Cultural Background," Pan-African Journal (Spring 1974), pp. 51-66.

Kaestle, Carl F. The Evolution of an Urban School System: New York City 1750-1850. Cambridge, Massachusetts: Harvard University Press, 1973.

Kaggia, Bildad. Roots of Freedom 1921-1962 (Nairobi, Kenya: East African Publishing House, 1975).

Kaunda, Kenneth. Letter to My Children. London: Longmann Group, Ltd., 1973.

_____. A Humanist in Africa: Letters to Colin M. Morris. London: Longmans, Green and Co., Ltd., 1966.

Keesing's Research Report. The European Communities: Establishment and Growth. New York: Charles Scribner's Sons, 1975.

Kenyatta, Jomo. Facing Mount Kenya. New York: Vintage Books, 1965.

Kerlinger, N. Fred. Foundations of Behavioral Research. New York: Holt, Rinehart and Winston, 1965.

Kerr, Alexander. Forte Hare 1915-1948: The Evolution of an African College. London: C. Hurst and Co., 1968.

Kilson, Martin L. Political Change in a West African State: A Study of the Modernization Process in Sierra Leone. Cambridge, Massachusetts: Harvard Universty Press, 1966.

_____. "Trends in Higher Education," in Africa and the United States: Images or Realities. Boston, 8th National Conference, United States National Commission for UNESCO, October 22-26, 1961, pp. 61-87.

King, Kenneth. "African Students in Negro American Colleges: Notes on the Good African," Phylon, Vol. XXXI, No. 1 (Spring 1970), pp. 16-30.

_____. Pan-Africanism and Education: A Study of Race Philanthropy and Education in the Southern States of America and East Africa. London: Oxford University Press, 1971.

_____. Education and Community in Africa. London: University of Edinburgh Press, 1976.

Kitzinger, Uwe. The Politics and Economics of European Integration. New York: Praeger, 1963.

Kofele-Kale, Ndiva. "Patterns of Political Orientation Toward the Nation: A Comparison of Rural-Urban Residents in Anglophone Cameroon," The Journal of African Studies, Vol. 2 (December 1978), pp. 469-488.

Koff, David and George Von Der Muhll. "Political Socialization in Kenya and Tanzania-a Comparative Analysis," The Journal of Modern African Studies, Vol. 5, No. 1 (1967), pp. 13-51.

Kofi, A. Teteh. "The Need for Principles of Pan-African Economic Ideology," Civilizations, Vol. XXVI, No. 3 (1976), pp. 205-229.

Kurtiz, Hyman. "Benjamin Rush: His Theory of Republican Education," History of Education Quarterly, Vol. VII, No. 4 (Winter 1967), pp. 432-451.

Labouret, Henri. "France's Colonial Policy in Africa," Journal of the Royal African Society, Vol. XXXIX, No. XLIV (January 1940), pp. 22-35.

Ladinsky, Jack. "Occupational Determinants of Geographic Mobility Among Professional Workers," American Sociological Review, Vol. 32, No. 3 (April 1967), pp. 253-264.

Langton, Kenneth P. Political Socialization. New York: Oxford University Press, 1969.

Laurie, Simon Somerville. Historical Survey of Pre-Christian Education (London and New York: Longmans, Green and Co., 1904).

Laye, Camara. The African Child. London: Cambridge University Press, 1966.

Lee, Everett S. "A Theory of Migration," Demography, Vol. 3, No. 1 (1966), pp. 45-57.

Legum, Colin. Pan-Africanism: A Short Political Guide. London: Pall Mall Press, 1962.

Lema, A.A. "The Integration of Formal and Non-Formal Education," Education in Eastern Africa, Vol. 6, No. 2 (1976), pp. 99-111.

Leon, Charles H. "Fifth General Conference of the Association of African Universities," World Higher Education Communique, Vol. 3, No. 3 (Summer 1981), p. 3.

Levine, A. Robert. "Western Schools in Non-Western Societies: Psychological Impact and Cultural Response," Teachers College Record, Vol. 79, No. 4 (May 1978), pp. 749-755.

Lewis, L.J. "Education in Africa," The Yearbook of Education. London: Evans Brothers, 1949, pp. 312-337.

_____. "The Universties and Teacher Education," in Society, Schools and Progress in Nigeria, Institute of Education, University of London: Pergamon Press, 1965, pp. 105-117.

_____. Society, Schools and Progress in Nigeria. Institute of Education, University of London: Pergamon Press, 1965.

_____. "Getting Good Teachers for Developing Countries," International Review of Education, Vol. XVII, No. 14 (1970), pp. 393-405.

Lewis, M.I. "Pan-Africanism and Pan-Somalism," The Journal of Modern African Studies, Vol. 1, No. 2 (1963), pp. 147-161.

Lightfoote-Wilson, Thomasyne. "Teaching for National Development," West African Journal of Education, Vol. XIII, No. 3 (October 1969), pp. 145-146.

Lindberg, Leon N. "Interest Group Activities in the E E C , " i n R e g i o n a l I n t e r n a l Organizations/Structures and Functions, Paul A. Tharp (ed.). New York: St. Martin's Press, 1971.

Livingston, Thomas W. "The Exportation of American Higher Education to West Africa: Liberia College, 1850-1900," The Journal of Negro Education, Vol. XLV, No. 3 (Summer 1976), pp. 246-262.

London Christian Student Movement. Christian Education in Africa and the East. London: Unwin Brothers, 1924.

Long, Larry H. "Migration Differentials by Education and Occupation: Trends and Variations," Demography, Vol. 10, No. 2 (May 1973), pp. 243-258.

Lucan, Talabi Aisie. "Review of Education in Sierra Leone in the Last Five Years," Journal of Education (Ministry of Education, Government of Sierra Leone), Vol. 1, No. 1 (October 1966), pp. 12-19.

Makulu, H.F. Education, Development and Nation-Building in Independent Africa: A Study of New Trends and Recent Philosophy of Education. London: SCM Press, Ltd., 1971.

Malinowski, Bronislaw. "The Pan-African Problem of Culture Contact," The American Journal of Sociology, Vol. 48 (1942-43), pp. 649-665.

Marris, Peter. "Economics is Not Enough," East Africa Journal, Vol. III, No. II (February 1967), pp. 13-18.

Martin, Jane (ed.). Global Studies: Africa (Guilford, Connecticut: The Dushkin Publishing Group, Inc., 1985).

Mason, Melvin J. "The Purpose of Teacher Education in Developing Liberia," West African Journal of Education, Vol. XV, No. 3 (October 1971), pp. 184-190.

Mathurin, Owen Charles. Henry Sylvester Williams and the Origins of the Pan-African Movement, 1869-1911. Westport, Connecticut: Greenwood Press, 1976.

May-ParkerJudith. "Secondary School Dropouts-Girls," Journal of Education (Ministry of Education, Sierra Leone), Vol. 1, No. 1 (April 1980), pp. 1-8.

Mazrui, Ali A. Political Values and the Educated Class in Africa. Los Angeles: University of California Press, 1978.

_____. "On the Concept of 'We are all Africans,'" American Political Science Review, Vol. LVII, No. 1 (March 1963), pp. 88-97.

_____. "The Educational Implications of National Goals and Political Values in Africa," Education in Eastern Africa, Vol. 2, No. 1 (1971), pp. 38-55.

_____. The African Condition. (Cambridge University Press, 1980).

Mili, Mohammed. "Telecommunications in Africa," Africa (1969/1970), pp. 131-136.

Mills, T.M. "Power Relations in Three Person Groups," American Sociological Review, Vol. 18, No. 4 (August 1953), pp. 351-357.

Minogue, K.R. Nationalism. London: Batsford, 1967.

Morgan, Gordon D. "The Performance of East African Students on an Experimental Battery Test," The Journal of Negro Education, Vol. XXVIII, No. 4 (Fall 1969), pp. 378-383.

Mosely, Ray. "Education Not Meeting Today's Need: Black Africa, Land in Torment," African Press Clips. Washington, D.C. (October 23, 1981), pp. 16-18.

Mujaju, Akiiki B. "A Critique of Education for Development," East Africa Journal (June 1972), pp. 4-9.

Mumford, W. Bryant. Africans Learn to be French. New York: Negro Universities Press, 1970.

_____. "Malangali School," Africa, Vol. 3 (July 1930), pp. 265-290.

_____. "Native Schools in Central Africa," Journal of the African Society, Vol. XXVI, No. CI (October 1926), pp. 237-244.

Murray, Victor A. The School in the Bush: A Critical Study of the Theory and Practice of Native Education in Africa. London: Frank Cass & Col., Ltd., 1967.

Mwingira, A.C. "A Search for Relevant Teacher Education," Education in Eastern Africa, Vol. 1, No. 2 (1970), pp. 4-11.

Nasser, Gamel Abdel. The Philosophy of the Revolution (Buffalo, New York: Economica Books.... 1959).

Ngugi, James. Weep Not, Child. London: Heinemann Educational Books, Ltd., 1964.

Nkrumah, Kwame. Africa Must Unite. New York: International Publishers, 1970.

_____. Dark Days in Ghana. New York: International Publishers, 1969.

_____. Handbook of Revolutionary Warfare. New York: International Publishers, 1968.

_____. Conscientism: Philosophy and Ideology for De-Colonization. (New York: Monthly Review Press, 1964).

_____. Ghana: Autobiography of Kwame Nkrumah (Thomas Nelson and Sons, 1957).

Normington, Louis W. Teacher Education and the Agency for International Development (AACTE), 1970.

Nowzad, Habram. "Economic Integration in Central and West Africa," in Regional Internal Organizations/

Structures and Functions, Paul A. Tharp (ed.). New York: St. Martin's Press, 1971.

Nye, Joseph S. "Attitudes of Makerere Students Towards East African Federation," East African Institute of Social Research, No. 157 (Part A, January 1963).

_____. Pan-Africanism and East African Federation. Cambridge, Massachusetts: Harvard University Press, 1965.

_____. Peace in Parts: Integration and Conflict in Regional Organization. Boston, Massachusetts: Little, Brown and Co., 1971.

_____. "Unity and Diversity in East Africa: A Bibliographical Essay," The South Atlantic Journal, Vol. LXV, No. 1 (Winter 1966), pp. 104-123.

Nyerere, Julius K. Freedom and Socialism. Tanzania, Dar es Salaam: Oxford University Press, 1968.

_____. "A United States of Africa," The Journal of Modern African Studies, Vol. 1, No. 1 (January 1963), pp. 1-6.

Obidi, Sam S. "Towards the Professionalization of Teaching in Africa," West African Journal of Education, Vol. XIX, No. 2 (June 1975), pp. 239-246.

Ociti, J.P. African Indigenous Education. Nairobi, Kenya: East African Literature Bureau, 1973.

Ogunsola, A.F. "Teacher Education Program in Nigeria," West African Journal of Education, Vol. XIX, No. 2 (June 1975), pp. 229-238.

Okafor, Nduka. The Development of Universities in Nigeria. London: Longman, 1971.

Ola, Opeyemi. "Pan-Africanism: An Ideology of Development," Presence Africaine, No. 112 (4th quarterly, 1979), pp. 66-95.

_____. "The New Africa: Beyond the Nation-State," Presence Africaine, Vol. XXVI, No. 3/4 (1976), pp. 236-266.

Omijeh, Mathew. "Training Primary School Teachers in Nigeria: Problems and Prospects," Education in Eastern Africa, Vol. 6, No. 1 (1976), pp. 13-25.

Padmore, George. Pan-Africanism or Communism. New York: Doubleday and Co., Inc., 1972.

Park, Robert E. "Human Migration and the Marginal Man," American Journal of Sociology, Vol. XXXIII, No. 6 (May 1928), pp. 881-893.

Parker, Geoffrey. The Logic of Unity. London: Longman, 1968.

Parker, Porter T. Groledom: A Study of the Development of Freetown Society. London: Oxford University Press, 1963.

Patrick, John J. Political Socialization of the American Youth: Implications for Secondary School Social Studies. Washington, D.C.: National Council for Social Studies, 1967.

_____. "Political Socialization Research and the Concerns of Educators," The High School Journal, Vol. LIV, No. 2 (November 1970), pp. 63-67.

P'Bitek, Okot. Africa's Cultural Revolution (London: Heinemann Educational Books, 1984).

_____. Song of Lawino and Song of Ocol. (London: Heinemann Educational Books, 1984).

"Peace Corps for Ghana," West Africa (July 1961), p. 730.

Peil, Margaret. The Ghanaian Factory Worker: Industrial Man in Africa. London: Cambridge University Press, 1972.

_____. "The Expulsion of West African Aliens," The Journal of Modern African Studies, Vol. 9, No. 2 (1971), pp. 205-229.

_____. Conflict and Consensus in African Societies: An Introduction to Sociology. London: Longmans, 1977.

Phipps, B.A. "The Teaching Profession in Uganda: Some Preliminary Thoughts," Makerere Institute of Social Research - Conference Papers, No. 164 (Part B, January 1963).

Pifer, Alan, et. al. "Responses to Edward H. Berman," Harvard Educational Review, Vol. 49, No. 2 (May 1979), pp. 180-184.

Pirouet, M.L. "A Comparison of the Response of Three Societies to Christianity (Toro, Teso, Kikuyu)," Makerere Institute of Social Research - Conference Papers (December 1968-January 1969), pp. 36-50.

Prewitt, Kenneth. The Recruitment of Political Leaders: A Study of Citizen-Politicians. Indianapolis, Indiana: Bobbs-Merrill, 1970.

_____. Education and Political Values. Nairobi, Kenya: East African Publishing House, 1971.

Raven, J.C. "The Comparative Assessment of Personality," The British Journal of Psychology, Vol. XL, Part 3 (March 1950), pp. 115-123.

"Reorganizing Ghana's Colleges," West Africa (July 1961), p. 791.

Resnick, Idrian, et. al. "Tanzania Educates for a New Society," African Report, Vol. 16, No. 1 (January 1971), pp. 26-29.

Roberts, George O. "The Role of Foreign Aid in Independent Sierra Leone," Journal of Black Studies, Vol. 5, No. 4 (June 1975), pp. 339-373.

Rodney, Walter. How Europe Underdeveloped Africa. Washington, D.C.: Howard University Press, 1974.

Rodney, Walter. History of the Upper Guinea Coast, 1545-1800. New York: Monthly Review Press, 1982.

Rohrs, B.M.C. Educational Problems of a Continent. Reviewed by Brann, in Education in Eastern Africa, Vol. 5, No. 2 (1975), pp. 223-225.

Rossi, Peter H. Why Families Move: A Study in the Social Psychology of Urban Residential Mobility. Glencoe, Illinois: The Free Press, 1965.

Rotberg, Robert T. "An Account of the Attempt to Achieve Closer Union in British East Africa," Makerere Institute of Social Research - Conference Papers, No. 158, Part A (January 1963).

Sabot, R.H. Economic Development and Urban Migration: Tanzania 1900-1971. Oxford: Clarendon Press, 1979.

Sass, Ravenel. "Mixed Schools--Mixed Bloods," The Annals of America (Encyclopedia Britanica), Vol. 17 (1950-1960), pp. 373-378.

Scanlon, David G. Traditions of African Education. New York: Teachers College, Columbia University, 1964.

Selassie, Haile. "Towards African Unity," The Journal of Modern African Studies, Vol. 1, No. 3 (1963), pp. 281-291.

Shack, A. William (ed.). Strangers in African Societies. Los Angeles, California: University of California Press, 1979.

Sherman, W.L. "Some Problems of Education in the Provinces," Journal of Education (Ministry of Education Government of Sierra Leone), Vol. 1, No. 26 (October 1966), pp. 30-34.

Shirer, William L. The Rise and Fall of the Third Reich. New York: Simon and Schuster, 1960.

Shrigley, Robert L. "Student Teaching in Nigeria," Peabody Journal of Education, Vol. 46 (January 1969), pp. 203-204.

_____. "Teacher Education in Africa," Peabody Journal of Education, Vol. 47, No. 4 (January 1970), pp. 221-223.

Sifuna, D. "Some Factors Affecting the Quality of Teaching in the Primary Schools in Kenya," Education in Eastern Africa, Vol. 4, No. 2 (1974), pp. 215-222.

Simmel, Georg. "The Number of Members as Determining the Sociological Form of the Group," American Journal of Sociology, Vol. 8, No. 1 (July 1902), pp. 1-46, 158-196.

Simon, Julian L. <u>Basic Research Methods in Social Science</u>. New York: Random House, 1969.

Sinclair, M.E. "Education, Relevance and the Community: A First Look at the History of Attempts to Introduce Productive Work into Primary School Curriculum," in <u>Education and Community in Africa</u>. Kenneth King (ed.). University of Edinburgh: Center of African Studies, 1976, pp. 45-80.

Sklar, Richard L. "Political Science and National Integration - A Radical Approach," <u>The Journal of Modern African Studies</u>, Vol. 5, No. 1 (1967), pp. 1-11.

Slater, K. Mariam. <u>The Caribbean Family: Legitimacy in Martinique</u>. New York: St. Martin's Press, 1977.

Smith, Edwin W. "The Function of Folk-Tales," <u>Journal of the Royal African Society</u>, Vol. XXXIX, No. CLIV (January 1940), pp. 64-83.

Smith, Othanel. <u>Teachers for the Real World</u>. Washington, D.C.: The American Association of Colleges for Teacher Education (AACTE), 1969.

Smith, Robert J. <u>The ECole Normale Superieure and the Third Republic</u> (Albany, New York: State University of New York Press, 1982).

Smith, Stephen J. <u>The History of Alliance High School</u>. London: Heinemann Educational Books, 1973.

Sodhi, T.S. <u>Education and Economic Development: A Treatise on the Problems of Economics of Education</u>. India: Muk Publications, 1978.

Sorie-Conteh, J. "History as a Guide," <u>West Africa</u> (December 21-28, 1981), p. 3060.

Southall, Roger J. "The Federal University and the Politics of Federation in East Africa," <u>East Africa Journal</u> (November 1972), pp.38-43.

Spivey, Donald. <u>Schooling for New Slavery: Black Industrial Education 1868-1915</u>. Westport, Connecticut: Greenwood Press, 1978.

Stabler, Ernest. Education Since Uhuru: The Schools of Kenya. Middletown, Connecticut: Wesleyan University Press, 1969.

Stoller, Nathan. "The Teacher: A New Definition," Phi Delta Kappan (December 1960), pp. 133-135.

Stone, Lawrence. "The Educational Revolution in England, 1560-1640," Past and Present, No. 28 (July 1964), pp. 41-80.

Streeten, Paul. Economic Integration: Aspects and Problems. Netherlands, Holland: A.W. Sythoff Leiden, 1961.

Tamarkin, M. "The Roots of Political Stability in Kenya," African Affairs, Vol. 77, No. 308 (July 1978), pp. 297-320.

Tarver, James D. "Occupational Migrational Differentials, Social Forces, No. 43 (December 1964), pp. 231-241.

Tasie, G.D.M. Christian Missionary Enterprise in the Niger Delta, 1864-1918. Leiden, Holland: E.J. Brill, 1978.

Tembo, Lyson P. "The African University and Social Reform," African Social Research, No. 25 (June 1978), pp. 379-397.

Temu, A.J. British Protestant Missions. London: Longman, 1972.

Tharp, Paul A. Regional Internal Organizations/Structures and Functions. New York: St. Martin's Press, 1971.

Thrasher, Max Bennett. Tuskegee: Its Story and Its Work. New York: Negro Universities Press, 1969.

Tiberondwa, A.K. "The Status of African Teachers in Independent Africa," Education in East Africa, Vol. 6, No. 2 (1976), pp. 159-166.

Tomlinson, Leila. "Oxford University and the Training of Teachers: The Early Years (1892-1921)," British Journal of Educational Studies (October 1968), pp. 292-307.

Tucker, Theodore L. "Protestant Educational Enterprise in Africa," in Christianity and African Education, Pierce Beaver (ed.). Grand Rapids, Michigan: William B. Eerdman's Publishing Co., 1965.

Tumin, Melvin, et al. "Education, Prejudice and Discrimination...," American Sociological Review (February 1958), pp. 41-49.

Tyack, David. "Forming the National Character," Harvard Educational Review, Vol. 36, No. 1 (1966), pp. 29-41.

University of London Institute of Education. "The Practice of Community Education in Africa," in Education and Community in Africa, Kenneth King (ed.). London: University of Edinburgh Press, 1976.

Urch, George E. "Africanization of Schools in Kenya," Educational Forum, No. 34 (March 1970), pp. 372-377.

Wallerstein, Immanuel. Africa, the Politics of Unity: An Analysis of a Contemporary Social Movement. New York: Random House, 1967.

_____. "Background to Paga - I," West Africa (July 29, 1961), p. 819.

_____. "End of an African Frontier," West Africa (July 8, 1961), p. 751.

Wandira, Asavia. "Teacher Education for Mass Education in Africa," Teachers College Record, Vol. 81, No. 1 (Fall 1979), pp. 77-93.

_____. "Foundatin Studies in Teacher Education in Africa," Education in Eastern Africa, Vol. 1, No. 2 (January 1970), pp. 12-26.

Ward, C.J. "The Expatriate Academic and the African University," East Africa Journal, Vol. 7, No. 10 (October 1970), pp. 12-16.

Ward, W.E.F. Fraisier of Trinity and Achimota. Accra, Ghane: Ghana Universities Press, 1965.

Washington, Booker T. Up From Slavery. New York: Bantam Pathfinder Edition, Bantam Books, 1963.

_____. "David Livingstone and the Negro," International Review of Missions, Vol. 2 (1913), pp. 224-235.

Watkins, Mark Hanna. "The West African 'Bush' Schools," The American Journal of Sociology, Vol. XLVIII, No. 6 (May 1943), pp. 666-675.

Watson, T. and O.W. Furley. "Education in Tankanyika Between the Wars: Attempts to Blend Two Cultures," The South Atlantic Journal, Vol. LXV, No. 4 (Autumn 1966), pp. 471-490.

_____. A History of Education in East Africa (New York: NOK Publishers, 1978).

Wayland, Sloan R. "Socio-economic Problems and Teacher Training," in Beredy and J.A. Lanwery (eds.). The Education and Training of Teachers: The Yearbook of Education. New York: Harcourt, Brace and World, Inc., 1963, pp. 373-381.

Weatherhead, H.W. "The Educational Value Work as Illustrated in King's Schol, Burdo, Uganda," International Review of Missions, No. 3 (April 1914), pp. 343-348.

Weeks, Rocheforte L. "Inter-African Co-operation," in The Development of Higher Education in Africa, UNESCO: Report of the Conference on the Development of Higher Education in Africa, Tananarive, 1962, pp. 214-216.

Weeks, S.G. "A Preliminary Report on a Sociological Case Study of an Urban Day Secondary School," Makerere Institute of Social Research, No. 170 (Part B, January 1963).

_____. "A Preliminary Examination of the Role of Minority Students at a Day Secondary School in Kampala, Uganda," Makerere Institute of Social Research, No. 169 (Part A, January 1963).

Weeks, Sheldon. Divergence in Educational Development: The Case of Kenya and Uganda. New York: Teachers College Press, 1967.

Welch, Claude E. Dream of Unity: Pan-Africanism and Political Unification in West Africa. Ithaca, New York: Cornell University Press, 1966.

Westermann, Diedrick. The Africa of Today and Tomorrow (London: Dawsons Pall Mall, 1969).

Wells, Jeff. "City Students Get Brighter in Math," New York Post (June 16, 1982), p. 7.

Wickert, R. Frederick (ed.). Readings in African Psychology from French Language Sources. Lansing, Michigan: Michigan State University Press, 1967.

Wilde, Patricia Berko. "Radicals and Moderates in the OAU: Origins of Conflict and Basis for Co-existence," in Regional International Organizations/Structures and Functions, Paul A. Tharp (ed.). New York: St. Martin's Press, 1971.

Williams, Wilson C., et al. "Pan-Africanism and the Dilemmas of National Development," Phylon, Vol. XXV, No. 1 (Spring 1964), pp. 44-64.

Wiltse, Charles M. (ed.). David Walker's Appeal.... (New York: Hill and Wang, 1915).

Woddis, Jack. Africa: The Roots of Revolt. London: Lawrence and Washant, 1960.

Yardele, E.A. and A.E. Figbo, et al. The Growth of African Civilization: The Making of Modern Africa, Vol. 11. New York: Humanities Press, 1971.

Yates, Barbara A. "African Reactions to Education: The Congolese Case." Comparative Education Review, Vol. XV, No. 2 (June 1971), pp. 158-171.

Yoloye, E.A. "Educational Exchange Between West African Countries," West African Journal of Education (October 1970), pp. 172-174.

STUDIES IN AFRICAN EDUCATION